The British Foreign Service
and the American Civil War

THE British Foreign Service
AND THE
American Civil War

EUGENE H. BERWANGER

THE UNIVERSITY PRESS OF KENTUCKY

Copyright © 1994 by The University Press of Kentucky
Scholarly publisher for the Commonwealth,
serving Bellarmine College, Berea College, Centre
College of Kentucky, Eastern Kentucky University,
The Filson Club, Georgetown College, Kentucky
Historical Society, Kentucky State University,
Morehead State University, Murray State University,
Northern Kentucky University, Transylvania University,
University of Kentucky, University of Louisville,
and Western Kentucky University.

Editorial and Sales Offices: Lexington, Kentucky 40508-4008

Library of Congress Cataloging-in-Publication Data

Berwanger, Eugene H.
    The British Foreign Service and the American Civil War / Eugene H.
Berwanger.
        p.   cm.
    Includes bibliographical references and index.
    ISBN 0-8131-1876-X (acid-free)
    1. United States—Foreign relations—1861-1865.   2. Diplomatic and
consular service, British—United States—History—19th century.
3. Diplomatic and consular service. British—Confederate States of
America.   4. United States—Foreign relations—Great Britain.
5. Great Britain—Foreign relations—United States.   I. Title.
E469.854   1994
973.7'21—dc20   94-6468

For Betsy as always
and to Anne and Tad,
with love

Contents

Preface

In this book I describe problems encountered by British consuls and the British legation during the American Civil War and attempt to determine their influence on the British Foreign Office's attitude and policies toward the crisis. My discussion is limited solely to issues within the Union and the Confederacy and does not cover such topics as the *Trent* affair, the building of Confederate raiders and Laird Rams in British shipyards, or other issues that at times put the Union and Britain on the brink of war. These topics have been thoroughly covered in such seminal works as Ephraim Adams's *Great Britain and the American Civil War*, published in 1924, and in many fine diplomatic studies and essays since.

I originally intended to study the consuls only, but investigating their problems made me aware of the vital role played by the legation in Washington. The consular and diplomatic corps were separate departments within the foreign service, but foreign ministers supervised the work of consuls and the two worked closely on issues of common concern.

My interest in this topic began when I read William Howard Russell's diary, published in 1863. As special correspondent for the London *Times* during the first year of war, Russell traveled throughout the United States and remarked on the consuls and their problems in each major city he visited. He also made numerous references to Lord Lyons, British foreign minister to the United States. Investigation on my part revealed that very few historical studies had been done on the consuls or Lyons. Thomas Newton's two-volume biography of Lyons, written in 1913, devoted less than one hundred pages to the Civil War years and was based on limited sources and documentation. For the consuls there was only the work of Milledge Bonham Jr. on the British consuls in the Confederacy, written as a doctoral

dissertation at Columbia University during the first decade of
the twentieth century. Bonham's pioneering study was an excellent introduction but, like Newton's biography, it also was
based on limited sources. Major collections including Lyons's
papers, Foreign Office correspondence between the British
legation and the consuls, as well as diplomatic correspondence
between the U.S. State Department and the British legation
was not available to the public before the First World War. Historians now have access to these materials and their availability opens the way for a more comprehensive investigation of
British legation and consular problems with the Union and the
Confederate governments.

I have broadened Bonham's study by including consuls in
the North as well as the South, and this has given me opportunity to compare the similarity and intensity of their problems. The issues were comparable but established diplomatic
relations between Great Britain and the Union eased their severity in the North and ultimately provided a means for easier
solution, whereas the lack of any diplomatic channel in the
South caused increasing resentment and bitterness toward
Great Britain and its consuls.

I also attempt to reevaluate past impressions of consular attitudes, especially those of Robert Bunch, consul at Charleston.
Bonham accepted the general belief of South Carolinians and
the U.S. State Department that Bunch was pro-Confederate.
However, Bunch's correspondence—found chiefly in Foreign
Office records and the Lyons papers—indicates the reverse was
true. His attitude about the war, the South, and its leaders,
expressed to his superiors at the legation in Washington and at
the Foreign Office in London, was hardly pro-Southern.

I have been exceptionally fortunate in securing assistance
from many individuals and institutions while undertaking my
research. Grants from the American Philosophical Society, the
National Endowment for the Humanities, and Colorado State
University provided funds for travel to libraries and reposito-
ries in both the United States and the United Kingdom. Li-
brarians at the Library of Congress, the National Archives in
Washington, D.C., and at Duke University were helpful in lo-

cating materials and answering my many questions. Beverly
D. Bishop at the Emory University Library; Charles Reeves,
assistant director at the regional center of the National Archives at East Point, Georgia; and Michael Meier of the Military Records Division at the National Archives permitted me
to photocopy a significant portion of the information I needed
from their holdings and to study in leisure away from the archives. In England, Mrs. H.E. Jones, assistant keeper of the
records in the Public Record Office at Kew, and Mrs. Patricia
Gill, county archivist at the West Sussex Record Office, answered my many letters and aided me in numerous ways during my research trips to London and Chichester. The staffs at
Kew and Chichester did much to help an uninitiated American
become familiar with the English library system. Without the
assistance of all of these individuals this book might never
have been written. Extracts from the Lyons papers are repro-
duced with the permission of the Trustees of the Arundel Castle Archives, and with acknowledgment of the County Archivist, West Sussex Record Office.

Colleagues and friends also aided me by reading portions of
the manuscript and offering suggestions for improvement. Professors Robert W. Johannsen of the University of Illinois, Ur-
bana, and Mark T. Gilderhus at Colorado State University read
an early draft of the entire manuscript and saved me from a
number of mishaps. Carolyn Duff, a professional editor, made
suggestions for organizational refinement that improved the
book throughout. Interpretations found herein, however, are
solely mine and I take full responsibility for them. John C.
Inscoe, editor of the *Georgia Historical Quarterly,* granted permission to incorporate into chapter 6 portions of "The Case of
Stirrup and Edwards, 1861-1870," which appeared in the spring
1992 issue of the *Quarterly.* Finally, my thanks to Betsy, Anne,
and Tad for encouraging my research trips to England even
though they had to remain at home. Staying home was particularly difficult for Anne because her appreciation for British
culture is inexhaustible. To my family especially and to colleagues I express my deepest appreciation.

1

The Foreign Service on the Eve of the War

The British foreign service in the nineteenth century consisted of the diplomatic corps and the consular corps. The diplomatic corps represented the British government in foreign capitals, acting as diplomatc agent and transmitting correspondence. The chief diplomatic agent was either an ambassador, a minister, or an envoy, the title determined by the military and political importance that London placed on the foreign country. The head of the British legation in Washington was a minister; he was supported by a secretary of legation, who served as chargé d'affaires in the absence or illness of the minister, and a number of attachés, unpaid young men who assisted with daily business or worked as secretaries. To reduce expenses, the British government did not maintain a permanent diplomatic compound in Washington, and the minister rented a private house to serve as both legation and residence for the staff.[1]

The consular corps was larger but in many ways the stepchild of the foreign service. Sons of the aristocracy and landed gentry received diplomatic appointments, while members of the merchant class and retired military officers were assigned to the consulates. Moreover, consuls were never promoted to the diplomatic corps because the Foreign Office considered such advances inappropriate and unfair to attachés working toward promotion. Only once, at the beginning of the nineteenth century, was a consul elevated to the diplomatic corps.[2]

The first British consulate in the United States was established at Boston in 1790, one year before the two countries established formal diplomatic relations; by 1860 the number had grown to fourteen. Because a consul's peacetime duties focused on enhancing his country's trade and protecting individuals employed in trading ventures, most of the consulates were located in seaport cities: Portland, Maine; Boston; New York City; Philadelphia; Baltimore; Charleston; Savannah; Mobile; New Orleans; Galveston; and San Francisco. The only consulates in the interior of the country were in Richmond, Chicago, and Buffalo.[3]

In contrast to the British service, other European nations maintained much smaller consular systems. France had four consulates and Spain had three, all located in major port cities. Other European and most Latin American nations supported at least two consulates, usually at New York and New Orleans, but often one person acted as consul for several countries or consular agents (a rank below consul) represented one or more governments.[4]

The major distinction between the British and American foreign services was the professionalism of the former and the political nature of the latter. Presidents usually appointed individuals to diplomatic posts as a reward for party loyalty, whereas British diplomatic personnel began their careers as unpaid attachés. American consulates, too, were awarded as political favors or at the request of politicians seeking appointments for friends and supporters. Some Americans assigned to minor consulates retained their posts despite changing administrations at home and a few even passed them on to members of their own family, but more lucrative consular posts, such as London, Paris, and Liverpool, changed hands with the inauguration of every new president. In contrast, most British consuls began their careers as unpaid secretaries or vice-consuls before being assigned a consulate of their own.[5]

Diplomats and consuls were accorded different kinds of reception upon arrival at their new posts. In the United States, ministers presented their credentials at the State Department before undertaking their duties, and the secretary of state then accompanied them to the White House for an audience with the president. The length of the meeting depended upon the administration's opinion of the county's importance. William Howard Russell, correspondent for the London *Times* visiting the United States in 1861 and 1862, was introduced to President Lincoln following the audience at which the Italian minister had been formally presented. Russell noted that Lincoln's remarks to the minister were perfunctory, whereas his conversation with Russell was more lively and lasted much longer.[6]

Consuls did not receive personal acknowledgement from the State Department. It merely granted them an exequatur, a formal statement authorizing them to exercise their powers. Exequaturs varied, some stipulating the exact geographical limits of the consul's authority, others being less specific. The consul at Richmond, for example, could only perform his consular duties within Virginia, whereas the exequatur for the consul at Chicago placed no restrictions on the geographical area of his authority. Unlike ministers, consuls were not granted extraterritoriality and were subject to punishment for infringements of national and local laws.[7]

In addition to consuls, there were numerous British vice-consuls in the United States. Some worked at consular offices, others managed separate vice-consulates. Until 1843 the Foreign Office named vice-consuls, and they received exequaturs from the United States government. This procedure became less formal after that date; the Foreign Office continued to name the vice-consul at New York City but permitted other consuls to choose their own subordinates. Exequaturs were no longer required for vice-consuls. In most cases the British legation in Washington approved vice-consular appointments, but as the wartime predicament involving the vice-consulate at Fredericksburg, Virginia, indicates, consuls did not always seek the legation's approval. Whereas consuls received their appointments from the Foreign Office and were British citizens, vice-consuls were selected from the local population and tended to be naturalized American citizens of British birth. Usually men with commercial interests, they received no compensation but accepted the vice-consulship to further their own business concerns.[8]

Copies of exequaturs, now on file in the National Archives, provide accurate information on the locations of British consulates in the United States and the individuals who staffed them. Data on vice-consulates is less accurate because exequaturs were not required. During the Civil War both the Lincoln and the Davis administrations requested the names of consuls and vice-consuls functioning within their borders. Information supplied by British authorities indicates only a vague knowledge about vice-consular personnel. The legation in Washington submitted a list of all vice-consuls in the nation, and the consul at Richmond responded to the Confederate request. There are numerous discrepancies between the two lists regarding the spelling of names, the location of vice-consulates, and the individuals who held posts. But they do indicate the existence of eleven separate British vice-consulates in the United States, mostly located in smaller port cities such as Key West and Pensacola, Florida, and New Haven, Connecticut.[9]

While the duties of the legation staff were confined to diplomatic matters, the responsibilities of a consul were wideranging. Asked about the various tasks he encountered in his job, one consul replied: "With the exception of the administration of the Sacrament of baptism and exercising the business of executioner, it would be difficult to say what duties I can not be called on to perform." Because a consul's chief obligation was to oversee and enhance his country's commercial interests, his duties assumed a mercantile character. He kept close contact with British vessels in his port, offering vital information about shipping possibilities and complaining to local authorities when infractions of trade treaties occurred. He warned ship's captains of possible shipping dangers, inspected ships, and estimated the value of imported goods for United States customs officials. Consuls acted as advocates for sailors and civilians in trouble with the law and provided legal assistance if it was needed. They also made sure that British ships paid their bills before leaving port and arranged transportation on British ships for penniless or stranded sailors and civilians. Occasionally consuls in the American South were called upon to trace and secure the release of black British nationals kidnapped or sold into slavery by unscrupulous authorities or individuals. They notarized documents, issued passports and certificates of nationality to British citizens, and recorded the births and deaths of British nationals in their district.[10]

At the more personal level, consuls were expected to establish friendships with local commercial and political leaders and even to become members of social organizations to further their country's interests. They were also expected to entertain (usually at their own expense) prominent visiting Englishmen and to introduce them to social and political leaders within the district. The consulate at New York City virtually closed its doors to all other business in the fall of 1860 as the consul devoted his entire attention to arrangements involved with the visit of Edward, prince of Wales. When journalist William Howard Russell traveled throughout the United States at the outbreak of the Civil War, consuls from New York to New Orleans gave elaborate dinners that provided Russell with introductions to individuals knowledgeable about current affairs.[11]

During the Civil War the Union blockade relieved the Southern consuls of their commercial responsibilities. Instead, their major concern centered on protecting British nationals, some from mistreatment by local authorities because of their race, others from being conscripted into the Confederate army or the Southern militia. Northern consuls encountered many of the same problems. These were, however, in addition to their commercial duties, which expanded because of an upsurge in United States foreign trade and the increasing use of British merchant ships by American exporters in order to avoid Confederate raiders.

Considering the responsibilities of foreign service personnel—diplomats and consuls—their salaries were minimal and seldom covered the expenses of office. Both were expected to provide money from their own or their family's resources if expenses exceeded salary. Occasionally the British minister in Washington recommended small supplements to cover inflation or as reimbursements for exceptional expenses, but generally he rejected pleas for increased salary because he thought the consuls "received sufficient compensation."[12]

Paid members of the legation staff received their salaries from the Civil List, a parliamentary appropriation authorizing wages for political and foreign service employees. Unfortunately payment was often as much as three years in arrears. Consuls were paid in part from the Civil List and in part from fees they collected for their various services. There was no standard salary scale, and the government made different arrangements with each consul. As will be noted later, some received higher salaries, but the average compensation for most British consuls in the United States was between four hundred and five hundred pounds a year.[13] This amount included rental for office space, fuel, all supplies, salaries for vice-consuls and clerks, if any were employed, and the consuls' own living expenses.[14]

To save money, consuls sometimes sent their families to live with relatives in England and almost always rented office space in the least desirable districts. The consulate in New York City, the busiest in the country, consisted of two rooms that could be reached only by going through a back alley and climbing three flights of stairs. Even the *Times* of London thought that such quarters were "beyond what . . . republican plainness ought to demand."[15]

To compensate for their low salaries, the Foreign Office permitted all but two British consuls in the United States to trade; that is, to engage in private commercial venture of their own. Some in the Southern states served as cotton factors; others operated import-export businesses. Several Northern consuls were agents for Lloyd's of London or for English companies wishing to expand their business activities to America. In consenting to these arrangements, the Foreign Office stipulated that consuls so employed could never discuss political issues in correspondence with their employers back home. Consuls almost never mentioned their trading activities to the legation or the Foreign Office, but the one who did, the consul at Savannah, proudly announced that his investments in business and activities in land speculation netted him over twenty thousand pounds a year.[16]

The legation in Washington supervised consular activities in the United States; still, the system of communication between the consulates, the legation, and the Foreign Office was not firmly established. Consuls sought advice from the Foreign Office as often as they did from the legation. If the issue seemed pressing or one in which the Foreign Office had a vital interest, they sent copies of their letters to both places at the same time. During the Civil War, consuls in the North retained a close association with the legation and sought direction for pressing problems. Those in the South turned more often to the Foreign Office because they were encouraged to give the impression of acting without direction from the legation. The Confederate government considered the British minister in Washington accredited to a foreign government and lacking authority to direct consular affairs within its borders. But the slowness of communication with either the legation or the Foreign Office forced consuls in the South to cope without direction and to assume duties of a more diplomatic character, especially those connected with protecting British nationals from military service.

The British foreign service in the United States was undergoing a transformation on the eve of the Civil War. The State Department, in 1855, had revoked the exequaturs of the consuls in New York City, Philadelphia, and Cincinnati and requested the recall of the foreign minister for attempting to recruit Americans during the Crimean War. The new foreign minister, Lord Francis Napier, while highly respected in Washington social and political circles, remained only two years, and his replacement lacked the same professional stature and personal charisma. The consuls at New York City and Philadelphia were quickly replaced, but the Foreign Office closed the Cincinnati consulate in retaliation for an American effort to charge the consul with violating United States neutrality laws. The closure of the Cincinnati office would prove a serious disadvantage to British nationals attempting to avoid service in the Union army during the war.[17]

American reaction to British recruiting efforts during the Crimean War (which would be in sharp contrast to the British reaction to a similar issue some years later) created a certain tension between the Foreign Office and the State Department on the eve of the Civil War. Southerners hoped that these mutual British-American suspicions would capture Britain's sympathy for their cause. In the beginning the South appeared successful, but among the factors that determined Britain's final decision were consular problems and the Confederate response to them.

2

The Consuls

The Foreign Office considered the consulates at New York City and Charleston, South Carolina, the most important in the United States. Not only was New York City the nation's major import-export center, but the consulate there served as a filter for virtually all news about America sent to Great Britain. Both the British legation and the consulates forwarded their mail to New York City for transshipment across the Atlantic on fast mail packets. It was important that the New York consulate be headed by a man of competence, and the individual chosen to hold that post during the Civil War had proven his ability in his former career.

The consulate at Charleston, to the contrary, required a man with the personality and ability to secure the confidence of the local population. The British government kept a close watch on sectional difficulties in the United States and was aware that they would undoubtedly break out in South Carolina if a crisis erupted. Since Charleston, the state's major city, was also the center of states' rights thinking, the consul was in a strategic location for evaluating local response to sectional issues.

The preeminence of New York City and Charleston was evident by the different stipulations and duties placed on the consuls in those cities. Unlike other British consuls in the United States, the consuls at New York City and Charleston were forbidden to trade—that is, to engage in business activities in addition to their consular obligations.[1] To compensate them for this restriction, their salaries were substantially higher than those of the other consuls. The consul at New York City received twelve hundred pounds a year, from which he paid his own wages, all office expenses, and the salary of a vice-consul selected by the Foreign Office.[2] According to correspondence between the foreign minister in Washington and the consul at Charleston, he was paid—for "special considerations"—£950 annually, a sum which was to cover all of his expenses. Neither consul received any of the fees they charged for services.[3]

The two consuls were almost regarded as consul-generals, although they did not hold the rank. The Foreign Office elevated the New York City office to a consulate-generalship in 1863, after its wartime duties had increased tremendously and it assumed supervision over the vice-consulates at Key West and Pensacola, Florida, cities the Union held during the entire war. The consulate at Charleston never achieved any upgrade in status. Lord Lyons, British foreign minister to the United States, often consulted the two consuls about appointments and other personnel matters. He also informed them about problems other consuls were encountering and asked for their advice concerning them. Foreign ministers normally solicited such guidance from consul-generals, not from mere consuls.[4]

Finally, the men appointed to the consulates at New York City and Charleston attested to the importance of these cities in British opinion. The Foreign Office named Edward Mortimer Archibald as consul at New York City in 1857. Archibald had little consular experience but was well-known and well-regarded in both England and Canada as a public administrator and jurist. At the age of twenty-two, in 1832, he had been appointed chief clerk of the Newfoundland Supreme Court, an office he resigned in 1838 to become the colony's attorney general. Serving in that position for almost a decade, Archibald, in 1847, became advocate general for Newfoundland. He also served on the commission that drew up the Marcy-Elgin reciprocity treaty of 1854, which expanded American and Canadian fishing rights along the Atlantic coast and granted free navigation of the St. Lawrence River and Lake Michigan to citizens of both nations.[5] Given his efficiency and experience, Archibald could be expected to restore confidence in his office, recently lost by the expulsion of his predecessor for recruiting American youths to fight in the Crimea. The selection of Archibald was an excellent choice; he was so well-admired that he retained his consulship until his death in 1883.

Robert Bunch was consul at Charleston when the Civil War began. Not as distinguished as Archibald, still Bunch had a long and commendable career in the consular service. From 1840 until 1848 he served in various consular posts in South America, then in 1848 he was appointed vice-consul at New York City. In 1851 he advanced to a full consulship at Philadelphia and was transferred to Charleston in 1853, following a number of calls for secession from Robert Barnwell Rhett and the passage by a state convention of a resolution declaring that "South Carolina has good cause to secede from the Union."[6]

Bunch was the most outgoing of the British consuls in the United States. His correspondence to Lyons and Lord John Russell, foreign secretary in London, indicates a keen sense of humor, astute observation of events around him, and the ability to win the confidence of others.[7] But Bunch's success as consul may have been his downfall. It was his personal friendships as much as his actions that caused his problems with the Lincoln administration during the war.

Archibald and Bunch were to be the consuls most involved in wartime activities, but the others played roles. John Edward Wilkins, consul at Chicago, dealt with problems arising out of military activities in the western theater. Like Archibald, he had no previous consular experience, but he held the distinction of being a fellow in the Royal Geographic Society. In November 1861, as fighting intensified between Union and secession forces in Missouri, the Foreign Office sent Wilkins to St. Louis, where he could more easily "protect British citizens and their property"; at least, that was the reason given for the transfer. He remained there until after the war, when he returned to Chicago.[8]

The major problems faced by consuls in the Northern states involved keeping British nationals from being drafted into the Union army. Charles Kortwright at Philadelphia, Denis Donohoe at Buffalo, and John Henry Murray at Portland, Maine, contended with such problems, though Murray's wartime responsibilities differed little from those he carried on in peacetime, except during the Tully hearings of 1864.

Francis Lousada, consul at Boston, found his workload increased in 1861 and 1862 when many British sailors were incarcerated at Fort Warren in Boston harbor for attempting to run the blockade. Still, his additional duties never became as onerous as those of Archibald, who had to contend with the much larger number of British citizens sent to Fort Lafayette in New York City.

On the Pacific coast, in San Francisco, Consul William Booker carried on his normal peacetime duties. Separated from the fighting front by thousands of miles of mountains and plains, he only occasionally reported on pro-Union sentiment in California. He did send several letters detailing activities of five Russian warships in San Francisco Bay in 1863; otherwise, his correspondence to the Foreign Office said very little about American national events.[9]

Frederick Bernel's position as consul at Baltimore was overshadowed by the nearness of the legation in Washington, thirty-five miles away. He reported fully on the riot between local civilians and Union troops on April 19, 1861, but during most of the war his time was taken up with securing supplies for British warships sent to observe American naval activities along the Atlantic coast. They used Baltimore as a source for fresh food and other nonmilitary provisions.[10]

The war had greater impact on consuls in the Confederacy, especially those at Charleston, Richmond, and Savannah. Indeed, the additional responsibilities and difficulties eventually brought an end to all unofficial communication between the South and the British government. Bunch was the most competent consul, but his lack of discretion would be his downfall. George Moore at Richmond proved ineffectual but his vice-consul, Frederick Cridland, a British citizen hoping to advance in the consular service, more than compensated for Moore's incapacity. Moore suffered from his inability to adjust to Richmond after twenty years as consul in Ancona, Italy. Inflation and hardships in the Confederate capital only aggravated his dislike for the city and the officials he had to deal with.[11]

The consul at Savannah proved as ineffectual as Moore. Edmund Molyneux certainly found Savannah congenial, having lived there since his appointment as consul in 1832. But he also wished to escape wartime hardships. Independently wealthy and reaching retirement age when the war began, Molyneux spent the first months of the conflict at his mountain retreat in North Carolina. Upon returning to Savannah he requested sick leave and returned to England, where he died within a year. Unable to send a consul from England, the Foreign Office accepted Allan Fullarton, a local banker, as acting consul. Considering his lack of experience and the problems he faced, Fullarton coped as best he could but his efforts went unappreciated by the Foreign Office.

The consul at Mobile also encountered the disfavor of the Foreign Office. Lord Russell dismissed the regular consul just as the war broke out and, anxious to avoid a confrontation with the Confederacy over the granting of an exequatur, he quickly appointed as acting consul James Magee, a retired businessman of British citizenship. Besides lacking in experience, Magee had strong pro-Southern bias because of his twenty years' residence in Alabama. It was merely a matter of time before Magee embarrassed the British government and fled to England under a cloud of disapprobation.

The consul at New Orleans at the beginning of the war, William Mure, served only until the fall of 1861, when he turned his office over to George Coppell and returned to England because of ill health. After a brief confrontation with General Benjamin Butler following the capture of New Orleans, Coppell's responsibilities reverted to a peacetime pattern. Occasionally British citizens crossed the military lines from the Confederacy and reported the suffering of other Englishmen, but Coppell could do little but pass this information on to the legation.

Consul Arthur T. Lynn at Galveston never dealt directly with the Confederate government; it seemed unaware of his presence. Lynn at times had to confront state authorities, especially with regard to the induction of British nationals into the Texas militia, but his reports to the legation and the Foreign Office imply only mild protests. His lack of forcefulness in protecting his fellow citizens may have been due to his isolation, or it may be that Union Admiral David Farragut's assertion that Lynn, although a British citizen, was "openly avowed as a notorious rebel" had some basis in fact.[12]

The major question confronting the Southern consuls at the beginning of the war was its possible impact on their occupations. On the eve of South Carolina's secession, Bunch asked Lyons: "What is my position?" Did his exequatur from the president of the United States give him the right to remain in the state once it seceded? If war broke out and he withdrew, to whom could British citizens appeal if their rights were violated or their property destroyed? Caught up in the wartime fervor being exhibited by Charlestonians themselves, Bunch even suggested stationing a British warship in the harbor to evacuate British nationals if such action became necessary.[13]

In grappling with these issues, both the legation and the Foreign Office recommended caution and rejected the suggestion about warships in Charleston harbor. If hostilities broke out and the ships were fired upon, the results could be disastrous. Still, as Lyons pointed out, "I think the English [government] will find it necessary to . . . hold unofficial communications with the Southern Government on matters concerning the interests of their subjects. . . . It is a preposterous pretension to exclude Foreign Governments from intercourse with the authorities however illegitimate [when] their Subjects must in fact look for protection." In London the question was important enough to be referred to the prime minister, and he advised the consuls to remain and await action on the part of the Southerners themselves.[14]

In the end Jefferson Davis, newly elected president of the Confederacy, solved the problem by not making it an issue; he permitted foreign consuls to remain. The Confederate State Department did not question the exequaturs issued by the United States government before 1861, nor did it insist upon issuing its own. Davis's decision did not please a large segment of the Southern public, but Lyons found it acceptable. He even recommended the Southern consuls be instructed to communicate only with the Foreign Office and to give the impression that the legation had no authority over them.[15]

Davis's decision was influenced by the necessity of having a

British Consuls and Consulates during the Civil War

Individual	Title	Consulate
Edward Archibald	Consul	New York City
Frederick Bernal	Consul	Baltimore
William Booker	Consul	San Francisco
Robert Bunch	Consul (1860-61)	Charleston
George Coppell	Acting Consul (1861-65)	New Orleans
Frederick Cridland	Vice-Consul (1860-63)	Richmond
	Acting Consul	Mobile
	(May-June 1863)	
Denis Donohoe	Consul	Buffalo
Pierrepont Edwards	Vice-Consul	New York City
Allan Fullarton	Acting Consul (1862-63)	Savannah
Charles Kortwright	Consul	Philadelphia
Charles Labuzan	Acting Consul (1860-61)	Mobile
Francis Lousada	Consul	Boston
Arthur Lynn	Consul	Galveston
James Magee	Acting Consul (1861-63)	Mobile
Edmund Molyneux	Consul (1860-62)	Savannah
George Moore	Consul (1860-63)	Richmond
William Mure	Consul (1860-61)	New Orleans
John Murray	Consul	Portland, Maine
Wm. Tasker Smith	Consul (1865)	Savannah
Charles Tulin	Acting Consul (1860)	Mobile
H. Pinckney Walker	Acting Consul (1861-63)	Charleston
John E. Wilkins	Consul	Chicago (St. Louis after 1861)

* Dates given if tenure was less than entire war period

communication link with the foreign powers. Until diplomatic recognition was achieved, the consuls were the only source of information on England's attitude, and they might even influence opinion in the Foreign Office. Indeed, secessionists had attempted to gauge British sentiment through the consuls even before the Confederate government became a reality. The first such effort occurred as early as 1856. On the eve of that year's presidential election, several Southern congressmen indicated to George James, then consul for Virginia, that a Republican victory might well precipitate a Southern independence movement, and they stressed the advantages such a move could have for England. The conversation seems to have gone no further. James reported it to the Foreign Office, but there is no record of its reaction.[16]

The second approach came on the eve of the 1860 presidential contest when Consul Archibald in New York City received a letter from "Benjamin" requesting his cooperation in a plan to separate the slave states from the Union upon Lincoln's election, "which is almost certain." "Benjamin" requested an introduction to "Her Majesty's Ministers at Washington City, with a view to the accomplishment of this great end." Britain's reward for supporting the South, wrote "Benjamin," would be a *"return to our allegiance with Great Britain, our mother country!!!"* "Benjamin" sent the letter by courier because, as he explained, he was a native Southerner and a former congressman and revealing his true identity might be dangerous. Because of this statement and the signature on the letter, Judah P. Benjamin, senator from Louisiana at the time, was accused of being its author, but he vigorously denied the accusation. The true author never revealed himself, but it probably was not Benjamin. Why would a United States senator seek an introduction to the British minister through a consul in New York City when he could make it as easily, and less obtrusively, at a Washington social gathering?

Given the circumstances of its delivery and the author's desire to remain anonymous, Archibald thought the letter might be a prank, but he decided to respond, telling "Benjamin" that he had no interest in the scheme and would report him to Federal authorities if he knew his identity. Archibald then informed his own government of the affair.[17]

Two more attempts to gauge British opinion through the consuls were made following Lincoln's election in 1860. Consul Mure at New Orleans wrote of being approached by "several gentlemen" who promised reduced tariffs and a monopoly over the entire coastal trade from Virginia to Texas if Britain revealed "sympathy" for the Southern move toward independence.[18] But the Foreign Office took more seriously the overtures made by Robert Barnwell Rhett, editor of the Charleston *Mercury* and leading fire-eater in South Carolina. Through Bunch's previous correspondence, Russell was aware that Rhett spoke for the leaders of the secession movement. The fire-eater asked Bunch directly what Britain's attitude toward a Southern confederacy might be. Not only did Southern hopes center on England, declared Rhett, but a separate Southern nation had much to offer: free trade, minimal or no import duties, and a market for English manufactured goods and shipping. In reporting the "pow-wow," as he called it, Bunch claimed he "declined giving any opinions beyond the vaguest generalities," but he certainly was not as firm as Archibald had been with "Benjamin." According to his own report, Bunch told Rhett that the only "stumbling block would be the reopening of the [African] slave trade," an idea then being pushed by more fanatical Southerners. Bunch thought slavery itself would not preclude British support, but "I spoke for myself not the Government." Taken aback by Bunch's remarks about the slave trade, Rhett threatened to seek out the opinion of the French consul, whereupon Bunch reminded him that all European nations were intent on suppressing the slave trade. Still, Bunch's equivocal statements about slavery left Rhett with "the distinct impression that Great Britain could be persuaded to recognize the independence of the Confederacy, if it were offered attractive inducements." Some historians have concluded, moreover, that Bunch's remarks about the slave trade influenced the Confederate government to outlaw the practice in its constitution, written two months later.[19]

Britain's reasons for wanting to keep the consuls in the Confederacy were just as strong as Davis's for allowing them to remain: the consuls served as the major source of information about local events and attitudes. While the Foreign Office desired information about the entire country, its chief concern lay with the South. "You should address an instruction to all H.M.'s Consuls at the Southern ports pointing out the importance of accurate and complete information being furnished by them," Prime Minister Henry Palmerston instructed Lyons following the first battle of Bull Run.[20]

The best source of information about Southern events was Robert Bunch at Charleston. Even Lyons deferred to Bunch's ability in this respect: "Mr. Bunch is in a better situation than I am for obtaining accurate intelligence respecting these details. He is also in a better position for estimating their effect in the South, which is the principal point of importance with regard to them." By April 1861, Lyons exhorted Bunch "not to scrimp in getting the news to me" and to use the telegraph or private messenger if necessary.[21]

Bunch's assessments were both accurate and penetrating. Even before secession occurred, he predicted that South Carolina had no other choice but to leave the Union: "It is difficult to see how any truce is to be expected. The time for compromise or intervention would seem to have gone by, and it would appear certain that South Carolina must either secede at all hazards . . . or be content to exhibit herself to the ridicule of the world."[22]

Bunch's reports became more pessimistic as the war continued. Though he saw potential victory for the South in 1861, he began to realize by mid-1862 that the Confederacy had overextended itself and lacked the resources to carry the war to a victorious conclusion. He was especially concerned about the anti-British attitudes expressed in Southern newspapers and by the general population and warned the Foreign Office not to accept at face value pro-British expressions made by Southern advocates in England. His opinions on Southern leadership also changed as the war went on. In the beginning he wrote almost in jest: "they have an uncommonly good opinion of themselves," but he was soon referring to Confederate leaders as "dead level mediocrity" incapable of understanding any point view except their own.[23]

Other consuls in the South supported Bunch's assessments. Molyneux in Savannah and Mure in New Orleans both reported that conservative elements felt secession was too rash an act but were being silenced because "excitement is so great, passions so bitter." Like Bunch they regarded Southern leaders as lacking in tact and ability. Molyneux, although somewhat sympathetic to the South because of his long residence in

Georgia, confided to Russell that Robert Toombs, Davis's first secretary of state, "talks too much" for the sensitive position he held. Regarding Davis himself, Mure classified him as "an ultra . . . of the South Carolina School, and most of the thinking people would have preferred to see Mr. [Alexander] Stephens in his place."[24]

Northern consuls, too, kept the Foreign Office informed of significant events in the Union. Generally pro-Union in their attitude, they emphasized the material advantages of the North, its population growth and industrial advance even under the stress of war. Charles Kortright, consul at Philadelphia, predicted one major consequence of the war would be the emergence of the North as an industrial power and wondered why the South "entered into this struggle in which it has so much to lose and so little to gain."

Pro-Union attitudes of Northern consuls made it possible for them to reach easier solutions to problems encountered with Northern authorities. In 1862 Lyons informed Russell that Consul Wilkins, now stationed in St. Louis, had little difficulty keeping British citizens from being drafted into the Union army or in gaining the return of their property. United States military authorities in the western theater were well aware of his pro-Union attitude and seldom questioned the cases he brought before them.[25]

With the secession of South Carolina, the Foreign Office became concerned about the outbreak of war, and it was consuls Bunch and Archibald who kept London apprised of events that led to the surrender of Fort Sumter and the start of the struggle. Writing at the turn of the new year in 1861, Bunch informed his superiors about Major Robert Anderson's decision to transfer his troops from Fort Moultrie to Sumter. The move was totally unexpected, but it encouraged South Carolinians to seize Moultrie and the customs house. Not only that, Bunch concluded, but "publick excitement" was being kept alive by continual talk of bloodshed "and reasonable consels [sic] are entirely disregarded."[26]

Archibald kept the Foreign Office aware of preparations for the Sumter expedition at the Brooklyn Navy Yard, and he even sent a "confidential agent" to get more information from military personnel and workers stationed there.[27] Once Fort Sumter surrendered, Archibald sent a full report to London. Normally the foreign minister would have supplied this information, but Lyons was unable to get any correspondence out of Washington because Maryland secessionists had cut all communications between the capital and cities to the north.

Archibald was aware that he was usurping a legation function, and he even held the mail packet an extra day, hoping Lyons's report would arrive. But finally he decided that the news of Sumter's surrender was too important to delay. Thus it was through a consul that the Foreign Office learned about the surrender of Sumter even before official word arrived from the United States.[28]

Consuls also kept the Foreign Office apprised of the South's voluntary cotton embargo at the beginning of the war. Many Southerners believed that Europe's need for cotton, particularly England's, would force the powers to recognize the Confederacy and break the Union blockade to obtain the fiber. As early as December 1860, Bunch wrote from Charleston: the Confederacy's "great aim is to be recognized by Great Britain. They try to bluster about England wanting cotton and being obliged to get it from them. . . . It actually amounts to the belief . . . that to withdraw the supply of cotton for one year, would alter the whole condition of [England's] existence." Echoing Bunch's concern, Russell the journalist commented during his visit to Charleston: "The doctrine of 'cotton is king,' to them is a lively all powerful faith. . . . Here were these Southern gentlemen exulting in their power to control the policy of Great Britain, and it was small consolation to me to assure them they were mistaken."[29]

Given this Southern confidence in the power of cotton to sway English opinion in their favor, local and state politicians encouraged a self-imposed embargo in 1861, perhaps under the belief that England would blame their inability to get cotton on the Union blockade. Unfortunately for the Confederacy, the consuls kept the Foreign Office aware that the Union blockade in 1861 was having little impact on cotton exports. They agreed it was too ineffective to prevent some trade. Only at the mouth of the Mississippi River, wrote Consul Mure, was the blockade being rigidly enforced; other ports were relatively open. Even as late as July 1861, three months after the blockade had been proclaimed, the consul at Mobile noted that Union warships appeared only occasionally off Mobile Bay, and merchant and passenger ships freely left the bay to use the intracoastal waterway between Mobile and New Orleans. Reports elsewhere were similar. From Bunch at Charleston and Fullarton at Savannah came word that coastal shipping continued unabated and that the blockade of major ports was sporadic. Informing Foreign Secretary Russell of the Union occupation of Cape Hatteras in August 1861, Bunch assumed it might enable the Federals to make the blockade more effective.[30]

Europe failed to receive cotton, the consuls maintained, because of the self-imposed embargo and not the blockade. Ships could get through, Bunch informed Russell, but Southerners were not permitting the shipment of cotton. Charlestonians were pressuring shippers to keep it at home, and a "Committee of Safety" in Wilmington, North Carolina, was using force to prevent the loading of cotton on vessels. "The action of these citizens is suicidal," Bunch concluded, and "an inglorious retreat from [Southern] promises of free and unencumbered intercourse."[31]

Bunch was unsure where the blame for the embargo lay, but he assumed that Judah P. Benjamin, then Confederate attorney general, had devised the scheme and implemented it despite the opposition of other presidential advisers. Vice-Consul Cridland at Richmond also suspected Benjamin. At least, Benjamin had cheerfully told him about the burning of one million bales of cotton in the Mississippi Valley. It is doubtful that the Foreign Office placed blame solely on Benjamin; all the consuls in the South, including Arthur Lynn in Texas, reported massive destruction of cotton. Still, the consuls' comments about Benjamin indicated a critical attitude toward him that intensified as the war continued.[32]

If Southerners hoped Britain would interfere in the war to obtain cotton, some members of the British cabinet feared it might be forced to interfere if a slave insurrection broke out.

Indeed, influential newspaper editors in England and even

the chargé d'affaires in Washington insisted that Lincoln's purpose in issuing the Emancipation Proclamation was to encourage a slave insurrection: he hoped to achieve through a slave uprising what his armies were incapable of accomplishing in the field. Again, consular reports assured officials that an insurrection was unlikely. "No one [in South Carolina]," Bunch reported, "seems to contemplate that the Proclamation of Mr. Lincoln will produce any effect upon the Negro population. . . . The Document has been fully published, and doubtless circulated among the slaves, who are fully alive to all that is going on." Vice-Consul Cridland in Richmond, closer to the Union army than the other consuls, made the most perceptive comment. The slave insurrection had started almost as soon as the war began, he declared, and consisted of fleeing to Union troops. Most slaves had little interest in seeking vengeance on their masters when freedom was so near. "I don't think there will be insurrection among blacks," he concluded.[33]

Consul Archibald's office became the chief civilian source of information on military events. Great Britain and other European powers sent military personnel to observe technical aspects of the warfare, but Archibald regularly forwarded copies of New York newspapers, which contained detailed descriptions of battles. Occasionally other consuls sent newspaper accounts, but only Henry Pinckney Walker, Bunch's replacement in Charleston after 1863, described his personal impressions. As an eyewitness to the shelling of Charleston and its later capture by Union troops, Walker was in an excellent position to relay details of the devastation of war.[34]

In sum, the consuls fulfilled many different functions for the British government during the war. In addition to carrying on the normal consular duties, they took on extra burdens produced by the wartime situation. Throughout the war they provided valuable information about the Confederacy and the Union, keeping their home government informed of domestic and military events across the ocean.

3

The Foreign Minister

Lord Lyons—Richard Bickerton Pemell, second Baron Lyons and first Viscount and Earl Lyons—served as British minister to the United States during the Civil War. His father, Edmund, first Baron Lyons, had been elevated to the peerage as a reward for long service in the Royal Navy and at various diplomatic posts in Europe. Like many British aristocrats in the nineteenth century, the first Lord Lyons arranged celebrated marriages for his daughters and prepared his sons for service to their country. The elder daughter married a German baron and the younger, Minna, the Duke of Norfolk. The younger son, Edmund, entered the Royal Naval College and rose to the rank of captain in the Royal Navy before he met his death before Sevastopol in 1855. The father also planned a naval career for Richard, but the young man found military service unsuitable. After serving as midshipman on his father's ship, Richard entered Oxford where he earned an M.A. before joining the diplomatic corps.[1]

Lyons began his diplomatic career in 1839 as unpaid attaché under his father's tutelage in the legation at Athens, a post he held for thirteen years. After his father became minister to Switzerland, Lyons served as attaché at various posts in the Germanies and in Florence, Italy. He moved into higher echelons of the service in 1856 with his appointment as envoy to the Duchy of Tuscany. Two years later, at the age of forty-two, he succeeded to the peerage upon his father's death and soon after was named minister to the United States.[2]

Naturally reticent, Lyons's reserve caused him to be regarded as arrogant by some Americans, taciturn by others. Perhaps because he had served in his father's shadow for so many years, he was more inclined to listen than to speak. Even during the Civil War, Edward Bates, Lincoln's attorney gener-

al, continued to refer to Lyons as the "Admiral's son." Lyons
expressed himself freely to John Russell, foreign secretary in
London, on matters involving diplomacy and to his sister Minna on social affairs, but even then he seldom elaborated. He
was a compulsive worker, fastidious about his health, and a
worrywart. Often Russell found it necessary to caution Lyons
about hypothetical situations he raised. After Lincoln issued
his blockade proclamation in April 1861, for example, Lyons
fretted the fate of British merchant ships that might be unaware of the proclamation and sail into Southern ports. He
seemed mollified only when Russell assured him the Foreign
Office would handle such matters when they occurred.[3]

Perhaps Lyons's reserve was due, in part, to his reluctant
acceptance by the Buchanan administration and the fact that
he never grew to appreciate Washington during his six years
there. President James Buchanan considered Lyons's appointment something of an affront because of the new minister's lack
of experience. As former American minister to the Court of St.
James, Buchanan was aware of Lyons's low ranking as a diplomatic officer, and he felt that Britain should send a more expe-
rienced and distinguished individual to represent its interests.
The British mission in the United States, he wrote, "ought always to be filled by a first rate man whose character is known in
this country and whose acts and opinions will command respect
and influence in England."[4] If Buchanan did not regard Lyons
as "first rate," the feeling was reciprocal. Writing to Minna
upon the departure of the Buchanan administration from the
capital, Lyons could only comment, "I shall miss Miss [Harriet]
Lane, [Buchanan's niece and hostess] very much. [She] did
wonders towards making that House pleasant."[5]

Regarding Washington itself, Lyons found the city "hot and
dull," and he made continual references to "the heat of the
place." Given his tendency to put work before pleasure in addition to the fact that he and every staff member at the legation
was a bachelor, Lyons seldom entertained on a large scale.
Unlike his immediate predecessor, Lyons did not admire the
Southern-oriented society of Buchanan's Washington and preferred small dinner parties with only the legation staff and sev-

eral guests present. Charles Sumner, a leading abolitionist and chairman of the Senate Foreign Relations Committee during the war, was a frequent dinner guest at the legation. Commenting on the social scene in the capital, Lyons wrote: "This is the gay season here; the consequence to me is that I have sometimes to dine out. The dinners are interminable in length, miserable in quality and not often amusing in the way of society. I have a large one at home tomorrow, but here at least the eating and drinking parts are excellent."[6]

Following the Union defeat at Bull Run in 1861, when rumor of a possible Confederate invasion of Washington ran rampant, he informed Minna, "It is not likely to make much difference to me whether the Southerners get here or not. I should have to go if they did, but that might be rather agreeable." When Prince Albert died in December 1861, Lyons confided that he was refusing all invitations to dinners or parties out of respect for the Prince Regent, and "this has been no sacrifice as you may suppose."[7]

William Stuart was Lyons's secretary of legation. Although somewhat excitable and more sympathetic toward the South than Lyons, Stuart had the ability to assume sole responsibility for the legation and to serve as chargé d'affaires in Lyons's absence. Stuart had previously been secretary of legation in Brazil, Sicily, and Greece, and had a complete familiarity with diplomatic procedure. He arrived in Washington just as the war broke out in 1861 and would remain until mid-1864, when he was transferred to Constantinople.[8]

Lyons and Stuart were assisted by a small number of attachés, who served as secretaries or as copiers of documents. That their work became overwhelming is seen in Lyons's constant pleas for additional personnel and a description of their work day:

During the Civil War we had to be in the Chancery at nine—there was no time for luncheon, a few sandwiches were brought to us on a tray, which we mopped down with lemonade. At a quarter past seven we ran to Willard's Hotel and swallowed a cocktail, harking back just in time for dinner at eight. This was the regular routine, and it constantly happened that, in addition, we had to go back to the Chancery at night and work till twelve or one in the morning. Any quantity of letters arrived daily asking every imaginable question, and often making untenable complaints. They were all opened by Lord Lyons, who made a pencil note upon them indicating the tenor of the answer to be sent, and returned them to the Chancery. Draft answers were then written, which were again sent up to Lord Lyons with the letters. He would nearly always alter the wording. Then he put an "L" at the bottom, and returned them to be written out for signature. In this way not a letter issued from the Legation which had not been approved by the chief. It was a most valuable safeguard, for you can never be sure what a young man may say when he gets a pen into his hand.[9]

There is no record of correspondence to and from the legation for the entire the war period, but in 1864 alone Lyons received 6,490 pieces of correspondence and sent out 8,326 communications—or 14,816 total. Half of these dispatches, 7,143 pieces, consisted of correspondence to or from the U.S. State Department or the British consuls.[10]

Lyons's responsibilities included supervising the consuls, and he was painstakingly precise. His communiqués were detailed and left no doubt about the action he wished taken. Indeed, at war's end Consul Archibald criticized Lyons's replacement: his instructions were little more than informal notes and left many questions unanswered.[11]

In return, the consuls' relationship with their chief was correct and formal. Among the Southern consuls, only Robert Bunch seemed to break through the barrier of formality. On February 14, 1861, Bunch began a letter, "I do not write this for the purpose of requesting your Lordship to accept me as your Valentine. . . ." A month later he relayed the boast of a Charleston doctor regarding Anthony Copeland, a black man executed for participating in John Brown's raid on Harpers Ferry. The doctor claimed that he had severed the dead man's penis and sent it to a Northern abolitionist. Given Lyons's reserve and sense of propriety, Bunch must have felt confident in his association with his lordship to repeat the story.[12]

Lyons's attitude toward Bunch, in turn, was almost paternal. When Bunch remained in Charleston during the summer of 1861 to gain Southern consent to the Declaration of Paris,

Lyons insisted the consul should receive extra compensation. After he learned that Bunch's stay would cost the consul his life insurance policy, which required him to leave Charleston during the summer months, Lyons requested from the insurance agent a temporary suspension of the policy and its reactivation in the fall. No other Southern consul received such personal attention. Informed that Molyneux had managed a number of affairs in Savannah satisfactorily, Lyons attributed the consul's success to "his large fortune and his established position in Georgia."[13]

Among the Northern consuls, Lyons found Archibald at New York City to be "a valuable public servant" yet issued occasional "mild reproofs" to him for suggesting policy. Archibald made no secret of his pro-Union leanings, and frequently offered unsolicited advice to both Russell and Lyons. For example, in May 1861, Archibald wrote: "The Southern insurrection, is regarded purely as a rebellion, and it is considered an unfriendly act on the part of the Governments of the nations not to regard it in the same light." He continued, saying the war was not "one of vengeance on the South. . . . the maintenance of the Union and of the National Constitution is, I truly believe, the predominant motive which influences the course of action." Reacting to calls in Parliament to debate the issue of recognition, Archibald cautioned the Foreign Office in 1862 to retain its policy of strict neutrality. Neither recognition of the Confederacy nor an offer of mediation between the belligerents would be well-regarded by the North and "might embroil this country in a war with England." While the letter made some impression on Russell, Lyons did not appreciate such comments. In response to one of them, he wrote: "You usually end your letters with suggestions about what I should do. Since I cannot always follow your suggestions or don't agree with them, please stop doing this."[14]

Lyons's most trying time with the Northern consuls came at the beginning of the war. Shortly after the surrender of Fort Sumter, Governor John Andrew of Massachusetts requested from Consul Lousada at Boston the names of arms merchants in Canada. Lousada referred him to Sir Edmund Head, governor general of the provinces, who began to receive inquiries about the purchase of arms from other Northern governors as well. Head turned the requests over to Lyons because, in addition to its other duties, the legation in Washington was also responsible for British North America's relations with foreign nations. Immediately Lyons informed the consuls to discourage the idea of arms purchases and to maintain an attitude of strict neutrality. To Lousada he wrote a special plea: "I beg you to bear constantly in mind that Her Majesty's Government have not authorized . . . Diplomatic or Consular Servants in this country to take part in the unhappy dissension. You will conform to these views & language unless you receive contrary instructions." When Consul Donohoe at Buffalo failed to respond to Lyons's instructions over the matter, the minister inquired about his leanings in the conflict and his trustworthiness.[15]

Lyons demanded that public statements by the consuls and the legation staff about the sectional conflict be totally impartial, and he adopted the same objective stance for himself. As early as December 1860, on the eve the South Carolina secession convention, Lyons cautioned Lord Russell: "We should if [at] all possible give every impression of not wanting to become involved in this quarrel." Even after the fighting between North and South began, Lyons reported: "I have not expressed any opinion on the current crisis [and] have attempted to remain on easy terms with government officials."[16]

Lyons's insistence on impartiality was dictated by his fear that Britain might be dragged into war if too much favoritism was indicated toward either the North or the South. To Foreign Secretary Russell, he wrote: "My own opinion is that any interference in the quarrel . . . would only bring upon the hatred of both." When the British Cabinet was considering Napoleon III's proposal of mediation in November 1862—a step the British had considered earlier—Lyons responded: "I certainly desire that the settlement of the contest be made without the intervention of England . . . the less conspicuous the part she plays, the more quickly will [Northern] irritation [with us] subside." Strengthening his point, he then referred to increasing British fears about American interest in Canada: "it must be remembered, too, that if the war with the South last any considerable time, the United States may find themselves at the close of it with a numerous, and probably not inefficient, army, ready and eager for an invasion of British North America."[17]

His public expressions of impartiality aside, Lyons's private sympathy lay with the Union. This was so evident to Russell the journalist that he wrote: "There is no minister of the European Powers . . . who feels as much sympathy perhaps in the Federal Government." And Lyons wrote to Minna, "I am really grieved to see these people bent upon cutting each other's throats." Lyons's pro-Union attitude was apparent even before secession occurred. The Southern states, he surmised, were merely using Lincoln's election as an excuse to leave the Union, an idea that the more radical element had advocated for "the avowed principle of perpetuating, if not extending, Slavery."[18]

Lyons's intense dislike of slavery made it difficult for him to conceive of supporting the Southern cause. "The taint of Slavery will render the cause of the South loathsome to the civilized world," he declared. Responding to Consul Bunch's report of his interview with Robert Barnwell Rhett in December 1860, Lyons wrote: "The domestic Slavery of the South is a bitter pill which it will be hard enough to get the English to swallow. But if the [international] Slave Trade is to be added to the dose, the least squeamish British stomach will reject it." Nor did he criticize the South alone on the slavery issue. "The Northern States [were as much to blame] for the turn of events, for [they] are quite ready to yield on everything except the *extension* of Slavery." Still, he concluded, "the sympathies of an Englishman are naturally inclined toward the North. . . . If I had the least hope of their being able to reconstruct the Union, my feeling against Slavery might lead me to desire to co-operate with them."[19]

Given Lyons's disdain for slavery, the high point of his diplomatic career, for him, came with British-American cooperation in suppressing the international slave trade. Since the end of the Napoleonic Wars in 1815, Great Britain had signed treaties with European nations giving it the right to search ships along the African coast if it suspected they were engaging in slave traffic. The United States, however, refused to sign such a treaty. Although Americans patrolled the coast of Africa on their own, the issue remained a sore point because slave traders used American flags to elude visit and search by British officials. With the outbreak of the Civil War and the departure of the Southern states from Congress, the Senate approved a convention with Britain giving the right of mutual search and establishing courts for the punishment of offenders. Seward and Lyons signed the treaty on April 7, 1862, and it was ratified in London several months later. In transmitting the document to the Foreign Office, Lyons indicated his pride in the achievement by writing: "Yesterday was the anniversary of my arrival three years ago at Washington. Weary years they have been in many respects. But if I am as fortunate in obtaining your approbation for this last proceeding as I have on former occasions, I should be very ungenious [ungenerous?] and ungrateful to grumble about the arrogance and disagreeableness of the post." [20]

Lyons's antislavery attitude and his private inclination to side with the Union influenced his relationship and cooperation with Henri Mercier, the French foreign minister. Personal acquaintances ever since they had served at their respective legations in Saxony in the 1850s, Lyons and Mercier presented a united front at the State Department in the early months of the war. Mainly they defended their nations' positions of neutrality and their right to communicate with the Confederate government through the consuls. But Mercier's sympathy for the South was stronger than Lyons perhaps realized, and he soon found himself acting as a brake on his French colleague. In March 1861, soon after Lincoln's inauguration, Mercier asked Lyons to sign a letter to their respective governments suggesting diplomatic recognition of the South. His argument focused on France's need for cotton, but he added that recognition before hostilities broke out might ease the severity of the fighting or cause the Union to accept Confederate independence. Ever cautious, Lyons refused because he considered recognition at this time to be premature and beyond the scope of a minister's duty to recommend. Two months later, in May, Mercier suggested another joint statement, declaring that England and France would not observe the blockade after September 1861. Such a statement, Lyons responded, was inconsistent with the policy of neutrality and "not within the province of ministers to discuss."[21]

Mercier continued to press, however. In April of 1862, as General McClellan was beginning the peninsular campaign, Mercier requested permission to visit Richmond. In the hope that he would "see now that the insurrection is shrinking and shrivelling," Seward encouraged Lincoln to grant permission. But events on the peninsula and his talks with Confederate officials, many of whom had been friends during the Buchanan administration, convinced Mercier of the South's invincibility, and he returned to Washington persuaded that only mediation would end the conflict. Lyons took leave for health reasons shortly after Mercier returned; he sailed to England where he remained from June until November 1862. By the time he arrived back in Washington, Napoleon III was making overtures to England and Russia about joint mediation, and Mercier again urged the idea on Lyons. Based on his previous conversations with Seward, Lyons became convinced that the United States would never accept mediation and opposed any interference by Britain. After the British cabinet rejected Napoleon III's proposal, Lyons began to distance himself from his French colleague.[22]

While Lyons sympathized privately with the Union cause, he found much to criticize about American society and leadership. Like most upper class Englishmen, he thought Americans were too materialistic and placed too much confidence in their government.[23] And the reason for the nation's problems, he concluded, were the politicians' failure to respond to Southern secession. Lyons squarely placed the blame on Buchanan: his statements were equivocal, his actions to stem the tide of secession ineffective, and he shunned all responsibility by turning the matter over to a Congress that was incapable of dealing with the situation.[24]

But if Buchanan failed to measure up to Lyons's standard, "President Lincoln looming in the distance [was] a still greater peril." Lyons regarded him as a rude political unknown who "has not hitherto given proof of possessing any natural talents to compensate for his ignorance of everything but Illinois village politics." The incoming president might "be well-meaning & conscientious . . . but not much more." Lyons characterized Lincoln's inaugural address as disappointing because it lacked a clear statement of his intentions. At least, he added, Lincoln "does not declare as Mr. Buchanan did that the Government has absolutely no right to use force to bring a state back into the Union." In the month between the inauguration and the firing on Fort Sumter, Lyons surmised that "the President and his cabinet have determined no policy toward the South. *The policy, if there is one, seems to be of inaction.*"[25]

On the president personally, Lyons, in 1861, made only one comment: "I dined in company with him the day before yesterday. He is a little uncouth but mild and quiet. I don't perceive the shades of difference in American manners as they do themselves." Whether the minister's opinion of Lincoln improved in succeeding years remains unknown. He almost never mentioned the president in official or personal correspondence, nor did he mention any personal contact other than state dinners or formal receptions. Following Lincoln's assassination, Senator Charles Sumner told John Bright, the English reformer, that Lincoln seldom spoke of personal antagonisms, but on one occasion did express an extreme dislike for Lord John Russell. If the statement is correct, Lincoln may well have avoided contact with Lyons, Russell's agent in the United States.[26]

Lincoln's major failure as president, according to Lyons, was his lack of experience in foreign affairs and his appointment of William H. Seward as secretary of state. Seward would eventually gain Lyons's confidence, but in the early months of the war, Lyons considered Seward too aggressive in his dealings with foreign representatives and too confident in his own ability to find a solution to the national crisis. Seward's tendency to "bluster and bluff" caused Lyons to write: "It is a great inconvenience to have him as the organ of communication from the Un.[*sic*] S. Government." In addition to directing the nation's foreign policy, Seward believed he was going to establish all the policies of the Lincoln administration. And, concluded Lyons, in his "unbounded confidence in his own skill in managing the American people [Seward] is apt to announce as the fixed intentions of his Government what is in reality no more than a measure which he himself supports."[27]

Mainly, Lyons feared Seward's intentions toward Canada—that he might purposely engage in war to acquire the provinces. Although Lyons could at times write: "I do not think Mr. Seward would contemplate actually going to war with us . . . ," he was alarmed by Seward's boast of using a foreign war to reunite the country. He also recalled Seward's statements, made during the presidential campaign of 1860, about seizing British North America to compensate the nation for its losses should the slave states secede. Then, in June 1861, shortly after Britain declared neutrality in the crisis and Seward appeared most belligerent, Lyons received a disturbing communiqué that seemed to confirm his suspicions. Archibald had heard of a plot, supposedly formulated by Seward, to purchase a number of newspapers in Canada East (present-day Quebec Province) for the purpose of agitating a union with the United States. Informing the Foreign Office and the governor general of Canada about Archibald's letter, Lyons declared such a scheme "improbable"; still, he urged improving Canadian defenses to discourage the Americans.[28]

Lyons also was concerned that Seward might seek war to reunite the nation and to bolster his own declining popularity. He was probably unaware of Seward's "Thought for the President's Consideration," written to Lincoln on April 1, 1861, which suggested a foreign conflict as a means of encouraging the seceded states to return to the Union.[29] Still, Seward's bellicose statements, his seeming unconcern about the gravity of the secession crisis, his misstatements about widespread unionism in the South, and his lack of consistency had lost him the confidence of his party, claimed Lyons, and he was not above using foreign policy to rebuild his political popularity. "This," Lyons concluded, "is no new course of policy with Mr. Seward. He has ever regarded the Foreign Relations of the country as safe material from which to make, to use his own phrase: political capital at home." That Seward's actions and statements were often intended to appeal to public opinion, Lyons was well aware; still, he wrote, it was "a mode of reasoning, which I confess [surpasses] my diplomacy to understand." Undoubtedly, Lyons's alarmist correspondence distressed his superiors at home. Prime Minister Palmerston assured Lyons of Britain's firmness in any crisis, but he did not believe the American would pick a foreign quarrel. Lending his support to Palmerston's statement, Russell added that "Seward [would not] indulge the insolence of his nature and nation."[30]

Seward's behavior toward the British foreign minister became more conciliatory following the *Peerless* affair. Summoning Lyons to the State Department, Seward informed him that the *Peerless*, a ship with British registry but believed to have been recently purchased by Confederates, was about to leave its Canadian port and become a privateer on the high seas, and he demanded that Lyons order British authorities in Canada to impound the ship. Lyons refused. The ship's papers were in order, he declared, and there was no proof that she was about to engage in unlawful activities. Seward thereupon threatened to seize the ship once it reached the high seas, no matter what flag it was flying and no matter what its papers indicated. Bluster may have helped in this case, for the *Peerless* did not leave port, but Lyons was still "grieved at the arrogant spirit and disregard of the rights and feelings to Foreign Nations with which the American Government seemed to be disposed to conduct the Civil War in which they were about to engage." But the final humiliation fell to Seward when he learned that Federal agents, not Confederates, had purchased the ship. In his embarrassment he soon began to make a special effort to gain Lyons's friendship. Aware of the foreign minister's dislike for large social gatherings, Seward often invited him to dinners where the only other people present were members of the secretary's family.[31]

Lyons's anxiety about Seward remained strong during 1861, and perhaps he continued to be wary of him for the rest the war. Even as late as 1863, when rumor again surfaced about possible British recognition of the Confederacy, Lyons wrote of Seward's strong language. This time Russell assured the minister: "I don't think Seward means to quarrel with us, but perhaps he will bluster rather more when he has lost the support of Congress. . . . We have no thought of recognizing at present."[32]

Lyons began to note a change in Seward's behavior during June 1861. Reporting a conversation on June 17 between himself, Mercier, and Seward about the British and French neutrality proclamations, Lyons concluded: "Mr. Seward's language and demeanour throughout the interview were calm, friendly, and good-humoured." One month later, on July 20, Seward requested that Lyons pay a visit to the State Department for a "private" talk concerning the closing of Southern ports. "No bluster, no bossing," Lyons reported. "He just wanted to know my opinion." Then again on August 1, Seward called Lyons to the department to discuss the closing of the ports, and this time he seemed almost apologetic that the action had been taken.[33]

Not only did Seward's relations with Lyons become more agreeable, but the secretary may have been engaging in a deliberate policy of separating the British and French foreign ministers. Lyons's correspondence intimates that he and Mercier had always confronted Seward together before the solo visit in July. In late July and early August 1861 Mercier was escorting the Emperor's cousin, Prince Napoleon, on his travels throughout the country. If Lyons placed any significance in Mercier's absence, he failed to mention it in his accounts to the Foreign Office.

After Seward adopted a more conciliatory tone, Lyons began to find their relationship easier, and by war's end the two men would show genuine appreciation for each other. Following the settlement of the *Trent* affair in late 1861, Seward gave permission for British troops, unable to reach their Canadian destination because of ice on the St. Lawrence River, to cross through Maine. Later in the year, when Seward and Lyons worked out the treaty on the slave trade, Lyons reciprocated. He drew up the draft but, to avoid the impression that America was submitting to Britain, he agreed to let it appear as if Seward had initiated the agreement. The terms Seward presented were the same as Lyons's. Then in 1863 Lyons warned Seward of a rumored Confederate plot to release prisoners of war from Johnson's Island in Lake Erie, a warning that may have caused the perpetrators to abandon the scheme.[34] According to Lyons's own statement, it was not unusual for him, while taking his daily walk, to encounter Seward "accidentally," and the secretary often invited Lyons into his carriage to discuss pressing problems. So friendly did the two men become that Secretary of the Navy Gideon Welles characterized Lyons as "cool and sagacious" and claimed he "shapes and directs" American foreign policy. "This is humiliating but true," he wrote. Indeed, Seward's behavior changed so much from his early aggressive attitude that Lyons found "his friendliness has become actually embarrassing."[35]

Some historians mark this change in Seward's attitude as emerging from the *Trent* affair, which made it clear "that there were other roads to gaining diplomatic aims than being bellicose."[36] Yet it began earlier and occurred for several reasons. For one thing, Seward must have become aware that his aggressive tone was having a negative impact on Britain's foreign minister, if not the entire diplomatic corps in the capital. Moreover, individuals outside Washington's diplomatic circle were beginning to complain about Seward's irascibility. Charles Sumner, chairman of the Senate Foreign Relations Committee and a fellow Republican, publicly referred to Seward as a warmonger. Thurlow Weed, Seward's long-time friend and political ally, cautioned the secretary to be less aggressive. Criticism about Seward's undiplomatic demeanor even came from abroad. Edouard Thouvenel, France's foreign secretary, communicated his displeasure with Seward's tone and language to Mercier, and the French minister showed the letter to Seward. For his part, Lyons avoided any personal confrontation with Seward and took pains to hide his disapproval of Seward's manner. Evidently this made an impact, for Seward informed Charles Francis Adams, United States minister to England, that "Lord Lyons, who, although a man of prudent reserve, is, at the same time, entirely truthful."[37]

In addition, the president was taking steps to quiet his secretary. When Seward brought Lincoln a "bold and decisive" response to the British and French proclamations recognizing Southern belligerency in May 1861, Lincoln toned down the communiqué and permitted it to be sent only on the condition that Adams use the message as a guide to lodge his own protest. Lyons reported the incident with a note of satisfaction that Seward was "getting his comeuppance."[38]

Lord Lyons's appointment as foreign minister was fortunate for both the Union and British governments. His dislike of slavery and his reluctance to see Britain become involved in war encouraged him to recommend caution, and delay proved the wisest policy for Britain in the end. Lyons's refusal to be intimidated by Seward earned the secretary's respect. Along with adopting a less aggressive tone, Seward sought a personal rapport with the British diplomat. But other issues would interfere and the rapport Seward hoped for would not be achieved until the settlement of the Bunch affair.

4

The Unwelcome Consul

Abraham Lincoln called for seventy-five thousand troops to put down the rebellion in the Southern states on April 15, 1861. Two days later Jefferson Davis responded with a proclamation offering letters of marque and reprisal to persons who wished to engage in privateering against Northern shipping. Some individuals became privateers, but their activities were an inconsequential aspect of the warfare. England and France refused to allow privateers access to their ports early on, and by 1862 the Union blockade and profits to be realized by blockade running put an end to privateering. Confederate raiders, which plied the high seas from 1862 to 1865, were more destructive to Northern merchant shipping.[1]

Still, Davis's proclamation and fear that Lincoln might also authorize privateering caused consternation in London and Paris.[2] Greedy privateers seldom distinguished between goods belonging to belligerents and neutrals; as a result, British and French shippers faced the possibility of substantial losses. The only solution, Russell informed Lyons, was to gain Union and Confederate consent to the terms of the Declaration of Paris.[3] That agreement, signed by European nations at the end of the Crimean War in 1856, contained four major provisions: it outlawed privateering; declared nonmilitary goods belonging to belligerents exempt from seizure if being transported in ships of neutral nations; declared that nonmilitary property of neutrals was not liable to seizure; and finally stated that blockades were binding only if effectively enforced.[4]

The United States had refused to sign the declaration in 1856, but Seward expressed his willingness to become a signatory in 1861. He was probably only too eager to have the international community recognize Confederate privateers as pirates. The administration considered Southern privateers outlaws and threatened to hang them, but Lincoln backed down after Davis declared he would execute prisoners of war in retaliation.[5] Seward's one stipulation about signing the declaration involved the process of negotiation: he refused to discuss the issue with Lyons and Mercier and insisted that it be negotiated between the American ministers to England and France and the foreign secretaries of those countries. Discussion on the matter went smoothly in England until September 1861, when Russell incorporated a statement into the convention stipulating that American consent to the declaration would have no "bearing, direct or indirect, on the internal difficulties now prevailing in the United States." In recognizing Confederate belligerence the previous May, Russell declared, Britain had accepted the right of the Southern government to commission privateers, and it could not now treat them as pirates. Seward rejected the British qualification, and negotiations broke down. Still, the refusal to become a signatory made little practical difference. The United States had championed the rights of neutrals on the high seas in wartime since 1776, and it observed them during the Civil War.[6]

The European powers sought Confederate consent to the declaration at the same time as they negotiated the issue with the United States. Here, however, they faced several problems. Because of Davis's proclamation authorizing privateering, the best England and France could hope for was the acceptance of articles two, three, and four—those dealing with the shipment of nonmilitary goods and blockades. Since the objective was to protect their own international trade, they considered the limitation a slight matter. More complicated was the issue of how to gain approval from the Davis government without making it appear as if any negotiations had taken place. From the beginning of the war, Seward had warned England and France against communicating with the Confederate government; he considered any diplomatic contact as tantamount to recognition. The seceded states were in rebellion, he maintained; they were not a separate independent government, and diplomatic matters concerning them had to be handled through the U.S. State Department. Therefore, he made it clear he would refuse any request to send negotiators to the South.

Under the circumstances, the Foreign Office in London and the Quai d'Orsay, the French diplomatic bureau, each decided to entrust one of their consuls in the Confederacy with the responsibility of gaining Southern consent to the declaration. Their presence already in the region eliminated the need to seek any required permissions from the State Department, and if the consuls dealt with local officials only, the powers could not be accused of engaging in diplomatic maneuvering with the Confederate government. Thus, Confederate concurrence to the declaration might be obtained without any apparent involvement of the powers.

The immediate question was who should be chosen to undertake this delicate task. Russell's original choice was Consul William Mure at New Orleans, but Lyons championed Bunch. Mure had been on leave during the early months of 1861, Lyons contended, and was not fully aware of events in the South. This was not the case with Bunch. His reports indicated his understanding of the situation and, declared Lyons, he had greater influence and popularity with important political and social leaders. Not only was Bunch president of St. George's Society, a fraternal organization devoted to maintaining British cultural heritage, but he had already shown his political acumen in 1859 when he persuaded South Carolina legislators to defeat a reenactment of the 1822 "Coloured Seamen Law."[7] The clincher in Lyons's argument was that Bunch could carry out the mission without bringing attention to himself or his actions. M. de Belligny Ste. Croix, French acting consul at Charleston, was in Washington and about to return to the Southern city. He could take to Bunch the guidelines, recently received from London, for the consul to follow in his negotiations. Any meeting between the two consuls would raise no suspicions, and the two men could contact influential persons and persuade them to seek Richmond's consent to the declaration. As Lyons reported to Russell when the plan had been finalized: "The French consul in Charleston and Mr. Bunch will do the deed."[8]

In transmitting the guidelines, Lyons cautioned Bunch to be "very careful in what you are about to do." He instructed Bunch to "act identically" with de Belligny and to involve himself as little as possible; he was not to travel to Richmond or to confer with Confederate officials. In addition, he was to say nothing about Lyons's role in the affair. The two consuls were advised to approach Governor Francis Pickens of South Carolina and to encourage him to persuade Confederate authorities to signify their consent to articles two, three, and four of the declaration. Bunch was free to say that Southern acceptance of the declaration was the "sine qua non" of friendship between Britain and the Confederacy, but he was to "give no hint of [diplomatic] recognition . . . the southern government would take great advantage of giving the impression that they are discussing great issues with Britain and France and [are] on the eve of recognition."[9]

Bunch ignored the suggestion that he contact Governor Pickens and may have disregarded the warning about recognition as well. Instead of Pickens, he and de Belligny approached William Henry Trescot, former secretary of the American legation in London and undersecretary of state during the Buchanan administration. Bunch justified the choice, stressing Trescot's ability and Pickens's incompetence. In his official report, Bunch stated that Pickens was at his plantation in the upcountry when the instructions arrived, and he feared a trip outside Charleston might cause too much notice. Privately he wrote that Pickens was "quite demented [and] I regret to say, a very helpless sort"; certainly not an individual to be entrusted with such a sensitive mission. Trescot, to the contrary, was "a man of talent and an agreeable companion." Bunch also described him as "a particular friend of mine," and that may have been the deciding influence in selecting the South Carolinian.[10]

Bunch and de Belligny met with Trescot on July 19, 1861. Cautious about the nature of their request, Trescot insisted on copies of the consuls' instructions from their governments to show authorities in Richmond. More important, Trescot's recollection of the conference implies that Bunch ignored Lyons's instructions about recognition. "The consuls," he wrote "were free to say that they could only look upon this step as the initiative towards a recognition. . . . They said they could make no pledges about the results of the Confederacy agreeing to the

Declaration of Paris, but certainly the consequences would be agreeable and beneficial." If Trescot remembered the conversation correctly, Lyons's estimation of Bunch would have undoubtedly fallen. Certainly he never would have told Russell, as he later did, that Bunch managed the negotiations "with great tact and good judgement."[11]

On July 20, Trescot left Charleston for Richmond to meet with Davis and his cabinet. The group agreed to accede to the British and French request. On August 14, 1861, the Confederate Congress gave its consent to articles two, three, and four. The consuls' role did not surface during the cabinet or congressional discussions, but unfortunately Bunch's indiscretion caused the entire issue to become a matter of controversy almost immediately.[12]

Even before Southern consent became public knowledge, Seward began receiving reports about Bunch's pro-Confederate sympathies. Specifically, they concerned Robert Mure (sometimes spelled Muir), a Charleston merchant who had left the Southern city in early August and was making his way to New York City by way of Louisville and Cincinnati. In Louisville Mure was overheard telling a friend that he was acting as courier for the consul at Charleston. From Cincinnati, Seward received word that the letters Mure carried were from officials in Richmond to Confederate sympathizers and commissioners in Europe. Bunch had permitted them to be placed in his consular pouch to Russell, who would in turn send them to the addressees. The pouch also contained other voluminous papers, including several pamphlets defending secession and pro-Southern accounts of the first Battle of Bull Run. Moreover, the report concluded, Mure was reputed to be a colonel in the South Carolina militia and was traveling on a passport issued by Bunch even though he was a naturalized American citizen. Seward had recently circulated a regulation requiring all passports issued to persons leaving the country to be countersigned by him.[13]

Seward could hardly ignore such blatant accusations of Mure's questionable activities and ordered his arrest. When New York City police apprehended the South Carolinian they found two suspicious items: a passport on Mure's person and a diplomatic pouch in his luggage. The passport, signed by Bunch, described Mure as a "British Merchant" acting as courier for the Charleston consulate and requested that he be allowed to proceed without delay. The pouch contained pamphlets, a large number of personal letters addressed to various individuals in Europe, and two dispatch envelopes bearing the seal of the Charleston consulate. Seward wisely sent the envelopes on to London, where Russell opened them and reported that they contained no controversial material. The police confiscated and examined the publications and other letters in the pouch.[14]

As reported by the *New York Tribune*, most of the letters were personal and of little importance: discussions of crops, banking, and personal and everyday affairs. However, there was one unsealed, undated, and unsigned statement that recounted the consul's recent diplomatic efforts. It concluded:

Mr. B., on oath of secrecy, communicated to me also that the first step to recognition was taken. He and Mr. Belligny together sent Mr. Trescot to Richmond yesterday, to ask Jeff. Davis, president, to ___(accept)___ the treaty of ___(commerce)___, to ___(accept)___ the neutral flag covering neutral goods to be respected. This is the first step of direct treating with our government, so prepare for active business by January 1.[15]

Immediately upon Mure's arrest, charges were made and explanations sought. To squelch a rumor that the affair was a conspiracy among the Southern British consuls because Robert Mure was reputed to be Consul William Mure's brother—some reports said cousin—Lyons requested a clarification of the men's relationship. Undoubtedly he was relieved when William Mure reported, "he is no relation, but merely bears the same name because his family comes from the same part of Scotland as mine." To distance itself from Robert Mure, now imprisoned at Fort Lafayette in New York City, the Foreign Office refused to intercede on his behalf or to seek his release. When Mure appealed for assistance from Archibald because of his British birth, Lyons instructed the consul not to interfere. The Foreign Office told Lyons, "Lord Russell . . . does not mean to say anything about the interception of Bunch's messenger." Finally, two months after Mure's arrest, Seward released him on the condition that he contact no one in the Confederacy for the duration of the war.[16]

The Foreign Office also sought an explanation from Bunch. At first, he attempted to pass off the "intercepted letter respecting my communication to the supposed writer" as a fabrication. There had been no discussion about a treaty of commerce during the conversation with Trescot, and the writer's reference to one indicated the falsehood of his statement. Bunch referred to the passport as merely a "certificate," which he had felt authorized to issue because Mure had only become an American citizen in order to purchase land from the Federal government. As Bunch explained the situation, Mure made a business trip to England every summer, and because the two men were friends Mure offered to convey the consular pouch to England. It was difficult, Bunch continued, to turn down "a good honest Scotchman, talking the grandest Doric . . . a president too of St. Andrew's Society—educating his children in Scotland and he intending to go & live there so soon as he shall be rich enough." Defending his decision to allow individuals to put private letters in the dispatch pouch, Bunch replied they were principally personal letters or letters that contained money from servants and laborers—all British subjects—who were helping to support relatives back home, and these people had no other way of getting the letters to Europe. Both Lyons and Russell found the explanation unsatisfactory. Russell demanded further clarification, and told Lyons to notify Seward that a British gunboat would be sent to Charleston to pick up the consul's statement.[17]

Bunch became more submissive the second time around. He still maintained that the anonymous statement was a fraud, "the work of a spy." He had only informed three individuals of his activities, and none of them would have placed such a letter in the pouch. He apologized for allowing Britons living in Charleston to send personal letters through diplomatic channels. He should have insisted that they use the one private mail service still operating but worried it might shut down at any time. Finally, Bunch admitted being wrong about the passport, particularly in describing Mure as a "British Merchant," and promised not to issue passports to American citizens in the future. This time Lyons accepted the explanation, but Russell remained unconvinced. He resented the forwarding of personal mail in the diplomatic pouch, contrary to instructions. Furthermore, Bunch never denied making the statement about Southern consent to the declaration being "a first step in the recognition of the so-called Confederate States." Russell was at least more charitable than Undersecretary Edmund Hammond, who confided to Lyons that Bunch was "a very perverse or stupid man . . . and not fit for his post."[18]

Despite his misgivings, Russell defended his consul against Seward's charges of inappropriate behavior and violations of United States law. First, Bunch had issued a passport, which Seward considered a diplomatic and not a consular function. Besides, Mure should have had the passport countersigned by Seward. His roundabout route of travel between Charleston and New York to avoid getting the secretary's signature only added to his guilt. Second, Bunch again engaged in a diplomatic function by negotiating with the Confederates and in doing so breached the terms of his exequatur. These limited his activities solely to consular functions in North and South Carolina. Finally, by his action Bunch had violated the Logan Act of 1799, which made it a crime for any citizen or resident of the United States to correspond with foreign governments about American foreign policy. Seward pointed out that Bunch was liable to punishment under the act because Britain and the United States did not concede extraterritoriality to resident consuls. Considering Bunch's impropriety, Seward demanded his recall.

Russell refused, declaring that Bunch's action to gain Confederate consent to the Declaration of Paris was taken at the direction of the Foreign Office. While what he did was not strictly a consular function, it was necessary to protect British trading interests. Since Bunch did not act on his own initiative, Russell questioned Seward's contention that he had violated the Logan Act. Moreover, in charging that Bunch had negotiated with a foreign nation, Seward was acknowledging greater recognition to the Confederacy as an independent state than

Britain herself conceded. Privately, Russell told Lyons that he was unconcerned about Seward's threat to charge Bunch under the Logan Act because the consul was free from punishment as long as Confederates held Charleston. If Russell was inclined to carry his argument further, he was dissuaded by the law officers of the Crown. They considered Mure's arrest and American complaints justified and recommended against a formal demand for restitution or apology.[19]

Given Russell's inflexibility, Seward took an extreme action: he revoked Bunch's exequatur, but in an almost casual manner. Calling Lyons to the State Department on October 28, 1861, Seward read his response to Russell's communiqué. It repeated previous assertions about Bunch's conduct, and the last paragraph stated that Bunch's exequatur "has been withdrawn." When Lyons inquired if the revocation had already been signed, Seward informed him that he was in no hurry; Lincoln would probably sign the order that evening.[20]

There is no evidence indicating that Lincoln ever signed a revocation order; even so, he was certainly aware of Seward's action. The two men conferred often, sometimes several times a day. During the late summer and fall of 1861, Lincoln stopped at the Seward residence almost every evening to discuss current issues. Charles Francis Adams, American minster to Great Britain, commented that Lincoln seemed to "have no idea about foreign affairs" and gave Seward a free reign. More likely, Lincoln was willing to entrust foreign policy to the secretary because of his confidence in Seward and his own concern about the military situation. As former chairman of the Senate Foreign Relations Committee, Seward was more aware than Lincoln of foreign policy procedures and practices. He often informed the president about attire to be worn at receptions when the diplomatic corps was to be present and whether or not Lincoln was expected to speak or merely to offer a greeting of welcome. Seward's continual references to Lincoln's views in his instructions to American diplomats, especially to Adams, indicates that he kept Lincoln informed about foreign policy issues and regarded his input as important.[21]

After his conversation with Lyons, Seward dropped the matter of Bunch's exequatur and never mentioned it again. This is indicated in a letter from Lyons to Bunch, telling him that revocation of his exequatur was a possibility but as of yet not a certainty: "Do not be surprised or annoyed if the U.S. Govt. revoke your exequatur. . . . Should it so happen I shall send you instructions as soon as I think it is desirable to give official notice to you of the fact." Lyons's correspondence indicates further that he did not raise the matter again with Seward until December 1861. The secretary then responded somewhat offhandedly that Bunch's exequatur had been withdrawn some time ago.[22]

Even though Seward announced the revocation of Bunch's exequatur in conversation, he never sent a formal statement to the Foreign Office or to the legation. Taking note of the fact, Russell remarked, "I hardly know how to deal with such a man." Nor did Seward take the usual steps within the United States: publishing letters patent revoking Bunch's authority and noting the revocation on Bunch's exequatur itself. In 1856 when the State Department withdrew the exequaturs of three British consuls for recruiting Americans to fight in the Crimea, it published letters patent in newspapers throughout the consuls' districts and in New York City. In addition—and Lyons would not have known this—no notification was made on Bunch's exequatur, then filed in the State Department but now housed in the National Archives. For the three consuls in 1856 there is a notation to the effect that their exequaturs had been withdrawn; there is no such statement on Bunch's exequatur. Because Seward failed to take any formal action, Lyons wrote as late as December 7, 1861, that he had still no reason to believe an official revocation had ever been signed.[23]

Despite the lack of these last formal steps, both the Foreign Office and Lyons accepted revocation as an accomplished fact. While on leave in the summer of 1862, Lyons wrote back to his chargé, William Stuart, that Bunch "is *not* Consul at Charleston either in the eyes of the British or the U.S. Govt."[24]

Seward also overlooked Bunch's failure to leave Charleston, and the consul remained in the city until February 1863, sixteen months after his exequatur was supposedly withdrawn. On advice from Lyons, Bunch no longer signed formal documents;

he turned that portion of the work over to his vice-consul, Henry Pinckney Walker. But he corresponded with Confederate authorities, chiefly over their attempts to conscript British nationals, and he continued to send detailed reports on conditions and events in the South. Lyons was undoubtedly relieved that Seward did not insist on Bunch's removal. Remarking on the possibility of Bunch's departure from Charleston, Lyons wrote: "I confess that I should greatly regret being deprived of the very valuable information which he furnishes on the state of affairs in the South."[25]

Possibly Seward temporarily forgot Bunch's presence in the Southern city, but he must have been reminded of it during the summer of 1862, when the *New York Herald* published an article about the consul. If Seward did not see the piece itself, surely someone would have brought it to his attention. The journalist noted that Bunch had left Charleston on H.M.S. *Racer* for a visit to Savannah, and along the way he stopped at Fort Pulaski, which had been captured by Federal forces the previous April. The writer wondered just how much information Bunch might have relayed to Confederates in Georgia, and he asked why Bunch was permitted to remain in the South.[26]

More mystifying than not demanding Bunch's removal was an order Seward signed in February 1862 permitting communications between foreign legations in Washington and their consuls in the South. It specifically stated that all correspondence had to be carried on national warships and taken only into those ports at which consuls were not permitted to trade. Bunch was the only British consul in the South who fell into this category, and thus his office became responsible for transmitting all correspondence between the Southern consuls and the British legation or the Foreign Office. Because these British ships conveyed messages frequently, it would have been easy for Bunch to leave the city if Seward so demanded. Bunch's departure from Charleston came at the insistence of Lyons, who feared a Federal attack upon the city. When Bunch departed, he left on the same British warship that brought his orders to leave and instructions for his replacement.[27]

Other events and actions imply that Seward used Bunch's

indiscretion to make a point without pressing it. He was aware that England and France were attempting to gain Southern consent to the Declaration of Paris despite his refusal to sanction an official visit by negotiators! Reviewing the entire chain of events for Russell, Lyons recalled a meeting he and Mercier had with Seward on May 18—two months before Bunch and de Belligny met with Trescot. Mercier showed Seward a letter from the French foreign secretary, Edouard Thouvenel, which "expressly stated that a communication with the Southern Govt. was to take place." Seward refused to receive it officially, so Mercier laid the document on his desk and, according to Lyons, the secretary "had the original for some time in his possession."[28] While Seward may not have been aware of the particulars, Bunch's activities could not have come as a complete surprise.

Other incidents indicate that Bunch may have been the object of special attention and punishment. For example, in 1864 when the Union naval commander in Florida was about to arrest Edward Rich, a Confederate sympathizer of British birth, Rich obtained a passport from the British vice-consul at Key West and fled the country. The State Department informed the British legation of Rich's escape but declared it had no wish to pursue the matter or punish the vice-consul in any way.[29]

More perplexing, Seward did not mention de Belligny during the entire Bunch affair. "Not the smallest allusion, that I recollect," Lyons wrote of his conversations with Seward, "was made anywhere to the share taken by the French Consul at Charleston in the communications with the so-called Confederate Government."[30] Russell was curious enough about this to make inquiries at Paris. Thouvenel informed the British ambassador to France that nothing had been said but, anyway, de Belligny was recalled shortly after the negotiations were completed. Thouvenel doubted that the negotiations over the Declaration of Paris had caused Bunch's problems; rather, it was the unsigned letter stating that "this was the first step to recognition."[31] Despite French involvement from the beginning, Britain was left to bear the entire responsibility once the matter became public. One wonders what effect France's lack of

support in 1861 may have had on Britain's refusal to join a
French-proposed mediation effort in 1862.

Thouvenel's assertion about the unsigned letter was probably correct, but Lyons believed that Seward singled out Bunch
because it was easier and safer to attack him than to make
extreme charges against the British government for its role in
securing Southern consent to the Declaration of Paris. Lyons
also saw Seward's actions as a "sop to public opinion." Recalling
his initial meeting about Bunch's activities with Seward on the
day of Mure's arrest, Lyons noted that the secretary emphasized
that "he was not seeking a quarrel. . . . a month ago he would
have taken away [Bunch's] exequatur." But Mure's arrest had
received so much notoriety that as time went on Seward was
forced to placate "the violent party here." He was taxing his
ingenuity, wrote Lyons, to avoid a disagreement with Britain
while, at the same time, trying to respond to the public call for
retribution. Thus, he built an argument that enabled him to
withdraw Bunch's exequatur, and, having achieved that, Seward demanded no further action against the consul.[32]

Seward's action was also prompted by anti-British sentiment within the country and by the belief that Bunch was far
too sympathetic to the Southern cause.[33] His residence in the
South for almost a decade and his friendships there undoubtedly swayed his early impressions of the South's ability to suc-
ceed. Shortly after Fort Sumter surrendered, Bunch predicted
the Confederacy would eventually consist of all fifteen slave
states, and even a year later he believed that the South was
"determined to prosecute the war to the utmost extremity."
Yet, Bunch doubted if the Confederacy would ever "rise to emi-
nence among the great powers of the earth." Its reliance on
cotton created an unbalanced and false economy, and "from the
day cotton comes into competition or is replaced, so this republic will diminish." The Confederate desire to preserve and extend Negro slavery was another factor. In the present age,
Bunch wrote, slavery deprived the South of "the sympathy and
encouragement which are as necessary to Nations as to Individuals." Further, Southern filibustering and expansionist
tendencies would have to be repressed by European nations.

Summing up his opinion of the Confederacy, Bunch concluded: "I believe the New Republic will be ostracized by public opinion of the world and only be regarded as growers of cotton and rice." [34]

Nor was Bunch's opinion of Southern leaders more complimentary. Reporting on the men who headed the new government, Bunch characterized Davis as a Southern extremist, a "manifest destiny supporter" elected only because of his military background. Bunch regarded the Southern cabinet as a "dead level of mediocrity," and he held a special antipathy for Judah P. Benjamin. While Benjamin served as attorney general and secretary of war, Bunch could only blame him for the cotton embargo. When Benjamin succeeded to the State Department in 1862, Bunch lamented the change as unfortunate, and he predicted difficulty with Benjamin in the future. Benjamin's British birth, Bunch believed, inclined him to expect too much from the English; indeed, Bunch predicted Benjamin might even expel the consuls if the South failed to gain support from Great Britain. [35]

Nor did Bunch have a high opinion of Confederate commissioners in Europe: William L. Yancey, Dudley Mann, and Pierre Rost. When the Confederate government sent them to gain diplomatic recognition and material support, Bunch wrote: "I am particularly anxious that the new commissioners, if received at all, should not be too warmly welcomed." Their belief in their "confounded cotton" and the idea that "we will do anything to get it," was not a "flattering estimate of us." Beneath the show of friendship and harmony expressed by Southern leaders, Bunch warned, was an intense dislike for Britain—"we have nothing to expect from the good will of the South." [36] Even though the U.S. State Department firmly believed that Bunch's sympathies lay with the South, Lyons and the Foreign Office were aware of his true feelings. Throughout the Bunch affair, Lyons found himself in a difficult position: he could not openly refute American charges regarding Bunch's pro-Confederate leanings despite his knowledge to the contrary. [37]

If Bunch indicated a distrust of Southerners, he was ambitious enough to become indiscrete. Intoxicated by his role in gaining Southern consent to the Declaration of Paris, Bunch began to hope for the impossible: advancing from the consular corps to the diplomatic. As stated earlier, British political leaders viewed the two services as separate and never transferred men from one to the other; yet, in reporting Confederate acceptance of the Declaration of Paris, Bunch asked Lyons to nominate him as foreign minister should Britain recognize the Confederacy. If that office was "too high," Bunch was willing to settle for secretary of legation at Richmond "with a salary not much above my present one." Somewhat taken aback by the request, Lyons replied: "I did not forward your letter for promotion. You have just had a great diplomatic success, but it is not good to ask for a reward at the same time that you send notification of your success."[38]

Bunch's exhilaration turned to depression in the months that followed, and he presumed his great achievement was being ignored only because he disobeyed the regulation about sending private mail. Lyons again came to the rescue, advising Bunch that the Foreign Office considered his conduct praiseworthy. "Don't," he warned, "assume the air of having been disapproved or harshly treated."[39] As he had in the past, Lyons championed Bunch's cause with the Foreign Office, and Bunch would be rewarded for his service. Perhaps to Bunch's regret, his promotion would be within the consular corps, and it would not be within in the United States.

Examined with historical hindsight, the Bunch affair points out several facets of Seward's diplomacy. He realized the limits of his power and did not press an issue he could not force to conclusion. As Russell contended, Seward lacked power to demand Bunch's removal, so he did not demand it. The Bunch affair further indicates that Seward's aggressive stand had moderated earlier than historians suggest. They date the change from the *Trent* affair, but Lyons's statements imply a more complacent attitude several months earlier. Whatever prompted the change in Seward's demeanor, it helped to foster a friendlier relationship with Lyons, who in turn presented a picture of a firm but not unreasonable secretary of state to the Foreign Office.

5

Arbitrary Arrests
and Property Rights

During the Bunch affair Secretary of State Seward asserted the
right to revoke the exequatur of a consul who had exceeded the
limits of his authority. Having made the assertion, he did not
press for Bunch's removal from Charleston and thus avoided
heightening tension between the British and American governments. Seward followed the same policy in regard to British
nationals arrested for blockade running or aiding the Confederacy in any way: he exercised his authority to incarcerate such
individuals but readily released them from prison.

From the beginning of the war in April 1861 until February
1862, Lincoln charged the State Department with ferreting
out and punishing anti-Union activities. These months were
also the period of most intense activity on the part of Confederate sympathizers, especially in the border states. The large
number of arrests in addition to the suspension of the writ of
habeas corpus in parts of the border slave states and the lower
North caused Seward's contemporaries and historians alike to
blame him for a harsh enforcement of the policy. One historian
wrote that Seward expanded his authority until he was ordering all the arrests in the free states.[1] Such a conclusion should
be reconsidered, for it does not take into account that Seward
was often unaware of individual arrests until after they had
occurred. While he supervised the program, the majority of arrests were made by local authorities outside the State Department. In addition, incarceration of civilians for pro-Confederate
activity was longer and more frequent after Lincoln transferred
the duty of stamping out dissent to the War Department.[2]

A review of Seward's response to the jailing of foreign nationals bears out the leniency of his policy. Indeed, the quick release

of foreign nationals caused one American, when informed about the arrival of a new prisoner in Fort Lafayette, to note in his diary: "I suppose as he is a 'British subject' he will be released as soon as the British Consul hears of his imprisonment; lucky thing now-a-days to have been born in England, or anywhere outside the 'Land of the Free and Home of the Brave!'"[3]

Seward not only discharged foreign nationals relatively soon after their arrest, but the State Department devised special oaths for them to sign in order to facilitate their release. American citizens had to swear an oath of allegiance to the United States but, depending upon the charges against them, British and other foreign nationals had to promise not to run the blockade again, not to travel to the South, or not to attempt to contact anyone there for the duration of the war.[4]

Arrests of foreigners accounted for 11.2 percent of the total of those engaged in anti-Union activities up to February 1862, and of these, 76.8 percent were British.[5] Most were caught attempting to get ships through the blockade or purchasing war materials for the South. Individuals arrested were sent to Fort Warren in Boston harbor or to Fort LaFayette in New York City; the majority ended up at Fort LaFayette. As a result, Consul Archibald received the majority of the pleas for help and soon found the work burdensome and time-consuming. Before he could visit a prisoner, Archibald had to obtain permission from authorities; then it took five and a half hours to travel to Fort Lafayette. There he had to ascertain the prisoner's citizenship, consider the reason for his arrest, and determine the probability of his guilt. Upon arriving back at the consulate, he would write a report to Lyons, who would then take the case before Seward.

Perhaps what disturbed Archibald most about his visits to Fort Lafayette were the conditions he encountered: "Prisoners are *never* allowed to go out of their cells, and from want of air and exercise are suffering extremely," he wrote in 1861. "The feeding of them is jobbed out at 43 cents a head per day, but not more than 10 cents worth, I am afraid, reaches the prisoners. The common men are barbarously dealt with." Nor did conditions improve as the war continued. Describing a prison cell to

Lyons in 1864, Archibald declared that "the place is not fitted to be a jail." Approximately twelve men were confined to cells that measured fifteen by eleven feet. Each cell contained only a small table, one wash basin and a bucket that served as toilet facilities for all the prisoners. The men hung hammocks from nails to sleep at night, and they were locked in their cells from sunset until seven o'clock the next morning.[6]

Once he obtained permission to visit a prisoner, Archibald had easy access to the fort because he was on friendly terms with the officers and because of his pro-Union attitude. He informed Lyons that he never wavered from his opinion that the North would subdue the South and reunite the Republic. Because Archibald was "northern in his leanings," as he phrased it, he did not sympathize with men who were obviously guilty. When two Britons, William McDonald and Alfred Phillips, admitted trying to discourage men from enlisting in the United States Army, Archibald refused to support their request for release. Nor was he particularly enthusiastic when he heard they were set free just two weeks later. He also refused to interfere when four British sailors on the captured privateer *Savannah* were charged with piracy. He believed them guilty and believed a jail sentence was justifiable punishment.[7]

Lyons was as judicious in his approach as Archibald. When Russell accused Lyons of being "too tame about the arrest of British Subjects," Lyons explained his policy. He sought release on a case by case basis rather than by following broad principles, because he believed this was the most effective approach with Seward. In addition, Lyons wrote, he never used "strong language" and never raised his voice; he merely stated the facts in each case and appealed for justice. As if to emphasize the success of his approach, Lyons added: "To judge from Mr. Seward's conversation, he is anxious, *in practice*, to avoid arresting British Subjects except by regular legal process. I dined with him the day before yesterday, nobody else except his own family being present."[8]

How successful were Archibald and Lyons at securing the release of British subjects? A check of the public record for individuals whose citizenship can be determined indicates that imprisonment of British citizens varied from three days to five months after their arrival at Fort Warren or Fort Lafayette.[9] For example, on October 4, 1861, military authorities caught Samuel Sharp attempting to cross army lines from the South, where he had engaged in commercial activities; he was released on October 7. Purcell M. Quillen came north from Charleston to purchase military equipment for the Confederacy and was arrested in Washington in late June 1861 and sent to Fort Lafayette on July 22. Even though he admitted to participating in the bombardment of Fort Sumter and his interrogators considered him a spy, Seward ordered him "quietly released" on August 7. Other cases include: William Patrick, arrested August 28, 1861, for trading with the enemy and released on September 13; William Williams and William Sims, who arrived at Fort Lafayette on August 21 after being caught attempting to run the blockade, were released on September 23.[10]

Individuals incarcerated for longer periods faced more serious charges or delayed their own release. Authorities in Detroit arrested John Shaver, a Canadian, on October 19, 1861, and charged him with using his position as a travel agent for the Grand Trunk Railroad to carry contraband letters and small arms to the Confederacy. Seward offered to release Shaver on October 28 if he would take an oath of allegiance to the United States, an offer he declined. Shaver finally gained his freedom on January 7, 1862, after he signed an oath not to travel into the South or communicate with anyone there for the duration.[11]

The charges against John C. Brain were more serious. Although a British citizen, he admitted being an officer in the Confederate army and a member of the Knights of the Golden Circle, a secret organization that encouraged Southern independence. In Michigan City, Indiana, where he was arrested in early September 1861, Brain distributed handbills encouraging men to enlist in the Southern cause and attempted to persuade Mary Fraley, a local resident, to transport small arms into Kentucky for transshipment to the Confederacy. Despite Lyons's pleas, Seward refused to release Brain as long as the loyalty of Kentucky was in doubt. Seward finally relented and discharged Brain in February 1862, a week before the fall of Fort Donelson.[12]

The *Official Records* imply that only one British subject remained in prison long enough to be transferred to the custody of the War Department in February 1862. Military authorities in St. Louis arrested Joseph Nolen, a minor, in October 1861 for engaging in "criminal acts." Consul Wilkins thought him guilty but appealed for Nolen's release on grounds of his youth. The local commander agreed to release Nolen if he would sign a statement promising to refrain from further "criminal acts." Because Nolen refused and demanded release as a "matter of right," he remained in prison and later was turned over to the War Department.[13]

If Lyons was inclined to deal with Seward on a case by case basis and to be cautious in his argumentation, Foreign Secretary Russell was not. It was the arrest of William Patrick and J.C. Rahming that prompted Russell to question Lincoln's authority to suspend the writ of habeas corpus and continue military arrests. Police apprehended Patrick on August 28, 1861, and charged him with carrying on commercial business with Southerners. Rahming was arrested after he tried to persuade a ship's captain to take cannon to Wilmington, North Carolina. Both men were freed within a month; however, Russell continued to complain about the illegality of Lincoln's and Seward's actions and pressed the argument even after Patrick and Rahming were released.[14]

Russell found support from a number of sources for his contention that the administration's actions were illegal: critics of Lincoln's policy within the United States itself, lawyers for the Crown, and the consuls. Just after Patrick and Rahming were arrested, Charles Kortwright, consul at Philadelphia, sent Russell a number of newspaper editorials that complained about Lincoln's arbitrary policies. "The mere suspicion of being engaged in treasonable intercourse with the South," Kortwright wrote, "renders a person liable to arrest . . . and he is carried off to prison, or to some neighboring Fort." Insisting that only Congress had authority to suspend the writ of habeas corpus, Kortwright declared the arrests of Patrick and Rahming a contravention of the Constitution. Shortly thereafter Archibald also sent editorials that presented much the same argument. Calling Patrick's arrest an outrage, Archibald contended that the government had no basis for holding him in prison.[15]

Russell's concern caused him to turn to Crown lawyers for support. The argument they devised stressed two points: first, that the suspension of the writ and arbitrary arrests "directly opposed the maxim of the Constitution of the United States, 'that no person should be deprived of life, liberty, or property, without due process of law'"; and, second, that the conduct of the executive department had not been authorized by Congress and, therefore, violated the Constitution and treaties of amity between Great Britain and the United States. Privately, Russell added that Seward does "as he pleases depriving British Subjects of their liberty." Russell then instructed Lyons to remonstrate against the administration's actions using the lawyers' argument as the basis for the protest.[16]

Seward's response came in a series of notes to Lyons but meant for Russell. The secretary began by writing, "The British government will hardly expect that the President will accept their explanation of the Constitution of the United States."[17] Shortly after he carried the argument further:

The duty of the President is to save the Government from being overthrown, and were the writ of *habeas corpus* to remain in full force till Congress could act, he might be rendered utterly powerless. . . . It may seem hard to imprison an individual, but it is harder for a nation to be destroyed. If foreigners come among us, they must share not only in our good fortune, but in the calamities which the rebellion has caused; and if they are found tampering with or encouraging it, they must be prepared to pay the penalty due to the gravest offenses against society.[18]

As Russell pressed further, Seward continued. When the foreign secretary again protested Patrick's arrest two months after the man had been released, Seward wrote:

I cheerfully consent to leave Earl Russell's protest on the record where it will lie side by side with the decisions of this government, which show that during a civil war, now of nine months' duration, no complaint of any kind has been denied a hearing, not one person has been pressed into the land or naval service, not one disloyal citizen or resident, however guilty of treason or conspiracy, has forfeited his life except in battle, not one had been detained a day in confinement who could not and would give reliable pledges of his forbearance from evil designs, nor indeed had one person who could or would give no such pledges been detained a day beyond the period when the danger which he was engaged in producing had safely passed away.[19]

Whether Russell was aware of Patrick's release when he sent his second protest is unknown, but he soon conceded that Seward's policy was not onerous. When Lord Carnarvon, in the House of Lords, protested the illegality of Lincoln's suspension of the writ and arbitrary arrests, Russell replied: "An innocent person being arrested and confined for several days in prison was undoubtedly a great grievance, and one for which he is entitled to compensation, but beyond the right to complain and beyond the constant remonstrances of Lord Lyons, the British minister, in every case, I do not hold that the circumstances warrant further interference."[20] This statement admitted the American right to jail subversives, but the words "confined for several days" acknowledged the leniency of Seward's enforcement policy.

Once the War Department was put in charge of ferreting out disloyal activities, arrests "outstripped anything Seward and the State Department ever managed to produce." Whereas 864 civilians were arrested during the ten months that Seward controlled the policy, Stanton apprehended 354 persons in August 1862 alone.[21] The case of J.M. Vernon shows that investigations also became more thorough. Picked up from a burning ship thirty miles from Charleston in February 1863, Vernon was imprisoned in Fort Lafayette. He demanded his freedom on the grounds of his British citizenship and claimed merely to be on a business trip to Havana. A four-month inquiry by the War Department indicated that Vernon had been selling arms to the Confederates. Stanton refused to release him until the end of the war or until he was exchanged as a prisoner of war. Both Archibald and Lyons blamed the new harshness on Stanton, and Lyons would now admit that Seward "is not at all a cruel or vindictive man."[22]

Lyons accepted the validity of War Department investigations and seldom challenged them regarding the arrest of British subjects. But the controversy between General Benjamin Butler and George Coppell, acting consul in New Orleans, proves he could be quite firm in cases of a truly diplomatic nature. Coppell replaced William Mure, who retired for health reasons in September 1861. After the Federal army captured New Orleans in April 1862 and Butler assumed command of the area, difficulties broke out between the commander and the foreign consuls. Butler presumed that because many of the consuls had lived in the South for years they were sympathetic to the Confederate cause, and he confiscated money and other property from the consulates.

Butler's conflict with Coppell began with the general's treatment of the "British Guard." This military unit had been organized at the beginning of the war for local defense and to quell any attempted slave insurrection; it was not established to fight Federal forces. Consequently, when Union troops entered the city, some members of the guard put away their weapons. Others gave their arms and equipment to Confederate troops abandoning the city. When Butler learned of their action, he ordered all members of the guard to bring their arms to military headquarters; those who did not comply were to be confined at Fort Jackson, near the mouth of the Mississippi River.

When Coppell complained, the general responded in what Lyons termed "gross and insulting language." After defending his policy, Butler told the consul: "I intend this order to be strictly enforced." In closing he added: "I note you sign yourself 'Her Britannic Majesty's Acting Consul,' but I have received no word of your right to act, and sir, your acts . . . have not been of such a character as to induce the belief on my part that you do rightfully represent that noble Government."[23] Offended by the tone of Butler's letter, Coppell threatened to stop carrying out his consular duties until he received assurance that his position would be respected and until Butler apologized. Lyons's protest and Seward's complaints to the War Department as well as an official statement from Lyons confirming Coppell as acting consul brought Butler around. He accepted Coppell's right to act as consul but gave him only a half-hearted apology: "If there was a misunderstanding in the past, remember, that all I have to go on were your two letters signed 'acting consul.'"[24]

Aside from arbitrary arrests, the most pressing complaint brought before the consuls and the legation by British nationals dealt with the destruction of American-owned property and with possible conscription into the Union or Confederate armies. These issues became so burdensome by early 1862 that Lyons remarked: "It seems to me that everybody North and South who gets into trouble discovers that he or she is a nonnaturalized British subject."[25] Conscription became in time the dominant issue; but, before that, consuls dealt with many complaints about the destruction of real or personal property.

The number of complaints were moderated by a several factors. For one, Britons residing in the Northern states did not incur destruction of property unless they lived in the path of Confederate raiding parties or in the way of Lee's army when it invaded Maryland and Pennsylvania. Secondly, Lyons drew up a list of circumstances under which cases should not be pressed, and it was fairly comprehensive. He saw little reason for British citizens to seek consular or legation help when Southerners had inflicted the damage. Since Great Britain lacked established diplomatic relations with the Confederate government, it had no means to negotiate these problems. Thus, when J. Hinton of Georgia protested that local officials forcibly closed his business and imprisoned him for refusing to serve in the Confederate army, his complaint went no further than the consulate in Savannah. In New York, William Argill, an alien resident of the state, wrote to Consul Archibald asking how to seek compensation for property he owned in Tennessee that Southerners had destroyed. The consul could only respond, "I see no means of securing redress for Argill and others owing to lack of communication with the Confederate States."[26]

Lyons was also adamant about not protesting the destruction of property belonging to Britons who had become naturalized American citizens or of those who sought to reclaim fugitive slaves. Responding to Consul Wilkins about an appeal for British protection from a man named Smith, Lyons called his argument "groundless." Smith had become an American citizen, and the legation would not complain about property damaged by his adopted country. In another instance, slaves belonging to an Englishman named Whelan fled to Union lines, and Whelan was unable to recover them. When Wilkins asked Lyons for guidance, the minister told him to put the matter aside: "I shall certainly give no countenance, support or protection to a British Subject who deals in Slaves. Is there not a statute making it penal for a British Subject to hold Slaves anywhere[?]"[27]

Lyons's list also prohibited consuls from assisting those who incurred damage during military action or damage done by unknown persons and those seeking relief because of extra taxation. In November 1861, Arthur Lynn, consul at Galveston, denounced a naval shelling of the city because the Union commander had given no prior warning. Noting damage inflicted on property owned by foreigners, Lynn published a complaint in the local newspaper against the Federal officers involved and sent a copy to Lyons. He duly forwarded the article to Russell but added: "It is quite true that a town *may* be bombarded . . . that British subjects may have their throats cut by the negroes in a servile insurrection, or be tarred and feathered by a Vigilance Committee. But we cannot keep a squadron at every port to protect them, and I do not know what points are particularly threatened."[28]

After General Benjamin Butler became the commander of Federal forces at New Orleans in 1862, rumor spread that he planned to impose a 10 percent tax on the people in the city. Apparently the rumor caused some British citizens to question Consul Coppell about the legality of such a tax, and he made inquiries to the legation. In response, the legation wrote that people opposed to the tax could question its legality because Congress or the state legislature had not levied it, while those in favor could contend that it was a tax placed on a conquered city. But it ended by suggesting compliance in order to avoid trouble.[29]

Finally, Lyons would not support exaggerated claims for compensation. In the late spring of 1861 army officials imprisoned John Stovin, a Briton living in Maryland, for threatening to poison a well from which Union soldiers took their water. After his release in the fall Stovin filed a claim for $150,000, basing the demand on loss of income because of his inability to plant crops. The State Department rejected the claim, and Stovin appealed to the legation. When Lyons learned that Stovin's farm was really the property of his recently deceased father-in-law and that Stovin had never worked it, he decided not to support the claim. He thought Stovin was entitled to some remuneration, but the amount he was requesting far exceeded any loss of income.[30]

Compensation from the United States government for damaged property, even when the British Foreign Office backed the claim, was difficult to obtain. At least this was true in regard to claims made on behalf of the estate of Edmund Molyneux. Consul at Savannah from 1832 to 1862, Molyneux, for all practical purposes, stopped functioning as consul when the war started. In the spring of 1861—the beginning of the warm season in Savannah—he traveled to his mountain retreat in North Carolina, where he stayed until December. Upon his return to Savannah, he requested and received an extended leave of absence for health reasons and returned to England, where he died within a year. During his absences Molyneux turned his office over to acting consul Allen Fullarton, who was also his personal banker. In the prewar years Molyneux had conducted consular business from his home, and upon his departure he permitted Fullarton to live in and use the residence for the same purpose. In October 1863 Confederate Secretary of State Benjamin ordered Fullarton to leave Savannah. Before departing, however, he secured the house, boxed and sealed all consular records, and hung a British flag over the main doorway to inform invading troops that the property was under British protection.[31]

Following the capture of Savannah in late 1864, neighbors in the city informed Mrs. Molyneux, living in England, that Federal troops were using the house as a headquarters and doing extensive damage. Shortly afterward she received similar news about damage to her mountain retreat in North Carolina. She complained to the Foreign Office and made pleas for compensation, but the response was cool. Given the heavy military activity around Savannah, Russell was reluctant to press Mrs. Molyneux's claim. He finally agreed to request compensation if she could provide proof that the house had been used as the consulate, supply a list of missing or damaged property, and present an estimate of damage. Through Fullarton and other individuals she was able to comply. According to her claim, Consul Molyneux's ten-thousand-dollar wine collection was stolen or consumed; most of the furniture, clothing, jewels, china, glassware, and packed trunks were missing or destroyed beyond repair; physical damage to the structure itself was almost irreparable; and what was left of the consular archives had been scattered throughout the house. On the basis of the information she received, Mrs. Molyneux filed a claim for twelve thousand dollars. Following an investigation by the U.S. War Department, the government refused to accept responsibility for the damage. Mrs. Molyneux continued to demand compensation in a series of highly emotional letters until 1871, when the Foreign Office informed her that it could do nothing if the American government refused to recognize her claim.[32]

Arbitrary arrests and mistreatment of civilians in the Confederacy were in sharp contrast to those in the North. Few cases were appealed to the Confederate State Department because there was no channel of communication between it and the British government. Few involved activities that threatened Confederate security. If the complaint of John Sullivan, a British resident in the Confederacy, is valid, foreigners in the South faced greater danger from local authorities than from the government at Richmond.[33] Records dealing with the arrests or harassment of British citizens indicate that most circumstances involved the issue of slavery or the confinement of free blacks. And if the cases of Tom Winnesfield, a West Indian black, and Captain Vaughn are any indication, justice was often frustrated.

Local authorities in Wilmington, North Carolina, accused Winnesfield of attempting to help a slave escape and arrested him in 1859. They never brought Winnesfield to trial but held him in jail for two years. He might have remained there longer except he became ill enough in April 1861 for his jailers to call in Edward Anderson, a local physician. When Anderson learned the circumstances of Winnesfield's arrest and imprisonment and his status as a foreign national, he informed Donald McRae, vice-consul at Wilmington. With Consul Bunch offering moral and financial support, McRae persuaded local authorities to free Winnesfield; he threatened to embarrass them by demanding a trial that would expose Winnesfield's confinement and the shaky evidence against him. Winnesfield's release came early enough in the war to enable McRae to send him back to the West Indies before the blockade became effective.[34]

The Vaughn case also took place just before the outbreak of war, and occurred because Vaughn socialized with blacks. Captain of a British merchant ship, *Kalos*, docked in Savannah, Vaughn invited several black stevedores to dine in his cabin. Hearing about Vaughn's invitation, members of the Rattlesnake Club, a local secret society, seized the captain and took him to the edge of the city; there they shaved his head, tarred and feathered him, flogged him, and forced him to walk back to his ship. The incident created a great deal of local indignation. The mayor of Savannah offered a five-hundred-dollar reward for evidence leading to the arrest of the perpetrators, and Consul Molyneux added one thousand dollars to that amount. In retaliation the criminals threatened to repeat the punishment, and Vaughn, apparently frightened, weighed anchor and fled. Eventually the guilty parties were caught, charged with riot, and released on bail. None of them showed up at their trial. When Molyneux complained to Georgia's governor, Joseph E. Brown, the governor expressed regret but stated that the men were now in the army and could not be brought back. The law had done all that was required in this case, and he considered the matter closed.[35]

The outbreak of war caused authorities in New Orleans to undertake a policy of incarcerating free blacks who were not local residents. The Foreign Office condemned the action on several grounds: it violated commercial treaties between Great

Britain and the United States, and it interfered with the men's freedom of movement. Louisiana authorities ignored British objections. Journalist William Howard Russell noted the large number of free blacks on his visit to the New Orleans city jail in June 1861; he especially pitied those from the Northern states, for they could appeal to no one. Russell was unaware that jailers seldom permitted imprisoned free blacks, American or foreign, to appeal to any authority. During a visit to the parish prison, Consul Mure found a West Indian who had been held for five weeks and refused permission to contact the consul. He also discovered that unscrupulous captains of cargo ships were encouraging the imprisonment of their black crew members when they docked at New Orleans to avoid paying their salaries. When Lord Russell suggested that Mure seek legal redress in such cases, Mure decided against it: "I am reluctant to follow Russell's instructions," he told Lyons. "The local courts certainly would not side with [the blacks] and, under the present state of things the [state] Supreme Court might not either."[36]

In July 1861, three West Indian sailors taken from a Union merchant ship by a Confederate privateer were brought to New Orleans and imprisoned. After local authorities ignored Mure's appeals for their discharge, he hired a lawyer to confer with Governor Thomas Moore. The governor seemed sympathetic but the conditions he stipulated for release "amount[ed] to a refusal." Since the men could not get through the blockade, he would free them only if Jefferson Davis gave permission for them to travel North by land. So outraged was Lyons by this stipulation that he suggested demanding indemnity "either from the Government of the so-called Confederate States, or from the State of Louisiana." Negotiations between Mure, and later Coppell, and Louisiana authorities finally led to the sailors' release in January 1862. New Orleans police put them on a small craft and sent them into the Gulf of Mexico, where they were picked up by a United States warship.[37]

Cases involving the arrest of British civilians were most numerous during the first year of war. Although a larger number of individuals were apprehended in the North, their cases were

settled with relative ease. The established diplomatic structure and Seward's willingness to cooperate with British authorities made this possible. Lyons found Seward more than
willing to avoid difficulties over mundane matters. Arrests in
the South were fewer but they caused greater frustration; most
of the individuals detained were not guilty of a crime in British eyes. Yet the settlement of these difficulties arising during
the first year of war indicated which of the two governments—
the Union or the Confederacy—would be the more obliging in
future controversies.

6

Searching for
Stirrup and Edwards

John Stirrup and Samuel Edwards were abducted from their home in Nassau and sold as slaves in Georgia on the eve of the Civil War. They were sixteen or seventeen years old at the time.[1] Stirrup and Edwards were not the only West Indians to be forced into human bondage in the United States before the Civil War. In March 1860, authorities in Brunswick, Georgia, seized William Brodie, a West Indian sailor, for attempting to help a slave escape and sold him into slavery. Consul Molyneux spent eight months trying to locate Brodie only to discover that he was an American citizen who had merely lived in the West Indies and that he was not eligible for protection. Several months before Stirrup and Edwards were seized, Lyons informed Lord Russell that a black named Martin Chartton had been abducted from Jamaica and was believed held in Virginia, and he requested permission to purchase Chartton if he could be found. Undoubtedly the outbreak of the Civil War impeded any progress in locating Chartton. At least there is no mention of him in subsequent correspondence between the legation and the Foreign Office.[2]

Free blacks in the slave states and in the North faced a greater possibility of being abducted and illegally sold into slavery.[3] Kidnappings of free blacks were reported as early as the 1790s, and they continued well into the antebellum period.[4] While the kidnapping of adults caused little public indignation, the abduction of minors did create noticeable compassion for the victims. In Belleville, Illinois, approximately fifteen miles southeast of St. Louis, for example, local townspeople took up a collection in 1823 to send Rachel, a black resident, to a more Northern city after all but one of her teenage children (unfortunately the report does not say how many) had been abducted, and kidnappers attempted to seize her youngest son. In a similar case involving the abduction of a minor the court ruled that "when one takes . . . a free negro boy of eight, with the criminal intent to appropriate him, the consent of such a boy does not excuse or lessen the offense," and the judge imposed a two year prison term on the kidnapper.[5]

And so it was with Stirrup and Edwards. Possibly because their youth created strong feelings of sympathy among those individuals who heard of their plight, efforts to free them continued throughout the war. The attempts seem somewhat haphazard, but considering the chaos in the wartime South they were perhaps the best that could be made at the time. Involved in this "quest for freedom" were the U.S. State Department, the British legation, and the British consul at Savannah as well as the U.S. War and Navy departments. Stirrup would escape from slavery after one year; Edwards remained in bondage during the entire war. Once he secured his freedom, United States officials, urged on by the British consul at Savannah, sought to bring his kidnappers to justice. Following is an account of the kidnapping, the search by British and American officials to find the adolescents, and the subsequent trial of the kidnapper. It is important because it is further evidence of Union cooperation with British authorities at the same time the two countries were encountering difficulties arising from the war.

Until evening of that spring day in 1861 when Stirrup and Edwards went fishing off the Bahama Banks, they certainly thought fortune must be smiling on them. Clouds were slowly gathering, but Stirrup and Edwards did not need to hurry to avoid a storm. The catch had been good; indeed, the youths had caught more fish than they needed. As they were returning to shore a gentleman called out from the *Hebe*, a schooner lying at anchor, asking the boys if they wanted to sell some of their fish. "We had seen the schooner for two or three days," recalled Edwards, and so they felt little concern as they climbed aboard. Besides the crew, two other black youths, Sampson and Kemp, had been brought on board by their employer, the captain of the British *Lazer*. The group seemed to be having a very cordial time, talking, laughing and imbibing heavily in liquor.[6]

According to his later testimony, Edwards's suspicions became aroused when one the crew members insisted that he take a drink, which he firmly refused. Then, suddenly, the white men who had accompanied Sampson and Kemp climbed into their boat, leaving their charges behind. Almost immediately the captain of the *Hebe* ordered the crew to weigh anchor, explaining to his youthful guests the necessity of taking the ship closer to shore to avoid possible damage from the coming storm. Edwards now insisted on leaving, but as he went aft he noticed that his boat had been set adrift. He shouted this news to the other three youths who instantly became alarmed. During the confusion that followed, Sampson and Kemp jumped overboard. A later report noted that Sampson drowned; however, he may have been shot. Edwards recalled that a crew member fired at least two shots after the fleeing youths as they swam away from the ship. "I was going to jump overboard [too] when a man caught me," Edwards told a jury many years later, "put a pistol at my head, saying, 'if you go any further, I'll blow your brains out; you are mine.'" Then "he put me [and Stirrup] down in the forecastle in the schooner." No sooner were the boys confined then they heard the ship heaving ahead, heading out to the open sea and not toward land as the captain had claimed.[7]

Two days later the *Hebe* arrived off the coast of Florida and spent the next week on the Indian River, an intracoastal waterway running from present-day Stuart to Titusville. Overcoming their initial confusion, Stirrup and Edwards began to become more aware of their surroundings, even though they were forced to spend many hours below deck. The captain also gave them strict instructions to go below if any strangers approached by either land or water. Stirrup and Edwards also noticed that Frederick Clark, whom they had been told was a passenger, had a great deal of influence with the captain; he conferred with Clark before making decisions or giving orders, and Clark began to take control of the boys.[8] When they asked Clark what he planned to do with them, he ignored the question. On the one occasion when they were permitted to go ashore, Stirrup told Edwards that the name of the schooner had been changed from the *Hebe* to the *Lavinia*.[9] Undoubtedly this step was taken to avoid detection.

Once the *Lavinia* arrived at Fernandina, Florida, Clark's role as master of the situation became evident. Taking Stirrup and Edwards with him, he immediately set out for Georgia. During the trip Clark instructed the youths to say they were from Florida, should anyone ask questions about their background. About twenty miles northwest of St. Mary's, he left the boys, telling them to wait until he returned. Stirrup attempted to return to St. Mary's but was apprehended as a fugitive by Henry Floyd, who then took both adolescents to his plantation, Bellevue. Three days later Clark arrived with an individual who interrogated Stirrup and Edwards about their backgrounds and skills. To the question of whether they wished to go with him, both Stirrup and Edwards answered "no." Despite their response, they were put into a wagon and taken away.[10]

Meanwhile British authorities in the Bahamas took action to recover the youths. Upon hearing of the kidnapping, W.C.J. Bayley, governor of the Bahamas, immediately notified the Foreign Office and Lyons. Giving Lyons all the particulars he knew about the case, Bayley concluded, "it is our belief that [the] *Hebe* was outfitted to capture defenseless Negroes. The captain knew the Islands well and gave different names to different people."[11]

Given his dislike of slavery, Lyons took a special interest in the case from the beginning. He reported the incident to Seward immediately but remained pessimistic about locating Stirrup and Edwards and bringing the kidnappers to justice. Apprising consuls in the South of the situation and asking them to use their influence with local authorities to apprehend the criminals, Lyons acknowledged the limited ability of the United States government to help because of the wartime situation. Also, given the current crisis, he did not expect the State Department to concentrate on finding the youths. His conclusion was correct. For the United States government, the outbreak of war overshadowed the abduction of Stirrup and Edwards. The State Department had more important issues to be concerned with, and Lyons realized that any demands on behalf of the kidnapped minors would be futile; consequently, no efforts to trace Stirrup and Edwards were undertaken in 1861.[12]

Stirrup's actions renewed the investigation. Hearing of the capture of Fernandina by United States naval forces in March 1862, Stirrup escaped from his master and made his way to Union lines. There he earned his living by working for the United States military, first the navy, then the army. Perhaps unhappy or simply just homesick, he wrote to his uncle in Nassau after several months. Briefly, he recounted his abduction—including the name of his kidnapper—his sale into slavery, and his escape. Stirrup also informed his uncle that, although he was working for the United States Navy, "I would like to come back home again if I can. I send my love to all." [13]

Unfortunately Bahamian officials forwarded the letter to the Colonial Office in London, and, by the time it arrived through channels at the State Department in Washington, Stirrup had left Fernandina and was now employed in the Sea Islands. Unaware of Stirrup's move, Seward requested a Navy Department investigation, which began to provide some concrete information. Checking with longtime residents in northern Florida, Admiral Samuel Dupont, commander of the South Atlantic squadron, was able to supply relatively accurate data about Stirrup and Edwards. Though S.L. Burritt, a Unionist living in Jacksonville, Dupont learned that Frederick Clark had lived in Fernandina but had fled the city at the approach of Union forces. He was well known and regarded as an unsavory individual. Burritt verified that Clark had kidnapped two minors from Nassau at the beginning of the war and had taken them to Georgia, where he had sold them in Camden County to a man named Malcolm Crawford for eight hundred dollars each. Burritt also noted that kidnapping was a crime in both Florida and Georgia but, since blacks could not testify in court against whites, convicting Clark would be very difficult. Probably the only way to bring the kidnapper to justice, Burritt assumed, would be to extradite him to Nassau. From subordinates within his own command Dupont learned that Stirrup, but not Edwards, had been employed on the CSS *Darlington* after it fell into Union hands. However, the army later took control of the ship and discharged all the civilian employees. Concluding his report, Dupont surmised that, in all likelihood, Stirrup was currently employed within the command of General Rufus Saxon, stationed around Beaufort, South Carolina.[14]

Seward now turned to the War Department, and the search for Stirrup began anew. At first the response was disappointing. Saxon reported his failure to locate Stirrup within his command but, thinking ahead, he asked what he should do with the young man if he were found. Instructions were forwarded to Saxon, but no correspondence regarding Stirrup took place for the next several months.[15]

Although he had been forewarned, Consul Archibald at New York City must have been somewhat surprised when in mid-April 1863, officers from the USS *Argo* arrived at the consulate with Stirrup in tow. As instructed, Archibald arranged to return the lad to Nassau, but he questioned the youth closely before his departure. Archibald was not aware of Burritt's memo, but Stirrup's answers verified the fact that he had been held as a slave on the plantation of W. Malcolm Crawford. Stirrup also told Archibald that he had escaped on March 3, 1862, and that at the time Edwards was still being held in slavery. Questioned about the location of Crawford's plantation, Stirrup replied that it was in Jefferson County, Georgia.[16]

Stirrup's information was only partly accurate. His unfamiliarity with American place-names sidetracked the next phase of the investigation. Malcolm Crawford's plantation was located near Jefferston, a village twenty miles northwest of St. Mary's; Jefferson County was located in the northeastern part of the state. Consequently, when Lyons instructed Allan Fullarton, vice-consul at Savannah, to locate Edwards and purchase him if necessary, Fullarton ran into a dead end corresponding with officials and residents of Jefferson County. Unable to find Crawford's name in recent tax books, the clerk in charge suggested that Fullarton contact George W. Crawford in Richmond City, head of the Crawford clan in Georgia. The response was negative there also. George Crawford advised Fullarton to search in another state as "Jefferson is a universal county name in the South." Fullarton even encouraged a friend to travel throughout several northern counties and question older residents, hoping that someone might remember Malcolm Crawford.[17]

By July 1863 any attempt to trace Edwards ceased. Fullarton became embroiled with Governor Joseph Brown of Georgia and the Confederate State Department in his efforts to keep British subjects from being conscripted into the Confederate army, and Secretary Benjamin took the drastic step of expelling him. No further efforts were made to find Edwards during the remainder of the war.[18]

The final search for Edwards began in 1865 when Edward Long of Lowndes County, Georgia, informed Samuel's father of his son's whereabouts. According to Long, he became aware of Samuel's plight in 1862 and purchased him with the intent of returning the youth to his home after the war. Long even offered to accompany Samuel on his return trip to Nassau. At first glance, Long's attitude appears very generous; however, several facts give the impression that he was attempting to protect Crawford and Clark from possible prosecution. He did not, for example, mention Crawford and implied that he had purchased Edwards directly from Clark. Nor did he mention Clark's name. Considering later events, what he wrote about Clark was a brazen falsehood: "His kidnapper, who lived in Florida, was hung because of his habitual practice of stealing negroes and selling them."[19]

Despite Long's correspondence to the Edwards family, the youth was not located until the fall of 1866. In part, the slow movement of official mail caused the delay: almost a year elapsed between the date of Long's letter to Edwards's father and the receipt of instructions by William Tasker-Smith, newly appointed British consul at Savannah, to trace Edwards and send him to Nassau. During that time Edwards had fallen in love, moved to Florida with his girlfriend, and lost contact with Edward Long. As a result, Tasker-Smith had to undertake his own search, but his efforts were lackadaisical.[20] Tasker-Smith's chief concern centered on getting himself reassigned to a different consulate. Before being named consul at Savannah, he had served as a member of the slave-trade commission in Africa, and he was disappointed at being given another "hot weather" post. Almost as soon as he arrived in Savannah, Tasker-Smith began a campaign for reassignment. For the next five years he

returned to England between May and November of each year
to plead his case.[21]

In time Tasker-Smith succeeded in bringing Edwards to Savannah, and almost immediately the youth spotted Clark in
the marketplace. On receipt of this news, the consul alerted
Henry S. Fitch, United States attorney for the southern district of Georgia. Fitch quickly apprehended Clark and brought
him before United States Commissioner Amherst W. Stone,
who under law was empowered to seek a grand jury indictment
if enough evidence existed to charge Clark with a crime.[22]

Stone considered two possible charges against Clark: engaging in the international slave trade and violating neutrality
laws between the United States and Great Britain. If found
guilty of the first offense, Clark could be punished under one
of two Federal statutes designed to curb the international
slave trade. The first, passed in 1818, provided for fines up to
ten thousand dollars and a prison term of three to seven years;
the second, an act of May 29, 1820, declared trafficking in
slaves from abroad to be an act of piracy, a capital offense.[23]
The charge involving British neutrality laws was mentioned
at the hearing but was never raised again.

That the hearing, held between May 6 and May 14, 1867,
created a good deal of public interest was evident by local
newspaper coverage. Normally the *Savannah News and Herald* reported legal proceedings on page three, giving each case
only a few lines. The case of the *United States v. Frederick
Clark* received front page coverage, with an entire column devoted to the first day's session. And the reporter took special
notice of the "English Consul in the Court." Indeed, Tasker-
Smith's presence caused Clark's lawyers to ask if their client
was being tried for the British government.

The high point of the hearing was Edwards's testimony.
Carefully guided by Fitch, Edwards told the story of his abduction and journey to Crawford's plantation. Although his account lacked specifics, it was still damaging. So much so that
the day after Edwards testified a friend of Clark arrived at the
British consulate and offered him one thousand dollars to return to Nassau immediately. When Edwards, on the advice of

the British consul, rejected the offer, the friend appealed to Tasker-Smith, claiming that Clark suffered from severe "heart problems" and probably could not endure the trauma of a trial and possible prison term.[24]

Clark's lawyers did raise several legal issues at the hearing. First, they contended that the Thirteenth Amendment negated all laws concerned with the international slave trade; since slavery no longer exited in the United States in 1867, the acts of 1818 and 1820 were no longer in effect. Thus, Clark had not violated them. Next, they maintained that "the offense, if any," was barred by the statute of limitations. Both the statutes of 1818 and 1820 required that the guilty party be apprehended and charged within five years of the alleged crime. Brushing the arguments aside, Commissioner Stone declared that his only duty was to determine if enough evidence existed to seek a grand jury indictment against Clark; he had no authority, he said, to settle legal questions. With that he requested the indictment, ordered Clark to post a bail of ten thousand dollars and to appear for trial before the next session of the United States District Court in August 1867.[25]

When the case reached the district court, Clark's lawyers again raised the same legal points; this time their argument made impact. Judge John Erskine sent the case on to the circuit court. The judge noted that an act of Congress in 1846 made district court decisions final in all cases involving the international slave trade.[26] Neither side, Erskine said, could appeal the district court's decision. Since questions of law were involved, Erskine felt it would be fairer to both sides to send the case on to the circuit court. If the judges there disagreed on legal fine points, their decision could then be appealed to the United States Supreme Court.[27]

For inexplicable reasons, the circuit court did not reach its decision until November 18, 1870.[28] Then it quickly accepted the arguments of Clark's lawyer and agreed to quash the case on demurrer.[29]

The focus of Clark's defense rested on the vagueness of the indictment. It did not give a specific date for the alleged kidnapping but merely stated that the incident occurred "on or about the tenth day of May 1861." Nor was the indictment clear about the exact nature of the crime committed. One clause charged Clark with aiding and abetting the kidnapping but failed to state specifically if he had masterminded the plot; another declared that he perpetrated the entire scheme "to hold, sell, or otherwise dispose of" Stirrup and Edwards. Thus one portion of the indictment charged Clark with a crime, while another declared that he merely supported the kidnappers. Finally, the indictment was drawn up after the five-year limitation set by the statutes. Clearly, the indictment stated that the alleged crime occurred in the spring of 1861, but the indictment itself was drawn up on May 14, 1867, which was six, not five, years after the crime was supposedly committed.[30]

Ironically, it was John Erskine, now acting as circuit judge, who agreed to quash the case.[31] Given the speed with which he sent the case from the district to the circuit court and his willingness to quash the case, one might suspect favoritism on the judge's part. Moreover, Erskine undoubtedly held nineteenth-century Southern values. Although he was a native of Ireland, Erskine had lived in the South since 1838 and had made close friendships with some of Georgia's leading politicians. Governor Brown had given Erskine a civil appointment during the war to make him ineligible for the draft, and later, in 1869, both Brown and Alexander H. Stephens, former vice-president of the Confederacy, backed Erskine's nomination to the United States Supreme Court. In decisions involving racial issues or the rights of white Southerners, Erskine revealed a Southern point of view. He declared, for instance, that Congress could not forbid former Confederates from practicing law, and he upheld Georgia's ban on interracial marriage;[32] yet, ultimately, Erskine made the only decision he could in the Clark case. The indictment was vague for several reasons. Under cross-examination Edwards could not remember salient facts, and several of his comments attenuated charges in the indictment. Also, documents that would have made the indictment more precise were filed at the Foreign Office in London or at the State Department in Washington and were not available to the prosecution. Probably because of his own confusion at the time of his abduction and his lack of understanding about how important certain facts might be later, Edwards could not remember specific information that would have strengthened the indictment. He could not recall, for example, the day on which he was kidnapped; the indictment, as a result, placed the incident in May 1861. However, Governor Bayley's report of the kidnapping, written shortly after it occurred, specifically stated that it had taken place on March 18, 1861. Nor could Edwards verify that he had ever been sold; he had never seen any money pass between Clark and Crawford. Still, Judge Burritt's statement to United States naval authorities clearly stated that Crawford paid eight hundred dollars each for Stirrup and Edwards. Neither Tasker-Smith nor Edwards's lawyers had any knowledge of the statement's existence, nor could they have called Judge Burritt as a witness; he had drowned at sea in 1865.[33]

On other points Edwards also proved to be an ineffectual witness: he admitted that he boarded the *Hebe* of his own accord, he did not know how his boat had been set adrift, he had never seen Clark acting as either mate or sailor on the *Hebe*, and no person on the boat had ever told him that he was being kidnapped for the purpose of being sold into slavery. Finally, Edwards did not know if Clark owned all or a share of the *Hebe*. Under the law of 1820, owners or shareholders of vessels engaging in the international slave trade were liable for the crew's actions.[34]

The vagueness of the indictment was also responsible for the failure of British authorities to follow certain suggestions as the case proceeded through the courts. Evidently U.S. Attorney Fitch realized the weak points in Edwards's testimony following his cross-examination, so he proposed two moves the British government might make to strengthen the case. He advised that it should consider returning Stirrup to the United States to serve as a witness against Clark and that it might instruct authorities in the Bahamas to check customs records to determine the *Hebe's* stated purpose for being at Nassau as well as whether Clark was listed as a passenger or in some other capacity. Clark's lawyers, Fitch thought, would build their defense on the argument that Clark was merely a passenger on the *Hebe* and had not been involved in the kidnapping.[35] There are several possible explanations as to why the British government ignored Fitch's suggestions. By the opening of Clark's trial in 1867, the personnel at the British legation and at the Savannah consulate had changed totally. By 1865 Lord Lyons and William Stuart had left Washington for new assignments. Both men had shown a keen interest in pursuing the search for Stirrup and Edwards during the war and probably would have proved valuable assets in Federal efforts to seek Clark's conviction. The new British minister to the United States was unfamiliar with the case, and in any case he died suddenly in September 1867. Allan Fullarton left Savannah in 1863; although he returned to the city and his banking business at war's end, he took no further interest in consular affairs. The British government also may have been unwilling to spend the money necessary to carry out Fitch's suggestions: between 1866 and 1870 the British cabinet passed from the Liberals to the Conservatives and back to the Liberals again. Plagued by problems at home and within the Empire as well as by pressing issues with the United States, neither political party might have been willing to focus much attention on a six-year-old kidnapping case.[36]

As of November 19, 1870, Clark was a free man. So was Edwards, but he had very little to show for the years he had spent in slavery and as a trial witness. At the conclusion of the case, the United States government paid Edwards $108.45 for travel and per diem.[37] He had been required to appear at the original hearing in May 1867 and at every court session until the case was quashed in 1870. He offered testimony at the original hearing only and was never called again to take the stand. He would have fared better financially had he accepted Clark's offer of one thousand dollars and left the United States.

The search for Stirrup and Edwards may have been the first time the United States government became actively involved in kidnapping cases involving black foreign nationals. No evidence in either British or American diplomatic archives indicates that Lyons sought Federal assistance in trying to locate

William Brodie or Martin Chartton, both kidnapped during the Buchanan administration. In appealing to the Lincoln government, Lyons hoped for a more sympathetic hearing, and he was not disappointed. True, wartime conditions slowed the investigation, but when fighting stopped the search for Edwards continued and Federal authorities in the South sought to bring the kidnappers to justice, demonstrating a commitment to protect blacks' rights during the early postwar years.

The case of Stirrup and Edwards was, moreover, another indication of Union cooperation to protect the rights of British nationals within the United States. While Seward pressed hard on issues of vital importance to American interests, he respected British concerns about the treatment of its citizens abroad. His willingness to cooperate in such matters stood in sharp contrast to the Southern attitude on similar issues.

7

Consular Problems in the South

Throughout the war, Lord Lyons insisted on impartiality from the consuls in their dealings 'with the two American governments. To avoid problems with the Confederacy, he asked the Southern consuls never to mention him or the legation in any way. He insisted that no reference to the Confederacy should imply actual or intended diplomatic recognition, and he suggested the use of the term "so-called Confederacy." Consuls in both the North and the South were to take no action or make any public statement that might indicate sympathy for either the Union or the Confederacy.

Northern consuls abided by these stipulations and caused few problems, but the situation was different in the South. There Lyons found himself in conflict with three men who evaded the rules and incurred his disapproval: Henry Pinckney Walker at Charleston; Peter Goolrick at Fredericksburg, Virginia; and James Magee at Mobile. Lyons's reaction to Walker and Goolrick revealed how he dealt with consuls who sidestepped his rules, but his response to Magee's action was the initial move that eventually cut all communication between Great Britain and the Southern government.

The foreign minister's difficulty with Walker came with the removal of Consul Bunch from Charleston. When Seward failed to issue formal notification withdrawing Bunch's exequatur and made no demand for him to leave the Southern city, Lyons encouraged the Foreign Office to let him remain. "You will not have failed to observe that it is on him that we are mainly dependent for information," Lyons observed.[1] As a result, Bunch stayed in Charleston where he carried on all consular functions except the signing of formal documents.[2]

But, as military activity became more intense in the Sea Islands and the surrounding regions, Lyons began to reassess Bunch's position. Suspecting a military move to capture Charleston, Lyons feared Bunch might be charged under the Logan Act if Federal troops captured the city, and he laid plans to remove the consul.[3] With Bunch's withdrawal pending, both the legation and the Foreign Office pondered the question of replacement and the major problem it created: how to avoid applying for an exequatur and offending either the Union or the Confederacy.

By late 1862 the British were aware that replacing any consul in South might be troublesome. The Davis administration had not officially changed its policy regarding consular appointments and allowed all prewar appointees to continue in office. But increasing anti-British feeling was causing a number of Southern newspapers and congressmen to question the presence of the British consuls, demanding that they request exequaturs from the Confederate government. If public sentiment forced the government to press the issue, the Foreign Office would be caught in a dilemma. An application to the Southern government would anger the Union, and the Confederates would certainly take offense if Seward granted an exequatur. Lyons guessed the situation correctly when he wrote: "It is almost certain that they would refuse to recognize a consul . . . who obtained an exequatur from the Federal government."[4]

Given the difficulty of the situation, the Foreign Office and the legation mulled the question of Bunch's replacement for several months. At first, James Murray, Russell's private secretary, suggested turning the Charleston consulate over to the French consul in the city. While putting a consulate into the hands of a consul from another country was a relatively common practice, a Frenchman might not be able to protect British citizens from being illegally conscripted into the Confederate army or state militia units. Murray then proposed sending the consul from Buffalo, who was already accredited, to Charleston and simply explaining the move as a relocation. But Russell and Lyons rejected this solution as too obvious. The third possibility was to promote Henry Pinckney Walker from vice-consul to acting consul. It was within Bunch's authority to make such an appointment, and it would appear as if Lyons had not been involved in the selection. Then, too, acting consuls did not need to apply for exequaturs. The only requirement was a notice informing Union and Confederate authorities of the change.[5]

Walker was born in England in 1820; he immigrated to the United States in 1839 and moved to Charleston. He became an American citizen in 1844 to meet the citizenship requirement for practicing law in South Carolina. From 1848 to 1860 he served as clerk of the City Court of Charleston but was forced to resign when he refused to take an oath of allegiance to South Carolina and the Confederacy. Out of concern for Walker's financial plight and his large family—he had eight children—Bunch named him vice-consul in 1861. The salary was small, but Walker accepted the position because he had no other means of support.[6]

Lyons had met Walker in June 1861 when he delivered some official correspondence to the legation and almost immediately took a dislike to the man. Lyons objected mainly to Walker's strong sympathy for the South. Even though Walker was not a secessionist, he defended slavery and other aspects of Southern life. Writing his impressions of Walker to Bunch, Lyons stated, "his having refused to become a citizen of the 'C' States does not amount to much," and he feared Walker was working at the consulate only to have protection from a foreign government if Charleston were invaded.[7]

Walker's action during the fall of 1861 only strengthened Lyons's suspicions. In August the *Alliance*, a British transport plying her way between Halifax and Havana, sailed into the harbor at Beaufort, South Carolina. Union blockading forces refused to let the ship depart. Merchant ships in Southern harbors or on the high seas at the time the blockade was announced were permitted to leave, as was evident in the case of the schooner *Eliza and Catherine*. That ship was on the high seas when Lincoln issued his blockade proclamation on April 19 and arrived in Charleston harbor at a time when blockading ships were temporarily absent. While the *Eliza and Catherine* was in port, the blockade was reestablished but the ship was permitted to depart because it had not known of the proclamation when it entered the harbor.

But the *Alliance* case was different. The ship had sailed directly from Halifax to Beaufort after Lincoln had issued his proclamation, and the captain had been aware of it; therefore, the ship was detained for failure to observe the blockade. In a letter to the British commander of the North American Station, Walker suggested the use of force to free the *Alliance*; Bunch imprudently attached a supporting statement to it. The commander forwarded the consuls' correspondence to Lyons, who responded immediately. Declaring that the use of force against Union blockaders would surely lead to war, Lyons rejected Walker's suggestion and asked the commander to say nothing about it to the Foreign Office. He recounted the details of Bunch's recent troubles and concluded, "the authorities are out of humour with Mr. Bunch. . . . It might almost ruin [him] if [Walker's letter and his statement] came before the F.O. at this moment." Lyons recalled Bunch's good work, "but this indiscretion about the use of force might upset him altogether." He also fired off a letter to Bunch, returning the correspondence and recommending its destruction. In addition, Lyons made his displeasure with Walker quite evident.[8]

Because of his misgivings, Lyons sought to defeat Walker's promotion to acting consul. Stressing Walker's American citizenship, Lyons declared that he could not claim protection as a British national if Charleston were invaded. An added problem was that Walker's two grown sons had joined the Confederate army and were stationed in the Charleston area, which would certainly create difficulty with Union authorities. Lyons predicted that Walker, because he had refused to take an oath to the Confederacy, would be ineffective in dealing with Southern authorities. Summarizing his objections, Lyons concluded, Walker "does not appear to me to be . . . a person to whom the protection of British Subjects and British interest could be confidently entrusted in critical and delicate circumstances."[9]

Lyons also responded strongly because he felt he had Bunch's support, and he did until the fall of 1862. Writing about a possible replacement in January 1862, Bunch declined to endorse

Walker. He was "a Southern advocate of the extremist type," who might be entrusted with the consulate in ordinary times, but Bunch doubted that Walker was a satisfactory choice at the moment.[10] Then while Lyons was on leave in England during the summer, Bunch changed his mind and pushed for his vice-consul's promotion. In a letter to William Stuart, chargé d'affaires, Bunch described Walker as the "natural person" to assume responsibility for the consulate: Russell and Lyons had already authorized Walker to sign all formal documents issued by the consul, and his experience would prove an invaluable asset. Bunch rejected the idea that Union authorities would find Walker unacceptable as acting consul. Walker "has strong prepossessions in favor of this section of the country," Bunch admitted, but he would not allow his sympathies to interfere with duty. Hearing of the change in Bunch's attitude, Lyons replied: "If Bunch is now pushing Walker, a remarkable change appears to have taken place in Mr. Bunch's mind on this subject." Later, when Stuart asked about forwarding certain letters to Walker, Lyons wrote: "If you want to send the Letters . . . go on and do so. I have written them chiefly out of civility and don't care whether they go on or not."[11]

In the end Bunch made the final decision about his replacement. Given only three days' notice to leave Charleston, Bunch merely turned over the consulate to Walker. Although he acted within his authority, Lyons remarked: "I am not entirely satisfied with this arrangement." In a last-ditch effort to keep Walker from assuming control, Lyons presented his objections directly to Walker and suggested that he turn the consular archives over to the French consul. Walker, Lyons believed, would have difficulty with Federal authorities if they captured the city. His refusal to swear allegiance to the Confederacy would mean nothing when compared to his former political position and his sons' service in the army. Finally, Lyons hinted that Walker and his family would be safer outside of Charleston.[12]

As one might expect, Walker defended himself. He failed to understand why he would be a special object of discipline by the Federal military. He informed Lyons that his sons were born in South Carolina and subject to Confederate and state law; further, they were eighteen and twenty years old, and he could no longer control their actions. He could not leave the city: he had no home in the country, transportation for his possessions was not available, and he could not afford a move because his sole income was his consular salary. As if to impress on Lyons the necessity of accepting his appointment, Walker notified him that following a bombardment of Charleston, the French consul had left for New York City. In a final plea of patriotic sentiment, Walker concluded: "I am actuated by duty and the circumstances of the time. I am really disappointed that you want me to turn the consulate over." [13]

Lyons bowed to the inevitable and concluded that Walker "will be as efficient as any person we can find." Still he could never bring himself to appreciate the efforts Walker would make on behalf of British subjects in South Carolina. Sensing Lyons's objection to him, Walker sent most of his correspondence directly to the Foreign Office for the remainder of the war.[14]

Although Walker remained in the consular service, Goolrick and Magee were quickly dispensed with. The elimination of Goolrick and his vice-consulate was facilitated by the fact that neither Union nor British authorities were aware they ever existed.

Much to the surprise of Federal troops temporarily occupying Fredericksburg, Virginia, in the spring of 1862, they came across Peter Goolrick, a storekeeper who claimed to be the British vice-consul. He hoisted the Union Jack over his doorway, declaring that he held one thousand barrels of flour in his cellar belonging to James Gemmill, a British subject, and that the flag and his official position protected his store and residence from search.

Conversations with Unionists in the city led Federal authorities to doubt Goolrick's story. Locals Unionists said he might be a British vice-consul but he was also an American citizen, a notorious secessionist, and the cellar contained more than flour. When Federal troops learned that Goolrick had two cellars, one in which he kept flour and another in which he hid military supplies that Confederates had been secretly removing since their evacuation from the town, they raided his store and seized the flour, supplies, and all of his official consular documents, including the British flag. When it was later discovered that he had received formal authorization to act as vice-consul in 1853, his papers—but not the flag, the flour, or the other supplies—were returned.[15]

At this time Lyons was on leave in England, so Seward raised several questions with William Stuart, chargé d'affaires: was the legation aware of Goolrick's position, and would it explain why a vice-consulate was needed at Fredericksburg when Washington was only fifty-six miles north and Richmond sixty-six miles south of the city? Seward also stated that he was willing to return the flour to Gemmill if it could be found. If not, Seward would compensate Gemmill if he were a British subject. In the event that Goolrick really was a vice-consul, the flag would be returned, but he doubted that Goolrick could claim British protection because of his American citizenship. Seward finally suggested that Goolrick be discharged and replaced with a British citizen or at least a loyal American.[16]

Stuart and Seward never developed the kind of relationship that existed between the secretary and Lyons, for Stuart tended to be much more critical of the Lincoln administration. He referred to the Emancipation Proclamation, for example, as a "cold, vindictive and entirely political" document designed to let friends of the Union keep their slaves while encouraging servile insurrection in the Confederacy. Still, Seward's letter caught Stuart by surprise. He responded that he knew nothing about Goolrick or the vice-consulate but would investigate the matter. He also requested Goolrick's continuance in office until the inquiry was completed because he had no authority to terminate any department within the consular service.[17]

The investigation was more time-consuming than complicated; it involved checking with the consulate at Richmond. But the response proved one thing: no one at the Richmond consulate had ever heard of Goolrick. "I will only here state that I conceive him to be of no use whatever," replied Vice-Consul Frederick Cridland to the question of Goolrick's effectiveness. "He has never made any report to this Consulate."[18]

Whether Lyons discussed the matter with Russell while he was in England is unknown. Upon his return to Washington, he reviewed the correspondence, assessed the situation, and short-

ly after informed Seward that the vice-consulate at Fredericksburg was closed and that Goolrick's services were terminated.[19]
This action would undoubtedly have been taken under any circumstances. British officials were unaware that the vice-consulate existed, and Goolrick was ineffective. Further, Fredericksburg was hardly large enough or far enough from a consulate to
justify a separate vice-consular office there. A few consulates or
vice-consulates had been established in the interior of the country, but they were located at active trading centers. But Lyons's
decision came much easier—and he made no effort to defend
Goolrick—because of the evidence indicating the vice-consul's
collaboration with Confederates.

Among the consuls, none was appointed with greater public
support than James Magee, and none left his post under a
thicker cloud of disfavor. Magee had no prior experience in the
consular service before his appointment as acting consul at
Mobile. The Foreign Office hurriedly named him to the post in
March 1861, just as the Confederate government was getting
under way, to avoid the exequatur question with the new government and because Magee had local popular backing. A
group of businessmen in Mobile had petitioned in support of
his appointment.[20]

When journalist William Howard Russell traveled through
the South several months later, he seemed impressed with Magee and implied that his performance was competent. Lyons,
however, referred to him as "incapable" and said he only sent a
few dispatches "recording the arrival and departure of vessels
running the blockade." Magee also protested against the conscription of British citizens into Alabama militia units, which
began shortly after the surrender of Fort Sumter, and into the
Confederate army following passage of the draft law in 1862.
His protests were so mild, however, that local recruiting officers ignored them.[21]

Magee's troubles began in November 1862 when Charles
Walsh, president of the Bank of Mobile, inquired if he could
arrange for the transfer of £29,806 ($155,000), in coin, to Eng-
land. The money, Walsh wrote, was payment on bonds issued
by Alabama before the war and was payable to British citizens
at several banking houses in London. Despite the conflict rag-

ing in the South, Walsh continued, "the state wishes to meet its obligations and remain in good standing with its foreign creditors." Magee immediately responded in the affirmative and wrote to Acting Consul Coppell in New Orleans requesting a British warship to take the money to Havana, from which it could be shipped to England. He did not inform Lord Lyons of his actions until six weeks later, at about the same time that the money was removed from the country.[22]

The warship arrived off Mobile on January 3, 1863, and was allowed to pass into the bay after informing the Union blockading squadron that it had private business to transact with the consul. That same day the vice-consul at Norfolk, Virginia, sent a telegram, under Lyons's signature, forbidding Magee to send the money out of the country. The British ship left Mobile with the money on January 5, and Magee later claimed he did not receive Lyons's telegram until the next day.[23]

Lyons refused to accept Magee's explanation. "Mr. Magee's conduct in the whole matter is . . . inexplicable," he informed Russell. Magee's failure to inform him of Walsh's letter, his own request for a ship to take the money away from Mobile, and his failure to keep the foreign minister informed of events as they occurred could not be explained away as "oversights," Lyons insisted. Further, Magee's dispatches for twelve days following the sailing of the warship failed to mention its departure or the receipt of Lyons's telegram. As far as Lyons was concerned, this was a "plan of the Confederate Secretary of the Treasury for sending specie to England by British Ships of War in payment for munitions of war." He suggested removing Magee before the United States government demanded his recall. Russell agreed, and on March 1, 1863—exactly two years after he had been appointed—Magee was dismissed from the consular service and instructed to turn over the archives to the French vice-consul in Mobile.[24]

Lyons attempted to arrange for Magee's departure from Mobile during the following months but canceled all arrangements upon learning that Magee had sailed out of New York City for Liverpool. Apparently he had made his own way out of the South; he had avoided Washington and Lyons entirely, and he made no attempt to contact the Foreign Office upon his return to Great Britain.[25]

The Confederate reaction to Magee's dismissal was quick and immediate and was, in fact, the initial step in the worsening of relations between the Southern government and the British consuls. Relating the entire incident to James Mason, Confederate commissioner in Great Britain, Secretary of State Benjamin concluded: "Debts due by a state are not subject to the laws of war and are beyond the reach of confiscation." More important, he resented Lord Lyons's interference, terming it "unjustified" because Alabama had the right and obligation to pay it debts. He also questioned Lyons's authority to direct consuls in the South because he was accredited to the United States, a foreign country in Benjamin's view. Confronted with Benjamin's letter several months later, Lyons called the Southerner's argument about Alabama's debt "a sophistry": "Benjamin knew at the time the great anxiety of the Confederates to get specie through the blockade to pay for their purchases of warlike stores in Europe, and [of] the great anxiety of the United States . . . to prevent this." But he acknowledged as sound Benjamin's comments about his authority over the Southern consuls. Lyons had always maintained that the Confederate government, even though it was not recognized, was within its rights to question his direction of consular activities in the South.[26]

Benjamin's complaint came, in part, because Governor John Shorter of Alabama demanded a formal protest, a strongly worded statement insisting that Britain did not have the right to remove Magee. Benjamin disagreed. "A nation places a consul in a port for her own convenience," he responded, "and she might withdraw him at pleasure, and decline to assign a reason." In addition, Shorter suggested that a new consul not be accepted at Mobile unless Britain extended diplomatic recognition to the Confederacy. While Benjamin was unwilling to commit himself immediately, he did ask to be informed if either Lyons or the Foreign Office assigned a consul to the city.[27]

The manner in which Magee was replaced indicates that British officials suspected difficulties. Proper procedures were followed in dealing with Seward, but Benjamin was deliberately deceived.

Lyons favored Frederick Cridland, vice-consul at Richmond, as Magee's replacement because he was already in the South and already a recognized vice-consul. If Cridland were sent to Mobile the only necessary action would be to notify Union and Confederate authorities. In May 1863 Lyons did inform Seward that Cridland was being transferred to Mobile as acting consul; no such statement was sent to Benjamin.[28] The first he read about Cridland's move was a brief paragraph in the *Richmond Whig* on May 18, 1863, stating that Cridland was to become the "Lincoln consul at Mobile." Cridland read it too and rushed to the State Department to assure Benjamin that the statement was erroneous. He had not been named consul, he assured Benjamin, but was merely going to Mobile as a private citizen to look after British interests. Cridland claimed he did not have a consular commission from the Queen or an exequatur from Washington; he had, he said, even asked the *Whig* to print a retraction. Benjamin accepted the explanation, telling Cridland that private citizens were free to travel in the Confederacy without restriction.[29]

Several weeks after Cridland left Richmond, the naval commander at Mobile informed Confederate authorities of his introduction to the new British acting consul. The French consul, who had been holding British consular archives, introduced the two men and showed the commander a letter, signed by Lyons, appointing Cridland acting consul. When informed of the incident, Benjamin took immediate action. His chief concern was the manner of Cridland's appointment, rather than the appointment itself: Cridland had been authorized to assume his position by Lyons who, according to Benjamin, had no authority to name Cridland to a post in the Confederacy. Benjamin also protested Lyons's action to the Foreign Office through James Mason. Russell ignored Lyons's role in the affair and stressed Britain's need to protect its citizens and their property in the area as justification for the appointment.[30]

Along with his refusal to accept Cridland as acting consul, Benjamin ordered him to leave Alabama and asked the local military commander to keep him informed about Cridland's movements. Later Benjamin relented when Cridland requested permission to remain in Mobile until he received instructions about the disposition of the consular archives. Then, following the sudden death of the French consul, who had entrusted Cridland with the safekeeping of the French archives, Benjamin permitted him to remain in Mobile but only as a private citizen.[31]

Four months after the Cridland episode ended, Benjamin expelled the British consuls in Richmond, Charleston, and Savannah and ordered them to leave the country. Because Cridland was the sole British consular official remaining in the South, although not recognized as such by the Davis administration, Russell tried to contact the Confederate government through him. In February 1864 he sent Cridland a communiqué and requested that it be forwarded to Benjamin. The Confederate secretary refused to receive it until Cridland presented his authority to act as a courier. But Benjamin also refused to accept Russell's instructions to Cridland as proper authorization and returned the correspondence unopened. At the same time, he informed Cridland to "refrain from further correspondence with this government until you are clothed with official character and recognized in such character by this government."[32]

Lord Lyons made every effort to discourage any show of sympathy for the Confederacy among his Southern consuls. If Walker still approved of the Southern way of life after his appointment as acting consul (and he undoubtedly did), it never came through in his correspondence. He had come to realize the limits of expressing his personal attitudes and feelings. Dismissing Goolrick proved no problem for Lyons; his post would probably have been eliminated even in normal times. Magee's case was different. Lyons's response to Magee's act of sending Confederate funds to England and his subsequent appointment of Magee's replacement brought into question his authority over the Southern consuls. It was the first step that would eventually eliminate any diplomatic contact, within the confines of the Southern states at least, between the Confederacy and Great Britain.

8

Conscription,
Confederate Style

William Mure had been consul at New Orleans since 1843. He retired in the late summer of 1861, but his last months in office, from April to August, were the most hectic of his entire career. Explaining the reason for this predicament, Mure wrote: "I have been so busy investigating cases of impressment . . . that I have scarcely time for any other subject." Several weeks before, he had taken the issue public in a statement to the *New Orleans Picayune*: "Since the 28th of April to this present day, with very slight intermission, many British subjects, some of whom [have been] only a few weeks in the country, were seized and forcibly carried off from the levee, steamboat landing, boarding houses etc., to the different places of rendezvous of military companies. When the men resisted they were frequently assaulted, knocked down, and being overpowered, carried off in furniture wagons to the headquarters of these embryo companies, where the most violent threats were used to compel them 'to sign the papers.'"[1]

Mure's experience served as prelude to the situation every consul in the South would encounter before war's end: forced or fraudulent enlistment of foreign nationals, appeals to consuls by victims, consular pleas to civil or military officials, and decisions whether to release the victims or retain them in service.

Although forced enlistments occurred in many areas of the Confederacy in the early months of the war, they appeared to be more blatantly carried out in New Orleans. Mure informed his superiors of the havoc and fear press gangs were causing in the city during April and May 1861. Hoping to protect British citizens from being forcibly conscripted, Mure wrote to Governor

Thomas Moore explaining that it was illegal to induct aliens by means of coercion. Foreign nationals, he wrote, might be called upon to maintain domestic order, but under international law they could not be compelled to participate in wars with other nations. Apparently the point was made, for Governor Moore issued a proclamation exempting from military service "members who are subjects of a foreign power and government." Several months later when Moore summoned all men between eighteen and forty-five years of age into militia service, he stipulated that foreign nationals would be used for local defense only.[2]

After Mure's retirement, George Coppell, the new acting consul, persuaded Britons in New Orleans to form the "British Guard," a unit designed to maintain order within the city. Within two months Coppell found himself opposing the governor's effort to incorporate the guard and other foreign military groups into the regular militia. Only a conference between Moore and the foreign consuls in Louisiana persuaded the governor to change his mind.[3]

Mure's tactic of dealing directly with the governor won praise from the Foreign Office, and the office instructed other British consuls in the South to follow his example. As a result, consuls received promises from a number of Southern governors agreeing not to induct foreign nationals into military units organized to fight Federal troops.[4]

The illegal conscription of foreigners was not limited to British citizens alone, nor was it confined solely to the South. Men from every national group in the Confederacy faced the possibility of forced service in the Confederate army or in one of the state militia units. To avoid conscription, French and Spanish nationals followed the British example and organized guard units to quell local disturbances. Germans, the second largest foreign group in the Confederacy, responded in various ways. Many, although not citizens, joined the Southern cause because they felt obligated to defend their new homes. Others went into hiding, while some even fled to Mexico. Constant pressure from military and civil authorities finally forced Germans in Texas, where the largest number lived, to submit. In January 1863 a

Texas recruiting officer wrote that Germans who had previously opposed the draft were now being quietly enrolled.[5]

Compliance was easier to obtain from non-British nationals because they lacked avenues of appeal. The number of non-British consulates in prewar years were fewer and mostly located in New Orleans. After Federal troops captured the city in April 1862 and the French consuls left Charleston and Mobile in early 1863, non-British citizens had no one to turn to. The few non-British consuls or consular agents in Galveston were too far removed from most of their countrymen to be of service.[6] Thus, the lack of European consulates left most foreign national groups vulnerable, while the presence of British consuls, until their expulsion in the fall of 1863, offered some means of protection, however slight, against conscription.

Conscription also became a more pressing problem for British nationals as the war continued because they were singled out as targets for special Confederate hostility. Southerners had great expectations of support and approval from the British government when the war began. As hopes for diplomatic recognition faded, they became antagonistic toward the European power. Even in the fall of 1862, when diplomatic recognition seemed most likely, Consul Magee complained about the anti-British attitude exhibited by the commander at a military camp in Mississippi. He patiently listened to French and Italian nationals and released them from any military obligations, while he ignored the pleas of Britons and destroyed evidence proving their alien status. Following the battles of Gettysburg and Vicksburg, when there remained little likelihood of British recognition, Thomas Wright wrote from Augusta, Georgia, "the white Subjects of Great Briton [sic] in the South are Exposed to all manner of Insult."[7]

Finally, British citizens, including Irishmen, were more affected by the conscription issue because they comprised the largest number of immigrants in the Confederacy: 138,067 out of 250,000 foreign-born nationals. While the 1860 census does not furnish detailed information on age, sex, and citizenship status of individuals born abroad, it is not unlikely that the majority of the unnaturalized males were of military age.[8]

Pressure brought upon British citizens to serve in the Southern military forced the British consuls to spend long hours safeguarding their fellow citizens. Frederick Cridland, then viceconsul at Richmond, apologized both to Lyons and to Russell in the spring of 1862 for not responding to their correspondence more quickly. He was spending sixteen hours a day at the consulate "protecting British Subjects who require passports and protections to prevent their being constantly annoyed by the military officers." In addition to working with individuals in person, Cridland sent "documents [to] numbers of counties where at present the ignorant militia officers are endeavouring to compell [sic] Her Majesty's subjects to muster into the militia."[9]

In the absence of a regular foreign minister in the Confederacy, the work of the consuls began to assume a diplomatic character. Unlike Northern consuls, who seldom, if ever, corresponded directly with the State Department, those in the South frequently appealed conscription cases directly to the Confederate government. The legation in Washington served as a channel of communication for Northern consulates; once a Northern consul asked for assistance from Lyons the case was, for all practical purposes, out of his hands. The lack of a legation in the Confederacy threw the burden of direct communication on the consuls themselves.

James E. Haley's induction under the Confederate Enrollment Act of 1862 shows the various steps that consuls had to take to secure an individual's freedom and the time it involved. Haley, an Irishman, was seventeen when an enrolling officer forced him to sign enlistment papers at Chattanooga in September 1862. Before he could be sent off to camp, Haley fled to Knoxville, where he was apprehended, arrested, and shipped to the front. When Consul Bunch heard of Haley's plight, he requested a discharge from his commanding officer on the basis of Haley's alien status and age. Bunch received no reply from the officer, but Haley wrote, complaining about further mistreatment as a result of the consul's request. Bunch next wrote several letters to George Randolph, Confederate secretary of war, in which he restated his original argument.

Randolph had recently resigned, so Assistant Secretary of War John A. Campbell responded to Bunch's appeals. The consuls, Campbell informed Bunch, had no authority in conscription cases. If aliens felt they had been illegally conscripted, they should seek redress through the courts, and not the consuls. Bunch immediately fired off another letter, insisting on his right to interfere, denouncing the treatment Haley had received, and demanding his release.

Bunch's response apparently caused something of a sensation in the War Department because one of its clerk's noted in his diary: "A Mr. Bunch, British Consul, has written an impudent letter to the Department, alleging that an Irishman, unnaturalized, is forcibly detained in one of our camps. He says his letters have not been answered, which was a great discourtesy, and he means to inform Lord John Russell of it. The letter was replied to in rather scathing terms as the Irishman had enlisted and then deserted. Besides, we are out of humor with England now and court a French Alliance."[10]

The curtness of Campbell's reply indicated his own irritation. He reviewed the provisions of the Enrollment Act, even though he did not feel it necessary to defend the measure. After all, he informed the consul, Bunch was not an accredited diplomatic agent. Campbell denied that Haley had been forcibly inducted and declared that the youth would have been given every consideration had he told the enrolling officer of his alien status. The proper time to appeal induction was before, not after it occurred, he wrote. To Bunch's complaint about his letters not being answered, Campbell replied that the War Department had treated Bunch with the same respect and "patience as if you had been regularly accredited to this Government. . . . Under the sense of what is becoming and proper it has replied to your letter without the slightest expression of complaint about the tone you have thought proper to assume."

The record indicates no further correspondence between Bunch and Confederate authorities on the Haley case. Perhaps Bunch felt he had reached a dead end, or perhaps he became absorbed with the details involved in his own departure from Charleston. Just as Bunch was about to leave his post, Confederate authorities acceded to his demand and discharged Haley on February 5, 1863, five months after his induction.[11]

Problems in the South were made more complex by the various draft laws the consuls had to contend with. Even after the enactment of the draft law of 1862, states continued to muster men into their own militia. Depending upon the law in question, a consul might find himself appealing to an enrolling officer, the commandant at a camp of instruction, a commanding officer of a military unit, a governor, the Confederate secretary of war, or the secretary of state. These laws affected white men only; the Davis administration did not make provision to enlist blacks until the last months of the war.

Before April 1862, every state called out militia units. The terms of the acts varied, but generally men between the ages of eighteen and forty-five were declared eligible for militia service. Each state, except Louisiana and Texas, provided for alien exemptions. Louisiana drafted foreign nationals to preserve local order, and Texas called out all men who had lived in the state for one month. On April 16, 1862, the Confederate Congress passed an act making all men between the ages of eighteen and thirty-five eligible for service; the bill contained provisions for various exemptions, including nondomiciled aliens. The following September, the Southern Congress raised the age limit to forty-five. In February 1864 it adjusted the age limits from seventeen to fifty, but declared that men over forty-five were to be used for local defense only. None of these acts provided for the drafting of foreign nationals living in the Confederacy. While debating the last act, a few lawmakers called for the conscription of aliens, but Congress rejected the demand. Some congressmen as well as members of the Davis administration feared such a move would anger European powers and in retaliation they might expel Confederates from their countries.[12]

The passage of the Confederate draft laws did not deter states from adding to their militia units after 1862. Following the fall of Vicksburg in 1863, South Carolina, North Carolina, Mississippi, and Georgia ordered all males not serving in Confederate or state forces into militia service to defend the states from invasion. The age limits varied, but included men from eighteen to fifty years old; in 1864 Georgia raised the age limit to fifty-five. None of these state laws exempted aliens for any reason, no matter how long they had lived in the state.[13]

If the various conscription laws in the South differed in specifics, they did establish a fairly uniform and direct process for inducting the men. An enrolling officer, usually a commissioned officer in the army, supervised conscription procedures in each state. Under his direction, noncommissioned officers oversaw enrollment at the local level. They ordered eligible draftees to assemble, typically at the county seat; there squads, each consisting of about ten men, were inducted and sent to camps of instruction. Local civil authorities arrested individuals who failed to report for muster and held them in jail for the enrolling officer. The new draftees received physical examinations at camps of instruction and, if accepted, were turned over to the camp commander for training. Training periods were not specified but were virtually eliminated as the need for men at the front became more acute. By 1863 camps of instruction became mere rendezvous points: men shipped out as fast as they arrived. Officers in charge of detailing assignments sent the new inductees to units containing men from their local area whenever possible. Serving with friends and neighbors, it was believed, created more camaraderie and discouraged desertion.[14]

As he reached each point during the induction process—the enrollment assembly, the camp of instruction, or the military unit—the alien inductee could present evidence of his alienage and request a release from service. He had to present proof of his foreign citizenship and evidence that he was not domiciled in the Confederacy. For those who needed proof of alienage, consuls supplied certificates of nationality; these were usually based on affidavits made by local residents. Consuls were so lax about questioning statements made by friends and relatives and so quick to grant certificates that military personnel considered many of them worthless. Consul Magee at Mobile claimed he issued five hundred certificates in the spring of 1862 alone.[15]

Proving that one was not domiciled was more complicated because the legal, Confederate definition of the word "domicile" was vague and not acceptable to everyone. Military personnel throughout the South defined the word to fit their immediate needs. With the passage of the Enrollment Act in 1862, Attorney General Thomas Watts decided that individuals were domiciled only if they planned to remain permanently in the Confederacy and did not plan to return to the land of their birth: "Long residence, of itself, does not constitute domicile. A person may acquire domicile in less than one year, and he may not acquire it in twenty years' residence." The "exercise of the rights of citizenship," marriage, and the acquisition of property, Watts continued, could be regarded as evidence of the intention to remain in the country, but they were not conclusive proof.[16]

Watts's definition caused confusion and resentment. British subjects wrote to consuls asking for clarification. Bunch complained to Benjamin because local enrolling officers were not abiding by Watts's definition. And, he asked, how could the Confederacy be certain that an individual planned to live in the country for the rest of his life? When officials in the Mobile area began to conscript aliens under the Enrollment Act, Consul Magee obtained an order from the War Department forbidding the action: "All enrolling officers are hereby expressly prohibited from enrolling as conscripts foreigners not domiciled in the Confederate States. By domicile is meant permanent residence." Within a short time the *Mobile Sun* declared that "it is astonishing to observe the great number of 'foreigners' in our midst and therefore exempt from the Conscript Act. . . . Nearly every town and city in the South is full of this class of persons—most of them able-bodied young men who ought to be in the tented fields in defense of the government of their adoption."[17]

Adding to this confusion was the fact that the official Southern definition of "domicile" did not conform with the British understanding of the word, which was broader and less restrictive. Law officers of the Crown declared that domicile should not be determined merely by an individual's intention to remain permanently within a country. Aliens who had voted, had served on juries, or had acquired substantial property might also be considered domiciled; they could be required to serve as long as they were not brought into contact with Federal troops. An individual who declared his intention to become a citizen but had not engaged in "activities of the state" was not eligible for military service until he officially changed his allegiance. If he refused to serve, however, he could be expected to leave the country.

In judging the question of domicile, British officials also considered length of residence. In June 1863, Charles Powers appealed to Consul Lynn at Galveston to secure his exemption from the draft. Powers had lived in Texas for over twenty years—since the days of the Texas Republic. During that time he had exercised the rights of a citizen by voting and serving on juries, and he had acquired $135,000 in property. Powers based his claim for exemption on his British citizenship and his stated intention not to become a citizen of the United States. Reviewing all the circumstances in the case, Lyons declared that Powers had not forfeited his British nationality but that he could hardly consider himself entitled "to Her Majesty's protection if he should find himself treated as a citizen."[18]

If Attorney General Watts and Crown lawyers differed on the meaning of "domicile" and their ideas about the obligations of aliens, so did Southern courts. Generally the courts agreed that aliens should be compelled to perform some service, but they differed on the extent and became more unyielding as the war continued. In 1861 the South Carolina Court of Appeals decided that resident aliens were only liable for militia and patrol duty for the maintenance of public order. Aliens who had voted, declared a Savannah court in 1862, could not claim exemption from military service. In February 1863, the Richmond Circuit Court declared a foreigner eligible for the draft if he had previously served in any Southern military unit, as either a volunteer or a conscript, no matter how short the time. Two months later the Confederate District Court of Mobile contradicted the central government, declaring all alien residents to be domiciled; it ordered consuls to stop claiming "domicile" as a basis for exemption. Finally in July 1863, Judge A.G. Mcgrath, former justice on the United States District Court, ruled that aliens who had voted or lived in the South for an extended time could not claim exemption from the draft. Assistant Secretary of War Campbell, who had served as an associate justice on the United States Supreme Court, disagreed with Mcgrath's decision. Possibly because of Campbell's opposition, the central government never adjusted its definition of "domicile" to conform to court decisions on the subject.[19]

In addition to the courts, Southern civil and military officials devised their own definition of "domicile." W.P. Miles, chairman of the committee on military affairs in the Confederate House of Representatives, opposed exempting aliens who had lived in the South since the beginning of the war. Most state governors defined "domicile" in broad terms and advocated the conscription of long-time resident aliens. Governor Joseph Brown of Georgia was so adamant about the subject that he took personal action in one case. When an Englishman applied to Brown for permission to leave Georgia in 1863, the governor ordered him into the state militia.[20]

Military commanders could be as rigid on the subject of alien service. In the spring of 1863, James Healy, an Irishman, led a movement for higher wages among his fellow workers at the Charleston Foundry and Machine Shop. The police took Healy before an enrolling officer, who forced him to sign enlistment papers. Consul Walker sought a discharge on the basis of Healy's alienage but got nowhere. General Thomas Jordan, the district commander's chief of staff, rejected the request, arguing that Healy's voluntary employment in a war industry negated his exemption because of alienage and made him liable for service under the 96th Article of War. But Jordan's true reason for Healy's induction slipped out: fears that his continued attempts to incite discontent about wages might upset the stability of the civilian community. In reporting the case, Walker expressed concern for the broader implications of Jordan's decision. Many British men, Walker wrote, worked in war-related industries and women worked in the quartermaster corps making uniforms because they could not leave the

Confederacy and were compelled to take any employment to earn a livelihood. The Confederates had use of their labor for wages far below the rate of inflation, and now Jordan's interpretation declared all the men liable for military service. Undoubtedly Walker felt a sense of relief several months later when the War Department rejected Jordan's reasoning and ordered Healy's release.[21]

Even military officers of a lesser rank than Jordan decided for themselves which aliens should or should not serve in the military. In June 1863, Consul Lynn at Galveston wrote to the officer in charge of recruitment in Texas, demanding the release of seven British subjects who had recently been taken to a camp of instruction. The officer agreed to release two of the men but insisted the others serve because they had either voted, sat on juries, purchased property, or married local women. In another case an enrolling officer refused to release an inductee because he had voted once.[22]

Some commanders became quite adamant about their refusal to release aliens. John B. Weems, commandant at the camp of instruction at Decatur, Georgia, complained bitterly to Consul Fullarton about his constant pleas seeking the release of British subjects. He agreed that these men had signed statements declaring their intention to return to Britain, but their past actions belied their declarations. They had enjoyed the protection of the government, Weems wrote, and they had appealed to its courts, invested money, voted, married, and engaged in other activities that gave more "intention as to permanent residence here, than can be disclosed by any affidavit to the contrary."[23]

Occasionally, high ranking military officers who came across injustices took pains to correct them. Henry Wayne, adjutant general of Georgia, for example, asked Consul Fullarton in 1863 to secure the release of an illegally conscripted teenager. Seventeen at the time of his induction, Frank Miller had come to the United States with an uncle in 1859 to engage in watchmaking. Within a short time the uncle died. Caught by the war and destitute, Miller became an itinerant laborer, hoping to work his way back to England. He came under Wayne's notice after he was fraudulently enrolled, and the officer appealed to Fullarton: "He is sober, steady, industrious, and faithful and in every way deserving. If you can't get him home, can you give him papers that will protect him?"[24]

Wayne's efforts on behalf of Miller indicate that higher level officers were easier to deal with than officers of lesser rank. Consuls felt this especially true when appealing conscription cases to enrolling officers and commanders at camps of instruction. "If we have to depend upon enrolling officers," wrote Bunch, "not one application in ten would reach the War Department. The sentiment of that office is decidedly in favour of forcing all foreigners into service. There is scarcely a day that I have not had to remonstrate *here* against it."[25]

A major complaint of the consuls was the failure of enrolling officers or camp commanders to reply to their protests. Consul Magee at Mobile informed the legation in Washington, at the end of October 1862, that he still had no response to communiqués he had written in early September about the conscription of seven British subjects. Consul Lynn in Texas spent seven months writing letters of complaint about the induction of several Britons to at least four different officials and never received any replies. "I am of the opinion," Lynn concluded, "that neither the Military or State Authorities intend to redress the grievances to which British Subjects are exposed or that any notice will be taken of the remonstrances I have made." Often when consular correspondence had not been answered for some months and the consul made another inquiry, the commander informed him that the individuals in question had been transferred and that he was unaware of their present location.[26]

In dealing with foreign nationals, military officers kept or "mislaid" certificates of nationality, jailed conscripts, or refused to let them contact friends or consuls. During his last months in Charleston, Bunch heard about two British subjects who had been imprisoned for the past nine months in Salisbury, North Carolina, for refusing to enlist, but he was unable to find out any details about the situation. Nor was this an isolated instance. An enrolling officer in Atlanta jailed Michael Greenan for refusing to enlist and did not allow him to change clothes, bathe, or contact friends. When Greenan demanded his certificate of nationality, the officer said it was lost and could not be found. Enrolling officers dealt with Thomas McCormick more harshly. After being jailed for six months, stripped of all clothing except for a blanket, and deprived of adequate food, he agreed to enlist if he were assigned to an artillery company. Sometimes harsh treatment resulted in death. When Thomas Hearn, age twenty-two, was sent to the jail in Charleston, he contracted typhoid fever. His jailers refused to take note of his illness until it was too late; he died shortly after being admitted to the hospital. At the time of Hearn's death, Consul Walker's permission to act as consul had been with withdrawn, and despite his knowledge of the affair, he did nothing for fear of bringing attention to himself.[27]

Unfortunately, a potential conscript's problems were not over if he persuaded one enrolling officer of his ineligibility. Enrolling officers frequently changed, and when a new one came into the district, foreign nationals found themselves starting over. The new enrolling officer in Georgia revoked Henry Fetherston's previous exemption, tore up his certificate of nationality, and gave him fifteen days to obtain exemption papers from the War Department in Richmond.[28]

In several instances punishment for refusing to enlist became severe. One enrolling officer threatened to shoot Thomas Neill when he refused to enlist. Another did shoot Michael McNamara "clear through the body" after he declared he would not enlist for any reason. John A. Lee in Texas agreed to enlist after he was chained to a wagon and paraded through the town. Enrolling officers took R. Belshaw of Montgomery, Alabama, to a camp of instruction at Tullahoma, Tennessee, and hung him from a rafter by his thumbs, allowing only the tips of his feet to touch the ground. At the same camp, officers hung J.J. Kelly by his heels with his head just above a tub of water and lowered him into the tub periodically. Kelly nearly drowned before he agreed to enlist. An enrolling officer in Sullivan City, Tennessee, struck a British subject with an axe for resisting enlistment in the state militia.[29]

The most inflexible of commandants at instruction camps

was Major Clarke of Brookhaven, Mississippi. In October 1862 Consul Magee informed the legation in Washington that no British subject could expect consideration from the officer: "He defies all British protection, takes the men's certificates from them and places them in jail, feeding them on bread and water." Magee even complained to the War Department that Clarke had publicly declared that "he don't regard one British Protection." By January 1863 Clarke devised a somewhat grim method of chastising those Britons he released: on their certificates of exemption he wrote, "it is urged upon all persons not to give employment in any way to this class of exempts, they having become a nuisance to the Southern Confederacy." After James Nelson received his discharge from Clarke, he made his way to New Orleans and informed the consul that "many British Subjects" were being exposed to Clarke's cruelty but unable to get away.[30]

During the months that George Wythe Randolph headed the Confederate War Department, March 19 to November 22, 1862, the central government indicated a willingness to work with the consuls for the release of aliens from military service. "The Secretary of War," wrote Cridland, "seems determined not to allow any violation of the rights of aliens . . . and whenever I have laid a case before him showing that the party arrested was a British Subject and not domiciled, he has promptly ordered his release."[31] On a number of occasions Randolph sent instructions to commanders in the Deep South, informing them that nondomiciled aliens were not eligible for induction and to release any who had been enrolled.[32]

Within a month of Randolph's departure, the War Department began to reveal a less lenient attitude. The first indication came with Assistant Secretary Campbell's reply when Bunch complained about James Haley's conscription. Several months later Consul Moore of Richmond informed Lyons that he now communicated only with noncommissioned officers. When he called at the State Department, Secretary Benjamin required Moore to wait several days before he would see him. Subordinates made excuses for their superiors at the War Department and at Richmond military headquarters whenever Moore went to those offices. "The authorities are leaning very hard upon British Subjects for conscription," Moore told Lyons. They deprived them of their certificates of nationality or arrested them if they refused to enroll. Others were forced to work on public projects for resisting induction.[33] To an acquaintance Moore wrote "the apparent apathy and indifference with which the War Department seems to regard cases of the most atrocious cruelty, quite baffle all my preconceived opinions of my own kindred race."[34]

When in February 1863 Moore complained to Benjamin about General Henry Winder's policy regarding aliens leaving the Confederacy, he received a cold shoulder. Winder, commandant at Richmond, agreed to issue passports to foreign nationals wishing to leave, but he singled out Britons for special censure. They were required to list any service in the Confederate army or in a Southern state militia unit on their passports. This stipulation, Moore claimed, "places them in extreme danger if they are apprehended by Federal troops while traveling north." He considered the requirement partly a reaction to Britain's rejection of Napoleon III's mediation proposal but also a diabolical means of keeping British subjects confined to the Confederacy, where they would be subject to military service or forced to work in military-related industries. Benjamin was unconcerned and saw no major problem with Winder's policy. Moreover, he informed Moore, it was purely a military matter. On hearing of the affair, Lyons responded: "I have read your despatches with much concern. I learn with much regret of Benjamin's attitude. I cannot come to your assistance because Benjamin would be less disposed to deal with me than you. All I have been able to do is to refer your despatches to Russell."[35]

Moore was not alone in noticing a growing inflexibility in the South about the conscription of aliens and an increasing dislike of Britons in particular. Informing Consul Fullarton of his brother's murder in Columbus, Georgia, John O'Connell insisted that his only crime was being British. "They are all down on us here," he wrote. Authorities did not arrest the murderer, he lamented, "so you see there is no justice for us." From somewhere in Virginia, British citizens petitioned Lord Russell to intervene with the Confederate government so they could leave the country, and another group from Galveston, Texas, requested a man-of-war to take them to a British colony. Russell regretted his inability to help the petitioners; he suggested they try to solve their problems by working through the consuls. He was aware from correspondence from both the legation and the consuls that his oppressed countrymen would have little success. Growing anti-British sentiment was causing Confederate officials to become uncooperative on most issues raised by the consuls or by British nationals. Although he was disturbed by their harsh treatment, Russell could do little to prevent it.[36] What he could not know, however, was that Benjamin would shortly expel the consuls, and then British citizens would be without any avenue of appeal.

9

Expelling the Southern Consuls

Confederate Secretary of State Judah P. Benjamin expelled the British consuls during the summer and fall of 1863. Publicly he stated that the action was necessary because of the consuls' efforts to prevent the conscription of British nationals into the Confederate army and state militia units. Yet, that was not the sole reason. Behind the dismissal lay a growing antipathy toward Britain for its failure to extend diplomatic recognition and a Confederate desire to retaliate in the only way it could—by dismissing the consuls.

Most nineteenth-century Americans, in both the North and the South, harbored suspicion and distrust of Great Britain. In part a carryover of antipathy created during the Revolution and the War of 1812, the attitude flared up again over various boundary disputes between the United States and British North America, and was exacerbated by the arrival of numerous Irish immigrants, few of whom had any affection for the English. William Howard Russell, the journalist, quickly became aware of dislike for England when he traveled throughout America at the beginning of the war. Welcomed at first, Russell soon found himself an object of censure after he published remarks that Northerners or Southerners considered uncomplimentary.[1]

Animosity against Britain grew rapidly in the South during the war because Southerners expected more than the British government was willing to give. Confederates believed Europe's need for cotton would force both Britain and France to recognize their nation and break the blockade in order to obtain the fiber. Indeed, Russell commented after conversing with several Southern leaders: "They assume the British crown rests on a cotton bale."[2] But France would only extend diplomatic recognition in conjunction with Great Britain, and the failure of the Foreign Office to support such a move caused Southerners to place the blame on Britain alone.

The high point of Southern diplomatic success came early, on May 13, 1861, when Britain and France extended belligerent status to the Confederacy and declared their neutrality in the war. From then on, Confederates considered Britain's every action a setback. On June 1, Britain closed her ports—including those in the West Indies—to both Northern and Southern privateers. When friends of the South in Parliament tried to force a debate on diplomatic recognition in September 1862, Lord Russell squelched the attempt. Several months later, in November 1862, Britain rejected Napoleon III's suggestion to press mediation on the North and South. Then on September 4, 1863, the British government detained the Laird Rams and other ships being built for the Confederacy in English shipyards. The following month, on October 8, the Foreign Office ordered the seizure of the ships, the same day that Benjamin expelled the last remaining consuls.[3]

Throughout the war, Britain observed the Union blockade despite Confederate claims that it was ineffective. In January 1863, Confederate ironclads attacked the Union blockading squadron off Charleston and forced it to withdraw. Under nineteenth-century international law, foreign nations were permitted to send ships to ports where blockades had been broken. Other European nations followed Britain's lead in ignoring Benjamin's notification of the break, and the Union quickly reestablished the blockade. Months later Walker wrote: "Many people in Charleston [still] denounce England for her faithlessness in the blockade."[4]

Lord John Russell strained an already difficult relationship by refusing to receive James Mason, Confederate commissioner to Great Britain. That this treatment rankled was evident. During a meeting with Benjamin in the spring of 1863 when the secretary seemed particularly inflexible, Consul Moore asked why he was being treated so curtly. Benjamin made several comments about Russell's refusal to meet with

Mason and ended by saying: "The interview I give you now is more than Lord Russell accords Mr. Mason."[5]

Increasing anti-British feeling began to surface in the Confederacy about a year after the war started. When Henri Mercier, French foreign minister to the United States, returned from Richmond in 1862, Lyons quizzed him about Confederate attitudes toward foreign nations. Mercier replied, "there appears to be a very good disposition toward foreigners in general; . . . less good perhaps toward the English . . . because more has been hoped from that country than from any other, and the disappointment has consequently been greater." Nine months later, just after Britain rejected Napoleon III's mediation proposal, Consul Moore described the general dislike for England in Richmond and the growing appreciation for the French. At the same time John B. Jones, a clerk in the Confederate War Department, wrote, "we are out of humor with England now and court a French Alliance."[6]

Bunch's correspondence to the Foreign Office catalogues growing Southern antagonism. Even before the war began, Bunch remarked about Southern wariness of Britain because of its antislavery policy. Referring to South Carolina he wrote: "This commonwealth . . . is conducting itself in a truly Republican manner, by guaranteeing to everyone absolute freedom of thought and speech—provided the conclusion and language happen to be very much in favour of slavery." When the first group of Southern commissioners—William L. Yancey, Pierre Rost, and Dudley Mann—went to Europe in 1861, Bunch cautioned Russell that he might find them insincere, for Southern people dislike "us violently . . . on account of our hostility to Slavery." Three months later he wrote of Southern disappointment because England and France had still failed to recognize the Confederacy. But Bunch did not advocate quick recognition because be believed that "from the good will of the new Confederacy we have nothing to hope. Hating us, as it does, . . . it will gladly hail any opportunity of embarrassing us." As he was about to depart the South, Bunch continued in much the same vein: "Our known antipathy to slavery adds another element to Southern dislike. If, at times, in the earlier stages of this contest, some kindlier feelings have been expressed towards Great Britain, they have been prompted by the hope that we would be useful to the Southern cause, either by raising the blockade, or in some other way become embroiled with the United States. . . . We have nothing to expect from the good will of the South."[7]

Animosity toward the British grew as the South encountered devastating defeats on the battlefield. Consul Walker at Charleston noted heightened bitterness toward Englishmen following the defeat at Gettysburg and the surrender of Vicksburg. Britons were being discharged from their employment and harassed for not joining the army, or they were being arrested and freed only after enlisting. Nor did this antagonism cease after the consuls were expelled. "The hatred publicly expressed against England," wrote Cridland from Alabama in late 1863, "makes it far from pleasant to be known here as a British Subject and in some instances no language or threats seem sufficient to express the growing enmity."[8]

From the beginning of the war, Southern editors and congressmen raised questions about Davis's decision to accept the foreign consuls. Led by the *Charleston Mercury* and the *Richmond Whig*, newspaper editors began asking whether the Confederacy or the United States had granted exequaturs to the consuls, and if the latter, what right did it have to confer consular authority within the Confederacy? By early 1863, the *Whig* was demanding the expulsion of the British consuls as a "vindication of our self-respect."[9]

During the fall of 1862, members of the Confederate Congress began to question whether consuls sanctioned by the United States should be allowed to remain in the Confederacy. Benjamin, in response, admitted that only one consul in the entire Confederacy (Ernest Raven, consul for the state of Texas from Saxe-Coburg and Gotha) had received his exequatur from the Richmond government. In asking for the exequatur, Raven's government made clear that its request did not imply or extend diplomatic recognition. All other exequaturs held by consuls had been granted by the United States government and consuls in the South were still receiving instructions and transmitting correspondence through their nation's diplomatic agents in Washington, D.C. Benjamin discouraged Congress from demanding expulsion by pointing out that the presence of the consuls was beneficial: their correspondence permitted "correct information to reach foreign nations on matters which are highly important to the public interest."[10]

Despite Benjamin's argument, agitation in Congress caused the Davis administration to discuss the matter of expulsion. One month after his report to Congress, Benjamin informed Mason: "The President has further under consideration the propriety of sending out of the country all British consuls and consular agents, and I will give you early advice on his conclusion on this point." Indeed, Davis's cabinet met on several occasions to deliberate the issue but decided to take no action; however, it attempted to terminate consular connections with legations in Washington. Benjamin ordered all foreign consuls, in June 1863, to stop transmitting communications through their legations and to send all future correspondence to their home governments through neutral countries.[11]

The first indication of a more rigid attitude directed specifically toward the British consuls came when Benjamin refused to acknowledge Frederick Cridland as acting consul at Mobile in May 1863. Previously he had accepted Allan Fullarton and H. Pinckney Walker as acting consuls at Savannah and Charleston. Benjamin did question Walker about the source of his authority but seemed satisfied when he learned that Bunch had made the appointment. Benjamin objected to Cridland because Lyons had named him to the consular post, and in Benjamin's view Lyons had no authority to select consuls in the Confederacy. While Benjamin refused to recognize Cridland as consul, he permitted him to remain in Mobile as a private citizen.[12]

The first consul to be expelled was George Moore at Richmond. Moore had been consul at Ancona, Italy, for twenty years before being sent to Richmond, and he had immediately disliked his new assignment. He often complained of his own depression and of illness in his family.[13] As a consequence most of the work fell to his vice consul, Frederick Cridland. Magee's removal and Cridland's transfer to Alabama forced Moore to become more involved in daily affairs at the Richmond consulate.

U.S. Grant's military moves toward Vicksburg in early 1863 marked the beginning of Moore's downfall. In mid-February, as pressure against Vicksburg intensified, the Mississippi legislature ordered all men between eighteen and forty-five years of age, including foreigners, into the militia to defend the state against Federal invasion. Hearing of the order, Moore fired off a letter to Benjamin calling the Mississippi law a violation of the Confederate conscription acts. He presumed the exemption provisions in the Enrollment Act took precedence over state law. Moore also complained about a British citizen, Thomas Jones of Rankin County, who had been assaulted, imprisoned, and seriously injured in one eye for resisting conscription. He was presently housed in the jail at Jackson, Mississippi, and Moore demanded his release.[14]

Benjamin responded by putting Moore on the defensive. The consul quickly found himself being questioned about his right to deal with conscription problems outside of Virginia. On what basis, Benjamin demanded, was Moore involving himself with affairs in Mississippi? His exequatur limited his authority to Virginia only, "but since you are raising a question regarding the laws and actions of Mississippi, it is well you present your authority for the precise nature and extent of your function."[15]

Unable to present such a document, Moore obtained an interview to settle the controversy. Benjamin was unyielding; he refused to allow Moore to deal with problems outside of Virginia but agreed to permit enrolled Britons in outlying areas to correspond directly with the State Department. Finally, the secretary declared, he had no objection to appointments of unaccredited consuls in states where there were none. He also ordered Moore to take up any future matters involving conscription directly with the State Department and not to refer them to the War Department.[16]

Shortly afterward Moore received an appeal from J.B. Caldwell, an attorney in White Sulphur Springs, Virginia. Two of his clients, Nicholas Moloney (also spelled Malony) and Eugene Farrell, both British subjects, had been conscripted into the Confederate army and were seeking discharges. Ignoring Benjamin's instructions, Moore contacted James Seddon, secretary of war, requesting releases for the two men. An investigation convinced Seddon that the men were domiciled and not eligible: both had purchased land, voted, married, and raised families. Neither had ever indicated his intention to return to his native Ireland.[17]

During the time it took the War Department to investigate Moloney's and Farrell's backgrounds, Moore vented his anger to lawyer Caldwell: "I have lived thirty-two consecutive years in despotic countries, and I am compelled to bear witness that I have met in those foreign countries more official courtesy and consideration from the local authorities, on my representation of grievances, than I meet at the hands of my own blood and lineage." Apparently Caldwell was not sympathetic to such sentiment, for he forwarded Moore's letter to Seddon and Benjamin.[18]

It did not take Benjamin long to react. On June 5, 1863, he informed the consul that President Davis had signed letters patent revoking his exequatur. Moore, according to Benjamin, had disregarded the limits of his authority by undertaking consular functions outside Virginia, and he had demonstrated disrespect for the Confederate government by corresponding with the War Department, ignoring instructions to the contrary. Benjamin did not mention Moore's letter to Caldwell.[19]

In an emotional response, Moore informed Lyons that the Confederate government was ignoring the "sanctity of personal freedom" and becoming unnecessarily sensitive about any opposition expressed toward it. The demand that "our persecuted countrymen . . . serve in an army not their own" compelled British subjects to act contrary to the wishes of their own sovereign, but this was of little concern to the Confederacy as it moved forward in its "merciless career, of compulsory enrolment for its army." Moore ended his abusive denunciation with a request for permission to leave this "wretched place."[20] Two months after dismissing Moore, on August 4, 1863, Benjamin terminated Mason's mission to Great Britain.

The controversies involving Fullarton and Walker originated at the state level following the surrender of Vicksburg. On July 17, 1863, Governor Joseph E. Brown increased Georgia's militia to eight thousand men, and the state's adjutant and inspector general ordered enrolling officers in every county to fill their quotas by August 4. He also stipulated the enrollment of "unnaturalized foreigners," because they were "bound to defend [their] domicile, and liable to be drafted by the State and compelled to do so." Although the ostensible purpose of the draft was to defend the state, the order directed militia commanders to place the new inductees under the direction of Confederate commanders if the need arose.[21]

Fullarton complained to Brown as soon as the conscription order became public. He understood the purpose of the draft but strenuously objected to placing British nationals under the command of Confederate officers. "Her Majesty's Government accepts the proposition that British Subjects are liable to local defense and in some instances to protect from local invasion," Fullarton wrote, but because this was a civil war, British citizens should not have to face the possibility of fighting Union troops and being labeled as traitors.[22]

Brown excused Fullarton's brashness because the consul did not understand the intent of the draft. The men were being called for local defense only, but it might be necessary to muster them into Confederate service in order to achieve better coordination of military movements and to enable those captured by the enemy to claim the rights and privileges of prisoners of war. The main reason for increasing the state militia, claimed Brown, was to quell possible slave insurrections. Union forces urged slaves to flee from their masters and encouraged them to engage in depredations against white Southerners. In addition, Union military units were now raiding deep into Confederate territory. When Confederate army soldiers were not available to repulse these raids, it would be necessary to call out the militia. But Brown did not expect militia troops to come into contact with units of the United States Army because Confederate soldiers would hold them back. Finally, Brown informed Fullarton that British subjects who refused to serve in the militia could leave the state.[23]

Frustrated by his inability to persuade the governor to change his mind and exempt foreigners, Fullarton issued a public statement that "ordered British nationals conscripted to service . . . to throw down their arms if they come into contact with troops of the United States." Angered that a mere consul would presume to issue such a command, Brown responded in kind. Any militiaman who refused to fight Union troops, Brown wrote, "will be dealt with as a dishonorable soldier." Georgia's draft did not violate British policy regarding military service by foreign nationals, he insisted. Fullarton had admitted that British subjects could be required to put down local insurrection and to defend a state against foreign invasion. Since Brown regarded the United States as a foreign country (although Fullarton did not), he saw no discrepancy between the draft order and British policy.[24]

Walker's problems in South Carolina were similar, but they involved men already enrolled in the militia. Five British workers at the Charleston arsenal had previously been inducted into the "Arsenal Guard," organized to defend the arsenal itself. They were never called to active duty because the arsenal had never come under threat. Then in June 1863 the local militia commander decided to reorganize his force, incorporating the various segments of the militia in Charleston into one unit; the entire unit would be called out when necessary. The British members of the "Arsenal Guard" refused to participate in the reorganized militia, and Walker encouraged them. Briefly, he argued they might be brought into contact with United States troops and, if captured, treated as traitors. Like Fullarton, Walker encouraged the men, and all other British subjects serving in state forces, to lay down their arms should they encounter Union soldiers.

When the "Arsenal Guard" refused to serve in the militia, the local commander arrested them and informed the enrolling officer for the Confederate army of their availability. After they were inducted into Confederate forces, Walker took up their case with General Thomas Jordan, the local commander's chief of staff, but he proved unsympathetic. Arguing that the men had forfeited their claim to neutrality by working at the Charleston arsenal, a war-related industry, Jordan refused to release them. Walker next appealed to P.G.T. Beauregard, commander of the district, who also declined to issue discharges.[25]

While Walker was defending the members of the "Arsenal Guard" he was also working on behalf of Michael Barlow. A volunteer in the state militia, Barlow had been assigned to the *General Clinch*, a ship carrying military supplies between Charleston and outlying fortifications that were under attack. Because Barlow might be required to fire on Federal troops, Walker requested a change of assignment or a discharge. When authorities denied his appeal, Walker again issued a plea to British subjects in the militia, Barlow included, to lay down their weapons rather than fire on United States forces.[26]

Next, Walker petitioned Milledge L. Bonham, governor of South Carolina. Stressing former Governor Pickens's proclamation of November 1861, which forbade the use of foreign nationals in dangerous duty, Walker insisted that Bonham was still bound by the order. Unsure of himself, Bonham decided to seek an opinion from the state attorney general. In the meantime, the local militia commanders in Charleston and Georgia complained to Benjamin about Walker and Fullarton, and undoubtedly they complained to Davis when he toured the states' defenses in early October 1863.[27]

The blow fell on October 8, 1863. While Davis was away from Richmond visiting General Braxton Bragg's army at Chattanooga, Benjamin took an exceptional step: he called a meeting of the Confederate cabinet, and the group voted unanimously to expel those British consuls still resident in the country. Informing Fullarton and Walker of the decision, Benjamin lectured them about their assertion that soldiers could throw down their arms: "This assumption of jurisdiction by foreign officials within the territory of the Confederacy, and this encroachment on its sovereignty cannot be tolerated for a moment. . . . I am directed, therefore, by the President to communicate to you this order, that you promptly depart from the Confederacy, and that in the meantime you cease to exercise any consular functions within its limits." Because Walker and Fullarton were acting consuls and had never received exequaturs, it was not necessary to issue letters patent.[28]

Benjamin's action—calling a special cabinet meeting while Davis was not in Richmond—was an unusual step, and he would not have taken it unless he knew the president approved. Davis's opinion about expelling the British consuls is unknown, but he likely supported such a move. As secretary of war in Franklin Pierce's administration, Davis had expressed his distrust of Great Britain, an attitude strengthened by stories his brothers had told him about British atrocities during the War of 1812. Distrust grew to dislike during the Civil War. Davis resented references to his country as the "so-called Confederacy," even though they were diplomatically correct, and he came to believe that Britain's policy was a "hollow profession of neutrality." Every step the Foreign Office took with regard to the South drove a wedge between it and the Confederacy and increased his antipathy toward the power. Historians note that Davis was quick to reprimand members of his cabinet if he disapproved of their actions. Given his anti-British perspective and his apparent lack of comment about Benjamin's expulsion orders, Davis's silence indicated his approval.[29]

In expelling the consuls, Benjamin overlooked Consul Lynn at Galveston; his exequatur was not revoked and he never received an order to leave the Confederacy. It is possible that Benjamin was totally unaware of Lynn's presence. He had written only one letter to the Confederate State Department and merely received an acknowledgment from an assistant secretary. When he heard of Walker's and Fullarton's dismissal, Lynn decided to remain in Galveston. During the next year, he reported that some Confederate civil and military officials in Texas refused to recognize him as consul, while others treated him no differently than before.[30]

Benjamin defended his revocation of Moore's exequatur and his expulsion of Walker and Fullarton in a long, somewhat rambling letter to John Slidell, Confederate commissioner to France. Moore, wrote Benjamin, had deliberately ignored a request that he not correspond with the War Department and "his remarks touching the conduct of the Confederate authorities in relation to two enlisted soldiers" were offensive. The actions of Walker and Fullarton were more repugnant: they regarded their own certificates of nationality as proof of the fact that an individual should be exempt from military service. These certificates were based on statements by the interested parties themselves, and a number of them had proved to be fraudulent. The consuls were, in effect, deciding for themselves who was eligible to serve in Confederate forces. By encouraging soldiers to lay down their arms when coming into contact with Federal troops, Walker and Fullarton were denying military commanders control over their own forces and were encroaching on the nation's sovereignty.[31]

Much of Benjamin's letter also dealt with Britain's withdrawal of Consul Magee from Mobile and the financial obligations of nations at war. Southern newspapers published the letter and Walker sent Lyons a copy. After reading it, he informed Russell: "Mr. Benjamin's lecture on the duty of Belligerents to pay their debts is totally beside the purpose." But Lyons was not unsympathetic to Benjamin's action. "I do not think," he wrote Russell, "that [Walker] or Mr. Fullarton . . . managed their correspondence with the Confederate Authorities with all the tack and prudence which their peculiar position with regard to those authorities rendered advisable." Indeed, Lyons seemed more surprised by Benjamin's original acceptance of Walker and Fullarton as acting consuls than he did by their dismissal. Although he did not consider the Confederacy an independent nation, Lyons understood that Confederates regarded their country as a sovereign entity and would be offended by the presence of consuls approved by the Union and supervised by the British legation in Washington. On a number of occasions he suggested that the Foreign Office sever any connections between the legation and the Southern consuls and inform the Confederate government of its action.[32]

Lyons read more into Benjamin's reasons for expelling the consuls then the secretary himself was aware. He asserted that there "was evidently a predetermined manifestation" whose objective was contemplated before the action was taken.[33] Lyons's statement deserves attention even though it may not be possible to determine positively what he meant by "predetermined manifestation." Benjamin, according to one historian, "was one of the most secretive men who ever lived." He destroyed his private papers for the war period, and only a portion of his official correspondence—which later fell into Union hands—remains.

Not only was he secretive, but "few among the members of the Cabinet could hate as bitterly as Benjamin." He made diplomatic recognition from Great Britain his chief objective and turned against the country when he failed to achieve his goal. Ironically, he was born in the West Indies and by British law was still considered a British citizen during the Civil War. After the war he escaped to England and, using his rights of citizenship, established himself in a successful legal career.[34]

Some historians regard Benjamin's expulsion of the British consuls as an act of frustration resulting from his failure to secure British recognition, or they see it as a decision to give up on Britain and rely solely on France, with whom Confederate foreign relations had always been more favorable.[35] Contemporary evidence also suggests that Benjamin surrendered to public opinion. In June 1862, fourteen months before dismissing the consuls, Benjamin informed Cridland, still acting consul in Richmond, that it would be a "very unwise policy" to remove any of them. They conveyed "proper information" to their governments and were the only means of Confederate contact with foreign powers. In late 1862 and early 1863, as demands for the removal of foreign consuls mounted in both the press and the Southern Congress, Benjamin repeated his contention. However, cabinet discussions about expelling the British consuls weakened his determination. When he informed Davis of the special cabinet meeting and the decision to expel the British consuls, Benjamin wrote: "Several members of the Cabinet expressed the opinion that this action on the consuls was very fortunate, as it enabled us by sending them away for a cause that so fully warrants their expulsion to satisfy public sentiment, which would have been quite restive under their continued residence here."[36]

Another indication that the expulsion of the consuls came in response to public demand was Benjamin's inconsistent policy in forcing the consuls to leave. If a consul's continued presence might draw public attention, Benjamin required him to withdraw from his district; otherwise, he seemed unconcerned.

Moore did not even inquire if he might be permitted to stay in Richmond. Eight days after Benjamin revoked his exequatur, Moore left for Washington. There he informed Lyons that he had hired a lawyer to handle cases involving the conscription of British subjects, and he departed for England and retirement.[37]

A week after his expulsion, Fullarton requested permission to remain in Savannah. His nonconsular responsibilities as a banker, he wrote, required his presence to look after the affairs of his clients. At the same time the president of the Bank of Savannah made a similar request, and a group of citizens petitioned Benjamin on Fullarton's behalf. Benjamin rejected the request and ordered Fullarton to leave the country.[38] But when a British warship arrived off Savannah to remove the consul, the commander of the Union blockading force refused to let the ship through.

Where Fullarton lived for the remainder of the war is unknown; he did not correspond with the Foreign Office following his dismissal. Probably he simply went into the countryside. After the capture of Savannah in 1864, a resident informed the legation that Fullarton had left Savannah on December 21, 1863, and that no one had seen him since; however, he had returned to Savannah by September 1865, when he signed an affidavit detailing the damages to Consul Molyneux's home. He must have then devoted his entire attention to private business, for he is not mentioned after 1865 in British diplomatic archives.[39]

Walker remained in Charleston and the government at Richmond seemed unconcerned. In fact, Confederate action kept him there. In early November 1863 HMS *Plover* received permission from the Union commander to enter Charleston harbor and bring Walker out through the blockade, but the Confederates refused to let the ship dock because Walker had been expelled. Two months later Walker informed Russell that he was still in Charleston and that the consulate remained open. He refrained from any correspondence with the Confederate State Department or with local militia commanders but continued to advise British subjects about how to avoid conscription. To protect the consular archives he had moved them to a private home, beyond the range of Federal guns.[40]

Walker's letters to Russell during 1864 chronicle Southern steps to force eligible men, citizens or not, into military service. In January he reported that British subjects in South Carolina and Georgia who refused to enlist were being fired from their jobs and not allowed to leave the city or county in which they lived. By June he estimated that five hundred British subjects had been thrown out of work. Evidently the damage this policy might cause concerned Jefferson Davis, for he appealed to the governors to reconsider: "Men who are employed in manufacturing and preparing munitions of war or military supplies are as effectively engaged in the defense of the country . . . as the soldiers in the field."

Unfortunately there was nothing Walker himself could do for conscripted British nationals. However, he did engage a lawyer to make appeals to military authorities. In July 1864 Walker related that James Gorman, a British subject, was taken from his place of employment and jailed for fourteen days for refusing to enlist. When authorities released him and he returned to work, his employer fired him and refused to pay $147 dollars in back wages. According to Walker, Gorman's case was not unique. By August, governors in the Deep South were issuing declarations that required foreign nationals to enlist or leave the state. The policy forced virtually all foreigners to enlist because they could not pass through military lines into Union held territory or leave by sea. In their quest to find eligible men, local authorities even attempted to draft Walker, and the forty-eight year old consul was forced to appeal his own conscription on the basis of his British citizenship and consular status. In his last letter before the fall of Charleston, Walker recounted that thirty-one British citizens had recently applied at his office, asking him to intercede of their behalf.[41]

In retrospect, Benjamin's dismissal of the British consuls turned out to be an order to stop engaging in consular activities rather than outright expulsion. Only Consul Moore at Richmond left the Confederacy, and he was required to depart because President Davis had signed letters patent. Walker, Fullarton, and Cridland remained in the Southern states but as private citizens. Although he was not included in the expulsion order, Consul Lynn was unable to play any kind of role that might lessen tensions between Richmond and London. Before 1863 he was too far from Richmond to act as a means of communication; after Vicksburg fell he was totally cut off from the Southern capital. Both the Foreign Office and the Confederate State Department recognized this fact. Neither gave any indication of wanting to employ Lynn's services in the few diplomatic contacts attempted between them.

Following the expulsion of the consuls, Edwin DeLeon, confidential agent for the Confederacy in France, told Benjamin that his action was a great mistake. It was insulting to Britain and left little hope for British sympathy or intervention. De-Leon predicted that, as a result of Benjamin's expulsion order, Britain would cut itself off from the Confederacy; he was only partly correct. Perhaps because of Walker's letters or other information it received about the conscription of British nationals, the Foreign Office made three attempts in 1864 to contact the Confederate State Department. The first came in January with an appeal to Seward. Lyons requested permission for the consul general at Havana to pass through the blockade at Wilmington or Charleston to contact leaders at Richmond. Lyons stressed that the sole purpose of the trip would be to confer about the protection of British subjects. Seward appeared sympathetic, thought Lyons, but refused, saying, "the United States would never sanction any communication with rebels within or outside the country." The Foreign Office now turned to Cridland, sending him a communiqué and requesting that he forward it to Benjamin. After Benjamin rejected the British correspondence, Lyons again approached Seward and was again rebuffed. Thus, one appeal to the Confederacy and two to the Union got the British nowhere.[42]

The final diplomatic contact between the Confederacy and the Foreign Office came with the Kenner mission to London. In March 1865, Benjamin sent his friend and Confederate congressman from Louisiana, Duncan F. Kenner, to England with a last ditch proposal: the Confederacy would abolish slavery in return for diplomatic recognition.[43] The Confederate government was aware that slavery had long been a stumbling block to

English acceptance of the South as an independent nation; still, by 1865 the Southern offer was an impotent gesture. No matter how the war ended, slavery would not survive. In March 1865 the Confederate Congress authorized the enlistment of black troops and the Davis administration promised them freedom in return for military service. The end of the war in April prevented the legislation from becoming effective. Two years earlier, in 1863, the Union had begun recruiting black soldiers, and of the 178,895 that enlisted, some 134,000 had been slaves. None of these men would ever return to bondage. Lincoln's Emancipation Proclamation had freed all the slaves in areas captured by the Union since January 1863. Scores of slaves had fled from plantations and could never be forced back. The final stroke came on January 31, 1865, just before Kenner went to England, when the United States Congress approved of the Thirteenth Amendment abolishing slavery. In effect, the Confederacy played its trump card when the game was over. With slavery on the road to extinction and cotton likely to become available again when the South returned to normalcy, Britain had nothing to gain by recognizing the Confederate States of America.

10

Conscription, Union Style

The Confederate government designed its draft system to raise troops; the Union devised its enrollment policy to encourage volunteering. Under the Federal Enrollment Act of 1863, districts that reached their quotas through volunteers could suspend the draft until the next call. Out of the seven hundred thousand men who entered service after passage of the Enrollment Act, only ten thousand were actually drafted. The Union's conscription procedure differed from the Confederate's in other ways too. Both sides permitted substitution—paying another individual to take the draftee's place. In the South, however, substitution remained insignificant because, even if an individual found a substitute, he still remained eligible for service; in the North his name was removed from the roll. Both sides permitted exemptions, but the list was far more extensive in the South, where it included officeholders, members of the state militia, certain factory workers, college professors and teachers, and supervisors of twenty or more slaves. The only valid reasons for seeking exemption in the North were physical or mental disability, financial dependency of parents, and alienage. Northerners could also avoid service by paying a three hundred dollar commutation fee until 1864, when Congress repealed the provision. Southerners never established a bounty system; that is, paying men to volunteer for service. In the North the bounty system flourished and eventually lead to the worst evil of the entire system, the evolution of the bounty broker.[1]

The process of acquiring men in the Union underwent three distinct phases. During the first year of the war the government relied on volunteering. All previous American wars had been fought without resorting to a draft, and since both Southerners and Northerners expected the war to be brief, they thought a volunteer force would be sufficient. When volunteering failed to produce the vast numbers of men needed, Congress, in July 1862, authorized Secretary of War Stanton to draft state militiamen. Then on March 3, 1863, Lincoln signed the Enrollment Act making all eligible men between the ages of twenty and forty-five liable for military service.[2]

In the early months of the war local authorities used subtle pressure to encourage enlistment by foreign nationals. Shortly after the surrender of Fort Sumter, for instance, Consul Archibald complained that the chief recruiting office in New York City had just opened in the same building as the consulate and that anyone coming to his office had to pass by it. "The whole thing was done," he wrote, "to mislead British Subjects into believing that it was done with my knowledge and authority." Given the war fever sweeping the city, Archibald wondered how he might discourage British citizens from volunteering. He feared any public comment on his part would appear "ungracious and obnoxious to the whole community" and might be regarded as conveying sympathy for the South.[3]

When Britain declared its neutrality in May 1861, the government also invoked the Foreign Enlistment Act of 1819, which forbade British citizens from taking part in wars between hostile nations. As a result Lyons announced to his consuls that he did not consider British subjects who volunteered in either the Union or Confederate military "to have . . . any claim upon my good office." His only exception was seeking discharges for minors who had enlisted without parental consent. As he explained, his action was dictated more out of consideration for the parents than for the youths themselves.[4]

Most enlisted minors were caught up in the wartime fervor and hoped to find glory on the battlefield. But when the horrors of war became real and the hardships of life in the field became too much to endure, they implored their parents to get them out of an unbearable situation. Parents then appealed to the consul in their district or to the legation itself.

Seward seemed as willing to discharge British minors from

the army as he had been to release from jail British citizens accused of breaching the blockade or engaging in treasonable activities. In cases where he could not comply, Seward sent a copy of the War Department's investigation, which proved in most instances that the individual was not a minor. But correspondence between the State Department and the British legation between April and December 1861 indicates that Seward procured discharges for most British minors whose cases Lyons presented. On December 9, Lyons submitted a list of ninety names, and Seward responded that these youths would be discharged if investigation proved them to be minors and British subjects; however, he did warn Lyons that the War Department might be less obliging in the future.[5]

The policy changed abruptly after Stanton assumed direction of the War Department in January 1862. When in April Lyons asked why minors for whom he had requested discharges were still in service, he was told that the new secretary of war would be guided by the circumstances in each case and that "minority alone" did not make an individual eligible for discharge. Shortly afterward Stanton announced the War Department's new policy: the age an individual gave at the time of his enlistment was considered his true age. The army did not enroll anyone under eighteen without his parents' consent, and therefore "the enlistment of a minor cannot be contested." The policy held during the entire war. The War Department denied release to a Canadian youth in 1864 even though his father proved he was a minor. Besides refusing to consider his age, the department maintained the youth's acceptance of all bounties placed him under obligation to fulfill his commitment.[6]

Following the passage of the Militia Draft in July 1862, Lincoln called for three hundred thousand men for a three-year period; the next month he asked for three hundred thousand more to serve for nine months. These calls created panic among British nationals. William Stuart, chargé d'affaires supervising the legation during Lyons's absence, noted that increases in state and local bounties encouraged some British nationals to enlist, but the majority wished to avoid military service. Stuart persuaded the State Department not to detain British subjects wishing to leave the country, but he felt that the achievement was not enough.[7] The major threat to Britons lay in the Western states. The Militia Act required state governors to increase the size of their militia units, and governors in the West wanted to draft the foreign-born, a substantial element in the western population, to achieve the goal. Writing to Stanton, Governor Edward Salomon of Wisconsin asked for clarification on alien exemptions. Almost half of the able-bodied men in his state, Salomon claimed, were foreigners who had declared their intention to become citizens and were now demanding exemption because of alienage. Moreover, the governor declared, under Wisconsin law aliens could vote upon declaration of intention to become a United States citizen, and large numbers of these men had voted. Expression of intent, replied Stanton, did not make a man liable for military service, but exercising the right of suffrage did.[8] Despite this distinction by the Federal government, Governor David Tod of Ohio declared all foreign nationals who had signified their intention to become citizens eligible for the militia draft, even if they had not completed the naturalization process. Almost immediately Stuart began to receive complaints from British nationals about forced enlistments in the Buckeye state.[9]

To ease fears of his fellow countrymen, Stuart sent H. Percy Anderson, special British agent in the United States, to discuss the situation with Midwestern governors. During September 1862 he traveled from Columbus, Ohio, to St. Louis, and then south to Memphis. Governor Tod readily agreed to exempt those Britons who held certificates of nationality. At first he insisted that certificates should be issued by a consul, but when Anderson pointed out the lack of a consulate between the East Coast and St. Louis, Tod relented and agreed to accept affidavits sworn before a notary public. The governors of Illinois and Indiana and General William T. Sherman, in command of the Memphis Military District, agreed to the same stipulation.[10]

Anderson found the governors willing to cooperate, but real

implementation of his agreement depended upon local officials. And as Consul Wilkins wrote from St. Louis: "The outrages were not done by anyone occupying an official position, nor have they been directed against persons of any particular nationality." In Missouri, Wilkins blamed extreme Union partisans and the rabid German element for ignoring the agreement between Anderson and the governors. As a result, Wilkins made most of his appeals for discharge after a British national had been inducted into the army. He found General John Schofield, commander of the Military District of Missouri from 1861 to 1863, usually cooperative and willing to release British subjects.[11]

Britons in other Western states were not as fortunate. During the fall of 1862 Chargé d'affaires Stuart reported several instances in Kentucky and at least six in Ohio in which British nationals were deprived of all proof of their foreign nationality and forced to enlist on threat of imprisonment or personal injury.[12]

The Militia Act failed to produce as many volunteers as the government had wished. Lincoln's call for six hundred thousand men only resulted in securing 519,546. But the Midwestern states had been more successful in raising troops than those in the East, so by the end of 1862 the pressure on foreign nationals lessened somewhat. Still, the need for men remained, and Congress, at Stanton's urging, passed the Enrollment Act of 1863. With it came renewed and greater difficulties for aliens intent on avoiding military service in the Union army.

Under the Enrollment Act, the Federal government took direct control of the conscription process. No longer were state governors in charge of raising troops; instead, the Federal government levied quotas on enrollment districts, which could be met by supplying volunteers as well as draftees. The Enrollment Act also stipulated the conditions of alien eligibility: all foreigners were required to enroll if they had declared their intention to become citizens, had voted, or had held public office.[13]

Apparently this requirement caused some concern, for Lyons asked Seward for clarification. Compelling registration of aliens who had announced their intention to become citizens, the secretary told Lyons, was a concession to the Western states, where much irritation existed over the large numbers who had made citizenship declarations but were now finding their old allegiance too cherished to abandon.[14]

Concerning the franchise, the administration had decided earlier that men who had accepted the privileges of citizenship were now required to fulfill a citizen's obligations. The voting issue became troublesome because a number of Western states (Indiana, Wisconsin, Iowa, Illinois, and Kansas) permitted immigrant males to vote once they met the state residency requirement and announced their intention to become United States citizens. Moreover, in some of these states individuals were required to make declarations of intention in order to purchase public land. Until the ratification of the Fourteenth Amendment in 1868 there was no Federal definition of citizenship: states determined an individual's status by granting or withholding the right to vote. It must have been with surprise that Lyons read Seward's response to his queries about citizenship: "A person may be a citizen of a State and entitled to vote there, without being a citizen of the United States." The situation became more apparent to Lyons when authorities in Indiana refused to release two British nationals because they had voted. In Indiana and other Western states, authorities contended, voting was considered equivalent to naturalization.[15]

Governor Salomon pushed the voting issue even further by attempting to enroll draft-age children whose immigrant fathers had voted but had never completed the final steps toward naturalization; the children themselves had never voted. Local judges authorized Salomon to draft these youths, but the Foreign Office opposed the decision. According to Crown lawyers, minor children of British subjects became naturalized Americans when their father's citizenship became final. If, however, the fathers failed to take the final steps toward citizenship, the children remained British subjects.[16]

The section in the 1863 Enrollment Act making men who had declared their intention to become citizens liable for service was a complete reversal of previous policy. In 1862 both

the War and State departments announced that a declaration
of intention did not make a man eligible. As Seward wrote, the
State Department "would not give [such a man] a passport, so
it cannot require service of him."[17]

The change may have been a concession to the Western
states, as Seward claimed, but it was dictated as well by the
growing need for soldiers in 1863. Undoubtedly, the realization
that too many immigrants were using their alienage to escape
service encouraged the modification. Under the old policy many
long-time British residents in the United States, as well as other immigrants, remembered their alien status and rushed to
consular offices to apply for certificates of nationality. Consul
Kortwright at Philadelphia issued twenty-six hundred "protection papers" before the passage of the Enrollment Act. Consul
Wilkins even persuaded military officers in the western theater
to release conscripted aliens who had made declarations of intention but had not completed the citizenship process. So many
men began to rely on their foreign birth as a safeguard against
conscription that Seward informed the British legation, even
before the change of policy took effect, that a certificate was not
enough to exempt a man from military service.[18]

When Lyons informed the Foreign Office that the Enrollment Act made foreigners who had declared their intention to
become United States citizens eligible for the draft, Russell
voiced his disapproval. Aliens who had announced their intention to become citizens and who had voted, he responded, should
be allowed to leave the country before they were drafted. These
people had remained in the United States believing no military
obligation would be required of them; to demand it now was a
breach of faith and at variance with the "comity of nations."[19]

Russell's argument made some impression on Lincoln and
the State Department. On May 11, 1863—approximately one
month after Russell expressed his opinion—Lincoln issued a
proclamation announcing that foreign-born residents who had
stated under oath their intention to become citizens or who
had voted could no longer claim alienage in seeking exemption
from conscription. They were given sixty-five days to leave the
country or face the possibility of service. Harsh as the procla-

mation may seem, it satisfied both the Foreign Office and Lyons. "I have now to state to Your Lordship," wrote Russell, "that in the opinion of Her Majesty's Government, the period of 65 days is with reference to all the circumstances a reasonable period."[20] Thereafter Russell accepted the new Union policy. In August 1863 several British subjects asked Lyons to request their exemption, declaring they had only announced their intention to become citizens in order to purchase public land. In response to a query from Lyons, Russell replied: "The cases with which you are concerned do not call for any interference on our part . . . and it is not unreasonable to expect [these men] to perform military service." Russell's acceptance of the new American policy in turn hardened Lyons's attitude. Responding to a similar case, he wrote: "I do not think these declarers deserve any sympathy from *us*, though I think they have been severely treated by those for whom they intended to renounce us."[21]

Lyons not only accepted the American stipulations, but he added two of his own. He consistently refused to consider any appeal if the person had previously volunteered for military service or if he had accepted bounty money. Justifying his attitude, Lyons wrote, "those who voluntarily enlist lose the Queen's Protection during their enlistment period." With respect to bounties, he added: "There is no doubt that some of the persons who apply to me are not entitled to British protection [because they] enlisted with the intention of securing the bounties, and then obtaining their discharge by addressing the Legation as British Subjects." In addition, Lyons carefully investigated each appeal to ascertain its honesty. In 1862 he refused to intercede on behalf of a Canadian after learning that the young man "was drunk and took the shilling in the regular way [when he enlisted]. He now tired of the service and falls back on his being a British Subject."

Lyons received Russell's support in the stipulations he laid down. The foreign secretary informed Lyons, in 1864, not to pursue the request of several British sailors for discharges from the United States Army. Evidence indicated that each man received a "certain amount of bounty. It is questionable if men who receive a bounty are entitled to complain." Learning from his own exchanges with Charles Francis Adams, United States minister to England, whom he considered the "most frank and cordial" foreign representative he had to deal with, Russell urged Lyons to "continue to go on quietly with Seward. I think this is better than any violent demonstrations . . . which might sour like beer if there should be a thunderstorm."[22]

Under the Enrollment Act the Federal government placed alienage exemptions on a uniform basis and standardized the process of appeal. Like every eligible citizen, the alien was subject to call, and if his name was drawn on the day of the draft, he had to appear before the enrolling board in his district. There he requested an exemption and presented his evidence: his certificate of nationality along with proof that he had never voted or declared his intention to become an American citizen. If satisfied, the board discharged him; if doubt remained, it forwarded the papers to the provost marshal general in Washington, who transmitted them to the State Department for a final decision. Seward informed all foreign ministers that the induction of these individuals would be suspended until the State Department reached a decision and that all decisions would be made in consultation with the legation of the man's nationality. "All things considered," Lyons informed Russell, "I have formed the opinion that these regulations do not render the establishment of claims to exemption unreasonably difficult, nor impose any excessive burden on Foreigners." Lyons asked his consuls to abide by Federal government policy, and he rejected a suggestion by Consul Kortwright to procure exemption because of alienage before the individual was called before the board. Too many appeals would be made, and neither the consuls nor the legation had the time or staff to handle all the cases that would be presented.[23]

If Lyons admitted the fairness of Federal policy and the State Department in dealing with the question of alien exemptions, he soon came to realize that difficulty lay at the more local level, with district provost marshals, enrolling officers, and lower grade officers in the army and navy. One month after he informed Russell of the procedure aliens should follow to secure exemption, Lyons admitted, "the government here is certainly desirous of behaving fairly toward aliens in the matter of the draft, but it is difficult to keep the subordinates in order."[24]

Local enrolling officers were more interested in filling quotas than in dealing with requests for exemption. Then, too, many draft officials felt that long-term residents who had enjoyed the benefits of living in the United States should not be exempt. They distrusted most claims of alienage and often cast aside the evidence offered, ordering the man into service. "Extended experience," wrote an enrolling officer in Wisconsin, "fully satisfied the Board that persons, who, after having enjoyed the many inestimable blessings freely bestowed upon them by this generous Republic, will, in time of national distress, seek to screen themselves from the dangers of war under their shield of alienage [and] will not hesitate to commit no less mean or unmanly act of perjury."[25]

The most frequent complaint of British nationals about draft officials was their refusal to accept certificates of nationality and their attempts to make securing exemption as difficult as possible. Forced into the army by his enrolling board in Louisville, Kentucky, J.S. Shaw, a Canadian, attempted to show his affidavit of citizenship, embossed with the Canadian seal. The company commander directed him to headquarters where "the major there told me to get back to duty. He would imprison any British Subjects seeking exemption." When another British citizen, also forcibly conscripted in Kentucky, presented his certificate, his commanding officer threw it on the floor and said it meant nothing to him.[26]

Nor were such instances limited to Kentucky. From Boston, Consul Lousada wrote that none of his certificates were accepted in the 3rd and 4th draft district in the city. Enrolling boards there required aliens to seek assistance from certain lawyers, who charged enormous fees for useless advice. In addition, the boards used "obnoxious language" and made insulting statements about England and the British. "It works in this way," Lousada concluded, "that the person notified gets disgusted at so many hindrances and goes away home, then they pounce upon him for not having shewn [*sic*] valid cause of exemption & thus gain their point."[27]

In Philadelphia, Consul Kortwright reported that local draft officials paid little attention to Federal regulations. One enrolling officer refused to look at Thomas Armrod's protection papers. "I don't want to see them," he declared, "because they are of no use whatever." After the officer discovered that Armrod had lived in a number of places before finally settling in Frankford, a Philadelphia suburb, he demanded Armrod present affidavits from every county he had ever lived in or traveled through signifying that he had never voted in any of those locations. Kortwright pointed out, in addition, the intense hardship being encountered by British subjects who worked in more rural areas of Pennsylvania, especially those in the western mining and manufacturing districts. Their distance from the consulate made it difficult to obtain evidence of their alien status, even if it were accepted by local enrolling officers. Kortwright was thankful, he told Lyons, that Britons could appeal to the courts. But then in September 1863 Lincoln suspended the writ of habeas corpus in all cases involving the draft, and this action, Kortwright insisted, put foreign nationals completely at the mercy of the enrolling boards and military officers. "Unless the War Department at Washington be moved to issue stringent orders [compelling enrolling officers] to give due weight to the rightful claims of Aliens, the efforts to afford protection . . . will be ineffectual," he wrote.[28]

From New York to St. Louis, the consuls' observations were similar. In 1864, Pierrepont Edwards, acting consul at New York City, interviewed several British subjects at the induction center on Hart's Island, a rendezvous point for the area. At first they were reluctant to discuss their situation because military officers derided them as "Lord Lyons men" and "Consul men" and threatened severe punishment if they revealed too much. But finally the men informed Edwards that officers had been told of the consul's impending visit several days earlier and had shipped off a large number of soldiers who claimed to be British citizens.

Even Wilkins, whom Lyons regarded as the most successful consul in dealing with military officers, wrote of his difficulties in the St. Louis draft district after Schofield was transferred to the East. He kept track of the number of exemptions granted in 1863 and counted less than five hundred. "I am fully aware how difficult it is for the central power to keep in check outlaying [sic] subordinate officers," he told Lyons, "but at the same time I thought it prudent to inform Your Lordship of the independent position assumed by many Boards of Enrolment."[29]

When British subjects and other foreign nationals were not intimidated by verbal abuse or refusals to accept their proof of alienage, draft personnel resorted to more extreme methods. In late 1864, Robert Dickson, a visiting Englishman, struck back at a would-be robber on the streets of Cincinnati and was arrested. The chief of police encouraged him to enlist, but Dickson refused. The officer then placed him in a small cage and gave him "very little food over the next four days." After Dickson finally agreed to enlist, he received a hundred-dollar bounty. Later, Dickson learned that he was a substitute for a wealthy, local resident who had staged the entire scenario, and the police had received seven hundred dollars in bounty money that should have been paid to him.[30]

John Flynn's confinement lasted longer and was more brutal. When he refused to join the army, Flynn was taken to a military prison in Alexandria, Virginia. Prison officials refused to let him contact family members until someone accidentally or purposely allowed one of Flynn's letters to slip through to his brother, Patrick. In the months that followed, Flynn told his brother that military personnel at Alexandria had stolen his money, broken his nose, and kept him "almost naked" in their efforts to force his enlistment. Apparently he gave in, for in February 1865 John informed Patrick that he had been fined three months back pay by a court martial—but that he was unaware of any crime he had committed. Still, he was not surprised that the court deprived him of his salary because, "the whole crew of them . . . are a lot of robbers and swindlers . . . this war is being carried on to make money for themselves and [their] friends." A month later John wrote to

Patrick, telling him that he was now attached to the 3rd U.S. Infantry at General George Meade's headquarters and that he was hoping to bring his situation to the general's attention. At that point the correspondence between the brothers stopped.[31]

Most galling to the personnel at the British legation was the "shower-bath treatment," usually administered in cold weather. The man was stripped of his clothes and hosed down with forced cold water. Although the treatment was probably not used extensively, it still incensed Lyons when he became aware that British citizens were subjected to it. His objections did not put a stop to the practice, however. In April 1865, after Lyons had returned to England, Luke Riley finally got word of his suffering to the legation. Until the end of the war, his officers destroyed any mail Riley attempted to send. Riley was hired in New York City to transport horses to Washington, D.C. Upon his arrival in the capital, two army officers apprehended him as a deserter and took him to a military prison. He was subjected to nine cold showers a day in zero degree weather, he claimed, kept in solitary, and fed only bread and water. When Riley became ill he was transferred to Alexandria, where "Captain Petted" pistol-whipped him, handcuffed him with his hands behind his back, and hung him from the ceiling. Riley wrote that Petted "kept me in that position for three days up and down every half hour," before sending Riley to the New York Cavalry. As a last warning, Petted told Riley not to contact anyone in the British diplomatic or consular corps, "or he would send me where the British Consuls could not find me."[32]

In addition to confronting inflexible enrolling boards and ruthless military personal, Britons also faced the possibility of falling into the clutches of bounty brokers or runners. This group sprang up almost as soon as Federal, state, and local governments started paying bounties, but their numbers became greater and their methods more sinister after the passage of the Enrollment Act of 1863. Discontent over the draft caused local communities to increase bounties in order to encourage enlistment, and the prices wealthy men were willing to pay for a substitute increased as well. Bounty brokers did not prey on British subjects alone; they had little concern about the nationality of their victims. They tended, however, to hang around the docks of eastern cities looking for unsuspecting immigrants, and a substantial number of British citizens were duped by their methods. Indeed, some ships' captains allowed brokers to begin recruiting activities on their boats even before they docked.

The bounty broker's sole objective was money. He received payment from the local community for bringing in volunteers and took as much of the enlistee's bounty as he could get his hands on. Fees paid by states and local communities ranged from twenty-five to thirty dollars per volunteer, but Federal, state, and local bounties together could amount to seven hundred dollars or more. For example, men enlisting in Indianapolis in 1864 received the following bounties: three hundred dollars from the Federal government, one hundred dollars from Marion County, and $375 from the municipal government. As the chargé d'affaires remarked, "the large bounty offered is such a temptation to the worthless men who ply their infamous trade that it seems doubtful whether it can ever be effectively put a stop to." Brokers kept close track of bounties offered and engaged in running, taking their victims to localities that offered more money. Brokers also preferred to deal with state or local recruiting officers because they were less concerned with the volunteer's physical condition and paid bounties in lump sums, whereas the Federal government paid in installments to discourage bounty jumping and desertion.[33]

Brokers had no legal position in the recruiting process, but in time the more naive came to believe that their assistance was necessary to enlist. Some brokers hung around recruiting offices and offered assistance to potential recruits, and once the recruit received his bounty, the broker took his share. Others sought recruits in the city and brought them to enlistment centers. Until 1863 most brokers used persuasion, but as the demand for volunteers became higher and bounties larger, many resorted to giving their victims drugged liquor, enlisting them under false pretenses, and taking most of the bounty. By 1864 the system became so notorious that the *New York Times* reported: "these harpies [are] ever ready to fleece their victims. The recruit seems to have no friends. He is hustled off without knowledge of what he is entitled to, or how he is to get it, and if he is without a well-informed personal friend to look after him, he will very likely turn up minus his bounty money."[34]

Most brokers belonged to the criminal element of society, but they did not work alone. Bartenders provided drugged liquor, barbers made overaged men look younger, boardinghouse and hotel keepers informed brokers of likely victims, and unscrupulous women posed as mothers of minor children and consented to their enlistment. But perhaps the system flourished because recruiting officers, in their zeal to fill quotas, ignored the deceit and corruption—and often participated in it by taking a share of the bounty. When the brokerage system became so blatant that it could no longer be ignored, the War Department assigned detective LaFayette Baker to investigate. Recalling his investigation, Baker declared: "The lenity of our military authorities, in regard to the punishment of offences [sic] against the law and loyalty, was a fruitful cause of the boldness with which [bounty brokers] acted, and the air of respectability worn by the crime itself."[35]

The activities of bounty brokers became so widespread and affected British subjects so broadly that by May 1864 Russell considered it the most troublesome issue between the United States and Great Britain. And the situation was exacerbated by the bounty brokers' lack of conscience: they sought out any likely prospect. In the fall of 1864 an Englishman named Perkins frantically appealed to Lyons for aid. His fifteen-year-old Asian-Indian servant boy, who spoke no English, had been drugged and enlisted in New Hampshire and was about to be sent to the front. At almost the same time Lyons reported the case of another fifteen year old who had been kidnapped and drugged while on an errand for his father. Once inducted he was immediately shipped off, without any training, to the 67th Regiment of the New York Volunteers.[36]

The old and the sick could fall victim as well as the young and healthy. In June 1864, George Watson, age seventy, was drugged, robbed, and enlisted in the army. Lyons appealed for

Watson's immediate release, without the usual War Department investigation, after the man became seriously ill and was confined to a hospital in Washington, D.C.[37]

In one case, Lyons demanded monetary compensation for the victim's family. In September 1864, John Davis, a Canadian who had been gravely ill for six weeks, took a cruise on the Great Lakes to restore his health. Soon after Davis arrived in Detroit, a bounty broker drugged and robbed him, and persuaded local recruiters to accept him into the army. Unable to endure the rigors of military life, Davis died two months after his enlistment. When informed of Davis's death, Lyons's temper flared. The case had been "shamefully handled," he told Seward. The man was ill at the time of his physical examination and the doctor chose to ignore his physical debility. Not only did army recruiters induct the man, but the broker or the recruiters stole all of his Canadian money and the entire bounty as well. Because Davis left a wife and children without any visible means of support, Lyons demanded a search for the thieves and compensation for the Davis family. Davis's treatment so upset Lyons that, for once, he lost his composure: "The outrages practiced on recruits are too unjust to be borne and in some cases too loathsome to be detailed. Almost every imaginable form of outrage and deception has been developed. . . . there is no artifice or fraud which has not been resorted to in carrying out this system of pillage. Old men and boys and persons labouring under incurable diseases are in numerous instances thrust into the service under the system of public plunder alike fraudulent to the recruits and the Government."[38]

When the British legation received word of a fraudulent or forced enlistment, it demanded an investigation from the State Department. The War or Navy departments then conducted the investigations, such as they were. In most cases they merely queried recruiting officers and accepted their word as truth. The investigation of Patrick McCann's enlistment is typical. McCann claimed he was drugged and inducted at Buffalo, New York. During its investigation, the War Department contacted McCann's commanding officer and the recruiting board in Buffalo. The commanding officer believed McCann's charges, but the recruiting officer testified that McCann arrived by himself and was not under the influence of drugs or alcohol; at the time he answered all questions intelligently and did not imply that any pressure was being put on him to enlist. Using the latter testimony as its justification, the War Department refused to release McCann.[39]

British diplomatic and consular personnel had little faith in the investigative process. "In point of form," wrote Lyons, "there is little to complain of. . . . From the nature of the case there can seldom be any evidence, except that of the recruiting officer on the one side, and the enlisted man on the other, and commonly the United States Government gives credence by preference to its own officers and retains the recruits in service." Vice-Consul Edwards referred to the investigations as "unworthy of credit" and "difficult to deal with." To a friend Lyons wrote: "I receive endless complaints from men that they have been improperly enlisted in the U.S. Army, some apparently well founded, some clearly unfounded, the greater part doubtful. The usual result is that the U.S. officers declare the enlistment was perfectly correct and regular and that the Govt. believe its own officers and keep the recruit. From the value of the case, there can seldom be any evidence of third Parties in the man's favor."[40]

Other complaints of the British legation focused on the length of investigations, the slowness in releasing men, and the policy of keeping them assigned to their units while investigations were being carried out. It was not unusual for both the War and Navy departments to lose all evidence and request its resubmission. In May 1864, Lyons found it necessary to inquire about four Britons who had been granted discharges but who remained in service. One of them was still with his unit two months after the War Department had recommended his discharge.[41]

The case of Patrick Cunningham indicates that delay sometimes led to tragic results. Illegally inducted into the New York Volunteers in January 1864, Cunningham and his wife both applied for his release. The investigation went slowly because the War Department lost all correspondence and it had to be resubmitted. Six months after his induction, the War Department decided in Cunningham's favor, only to learn that Cunningham had been killed in battle a month before. The government extended its regrets and offered to make restitution to Cunningham's family, but correspondence between the State Department and the British legation indicates that none had been paid as late as February 1866.[42]

As the number of fraudulent enlistments increased, especially in 1864, the War Department began to demand return of any bounties received before releasing an alien, a decision that only added to the inductee's hardship. In many instances the money had gone to the bounty broker and could not be retrieved; thus, the soldier was forced to repay money he had never received. Even if the money was repaid, the process was cumbersome and the military kept the man in service all the while. The money was sent to Lyons, who turned it over to the Treasury and showed Seward the receipt. Seward then informed the War Department and the soldier was released within the next several months.[43]

Requiring repayment often resulted in additional foul-ups. When John Arthur Verner was killed in action in January 1864, his mother wrote a blistering letter of complaint about the runaround she had been given. Initially she was required to resubmit evidence about her son's fraudulent conscription. After the War Department agreed to a discharge, it required her to repay the son's bounty; still, she heard nothing more until she received news of his death. In this case, the fault lay not with the government: without telling his wife, Verner's father had never forwarded the money. In another case the money was paid by the parents of a fifteen year old inducted in May 1864. But the boy's commanding officers did not release him until a year later and then refused to pay him, claiming that he was not entitled to any compensation because he was a minor.[44]

Of the five hundred thousand foreign-born who fought for the Union, approximately 189,000 were English and Irish. Ella Lonn concluded that of these, 235 were fraudulent enlistments. This figure is somewhat low for several reasons. The legation asked for the release of over one hundred Britons in 1861 alone, and requests increased in the following years. In November 1863, Lyons received "more than nine hundred notes from Mr. Seward already this year" dealing with fraudulent enlistments. Lonn diligently researched correspondence between the State Department and the British legation and perhaps reached her conclusion by counting the number of letters. Frequently, however, individual letters mention three or more names and sometimes as many as six or seven. A more reasonable estimate of the number of British subjects who brought their cases to Lyons's attention would be somewhere between 450 and 500. Correspondence between British legation and State Department between January 1, 1862, and April 15, 1865, contains the names of 473 individuals who claimed to have been fraudulently conscripted into the Union army or navy.[45]

Ultimately, an accurate figure can perhaps never be reached. In his instructions to the consuls, Lyons urged them to forward only cases they could not resolve; thus, many were never entered into legation records. Lyons also understood that a definite number of forced enlistments would be impossible to determine. Many British subjects were unaware that they could appeal to their consuls or to the legation and made no efforts to do so. Others were prevented from contacting British officials. Both Edwards and Archibald wrote that Union army and navy officers kept foreign recruits from corresponding with consuls or relatives: they destroyed draftees' letters, threatened to assign draftees to arduous duty assignments, and even shipped off recruits when they knew a foreign consul might be visiting a rendezvous center. After a trip to Hart's Island in 1864, Edwards related that "in many of these cases even where the parties are aware that their proper course would be to have their complaints before the consul, . . . their short time on the island would preclude the possibility of application."[46]

Determining the exact number of forced enlistments of British subjects is further complicated by imperfect military record keeping during the Civil War era. Enlistment papers and service records indicate places of birth but fail to state whether a foreign-born individual was naturalized. In addition, bounty brokers declared aliens to be American citizens and even enlisted them under false names. That sometimes worked to the aliens' advantage. Lyons was able to secure the release of about a dozen fraudulently enlisted Britons "by reason that [their names were] never borne on the Records of the Army of the United States."[47]

Numbers aside, the tension that forced enlistment caused was mitigated by cooperation on both sides. Seward sought as best he could within War Department regulations to procure discharges for individuals whose complaints were valid. Nor did Lyons demand redress for every case brought to him, especially appeals from long-time residents in the United States.[48] Difficulty arose when Americans conscripted newly arrived immigrants or lured British citizens from their homeland under false pretenses. Even though the Federal government did not sanction such practices, they caused as much tension between the United States and Great Britain in 1864 as had the *Trent* affair in 1861 and the Laird Ram crisis in 1863.

11

Preying on the Innocents

Approximately eight hundred thousand immigrants arrived in the North during the Civil War, about two-thirds of them men between eighteen and forty-five years of age. Of these, 183,448 served in the Union army.[1] Few fought for ideals; many were attracted by huge bounties or were lured into the military by force or fraud. British subjects who fell into the "newly arrived" category came mainly from three regions: British North America, Ireland, and Great Britain. At the beginning of the war, bounty brokers and military personnel focused on Canada as a locality for obtaining fighting men. As the need for soldiers became more acute and bounties increased, brokers made greater efforts to entice newly arrived immigrants, and finally to transport them from their European homeland to the United States under false pretenses. Following is a summary of attempts to lure British immigrants into the Union military and efforts by Northern consuls and legation personnel to mitigate the problem.

The first group of recruiters consisted of state militia or federal military personnel who sought out British servicemen in Canada and encouraged them to desert. Because many were Irish, the Americans played on their anti-English feelings or emphasized monetary advantages to be gained by changing loyalty. They also hinted at rapid promotions because of the soldiers' experience. Whereas noncommissioned officers in British North America received only forty cents a day, the promise of collecting a Union army sergeant's pay of $1.00 to $1.60 was an attractive incentive. In addition, volunteers would receive Federal, state, and local bounties and money for serving as substitutes.[2]

These promises of money and advancement were successful. Desertions by British soldiers prompted Denis Donohoe, consul at Buffalo, to remark that "every Irishman would desert from the Sixteenth Regiment when there was an opportunity for doing so." By the fall of 1861, American recruiting activities in Upper and Lower Canada become so blatant that Sir Edmund Head, governor general, asked Lyons to discuss the issue with the State Department. Head estimated that Americans had distributed some eight hundred circulars, which offered unseemly inducements, among soldiers. They made appeals particularly to commissioned officers. One colonel from a Michigan militia unit tried to persuade several officers of a top British regiment to enlist in the United States Army. When Lyons raised the issue, Seward assured him that such activities were not authorized by the Federal government, but he gave no assurance that he could stop them.[3]

Within a short time, early in 1862, crimps—the Canadian term for bounty brokers—entered the recruiting scene to lure British soldiers and Canadian civilians into the Union army. Some worked alone, while others employed bartenders or boardinghouse keepers to be on lookout for likely prospects. Most crimps dressed well and gave every appearance of being gentlemen. Usually they struck up a friendship with victims and entrapped them through friendly conversation and drugged liquor. In 1864, for example, a landlord in Quebec City introduced three British sailors to another tenant. They accepted several drinks from their new friend and upon awakening found themselves in army uniforms in Lebanon, New Hampshire, fresh recruits in the United States Army. Of the seven hundred dollar bounty due each of them, the sailors received two hundred dollars apiece while the crimp, by then long gone, took the rest.[4]

If drugging failed to achieve their objective, crimps engaged in kidnapping. One official in Canada reported that men living near the United States-Canadian border found it unsafe to be out alone after dark, "while [citizens] protested that they would be awakened at night by the screams of people being kidnapped."[5]

Crimps brought their victims across the border by boat and overland. Frontier lakes and rivers, Donohoe reported, were crowded with small craft used by crimps to row their victims to the American shore. Others hired yacht owners to take their "cargo" to the United States. In winter, crimps resorted to sleighs and crossed the border in out of the way places to avoid both American and British customs officials.[6]

Crimps, however, preferred to entice likely prospects to the United States rather than to sneak them across the border, thus avoiding colonial officials, who were becoming increasingly alert to crimping activities. Usually they promised well-paying jobs, sometimes with attractive side benefits. Because immigration from Europe declined from its yearly 1850s levels during the early part of the war and an increasing number of men left civilian life for the fighting front, a severe labor shortage existed in sections of the North, and Canadians looking for work were easily persuaded to come to the United States.

Both Lyons and his chargés d'affaires—William Stuart and, after mid-1864, Joseph Hume Burnley—made frequent protests against the "nefarious practice" of enticing youths from British North America with promises of jobs and then forcing them to enlist in the army. Consuls became so suspicious of employers looking for workers that they discouraged Canadians from seeking employment in the United States. In 1863, when a Vermont quarry owner asked Consul Lousada in Boston to issue a public statement that unnaturalized aliens were not eligible for the draft, the consul refused. Lousada feared the workers might be fraudulently enlisted once they arrived in the United States. Following a similar request several months later, he suggested that Lyons warn colonial officials of a possible raid on military-age men.[7]

Instances of kidnapping or drugging of Canadians working within the United States were numerous. For example, when friends told John Casey, a newly arrived immigrant from Ireland, about job opportunities in Vermont, he left Canada for the United States. On his first day of work, Casey was drugged and inducted into the 2nd Vermont Regiment. Caught attempting to desert after he arrived at the front, he was court-martialed and sentenced to ten years of hard labor on the Dry Tortugas. It was from there that he was able to send an appeal for help to Consul Archibald in New York City.[8]

Another case involved James Fitzgerald, age fifty-seven, who obtained a discharge, but not his freedom, after his induction into the army. On his way from India to England, Fitzgerald stopped in Canada to earn passage money for the last leg of his journey. His Canadian employer requested his company on a business trip to the United States. When the men arrived in Battleboro, Vermont, the employer introduced Fitzgerald to the local provost marshal, who drugged and conscripted him into the army. After he arrived at a rendezvous and complained to his commanding officer, Fitzgerald recalled, "he laughed at me & said he was glad I was sucked in, and to say no more about it if I did not want to get a hole in my jacket." The officer also intercepted a letter Fitzgerald had written to Lyons; he confronted Fitzgerald and "told me that if I ever wrote another such, I would be kept from writing for some time." Finally sent to the Virginia front, Fitzgerald was caught attempting to desert. He exposed his fraudulent enlistment at his court-martial, and the court agreed to discharge him. Still, he did not gain his freedom. Military authorities confined him for a time to Old Capitol Prison in Washington, D.C., then sent him to the Dry Tortugas, where he was told he must stay for the duration of the war.[9]

Some historians claim that immigrants in the Union army were exemplary soldiers. Such may be case with those who enlisted willingly, but correspondence from soldiers forcibly conscripted indicates many tried to desert whenever possible. Their statements also indicate that they were closely watched and regarded as potential deserters. Provost Marshal General James B. Fry believed desertion was the most common crime of the foreign enlistee. Following the war he wrote: "It is a notorious circumstance that the great mass of professional [deserters] were Europeans."[10]

While deserters were usually apprehended, James Conway's account indicates how successful some could be. A sailor on the *Coral Queen of London*, Conway was drugged in a New York

City tavern and, upon awakening, found himself "in a village in the state of Ohio, dressed in the garb of an American soldier." When his commanding officer refused to release him because his bounty had already been paid, Conway gave the appearance of accepting his situation. Shortly thereafter he was assigned to a unit near Nashville, Tennessee. While on night sentry duty, Conway took off and hid among cotton bales on a steamboat headed for the Ohio River. He left the ship in Indiana and made his way on foot to Pittsburgh, where he worked until he saved enough money for rail fare to New York and passage to England.[11]

From the beginning of the war, the colonial government in British North America did all within its power to discourage crimping in Canada and to prevent its citizens from crossing into the United States. Fitzgerald remembered his employer telling the provost marshal in Battleboro how difficult it was to cross the border, even though both men were British citizens. In 1863 the colonial government authorized a fifty-dollar reward for the apprehension of crimps or their agents. The following year it raised the sum to two hundred dollars. Individuals found guilty of enticing Canadians into the United States military were liable to a six-month sentence at hard labor and a one hundred dollar fine. Finally, in November 1864, the colonial government placed special agents in the border counties to prevent men and boys from being taken into the United States. Informing Seward of the new measures, Chargé d'affaires Burnley said the colonial government would be forced to protect its citizens as long as the United States allowed "this source of evil" to continue.[12]

In the United States itself, New York City became the focal point for bounty brokers hoping to entice immigrants into the Union military. So flagrant were their methods and so willing were local recruiting officials to accept immigrants, that even General Isaac Wistar, commander of United States forces at Yorktown, Virginia, remarked about the quality of recruits he was receiving:

I think I am justified in saying that most of these unfortunate men were either deceived or kidnapped, or both, in the most scandalous and inhuman manner, in New York City, where they were drugged and carried off to New Hampshire and Connecticut, mustered in and uniformed before their consciousness was fully restored. Even their bounty was obtained by the parties who were instrumental in these nefarious transactions, and the poor wretches find themselves on returning to their senses, mustered soldiers, without any pecuniary benefit. Nearly all are foreigners, mostly sailors, and both ignorant of and indifferent to the objects of the war in which they thus suddenly find themselves involved.[13]

Consul Moore at Richmond, before the Confederacy revoked his exequatur, also complained about enlistment frauds in New York City. Men were enlisted under the influence of liquor and drugs and then sent to the fighting front without training. If they deserted, the men were too frightened to flee north; instead, they came into the Confederacy where they were arrested on suspicion of being Northern spies.[14]

Widespread induction fraud became so much a part of the enlistment process in New York City by 1864 that the Federal government found it impossible to rely on the urban police force to stop it. Many police officers, as well as recruiting agents, cooperated with brokers and received a share of the bounty for their collaboration.[15] The government finally assigned War Department detective LaFayette Baker to investigate the system, and his recollection of what he discovered was anything but encouraging: "It would be impossible to give a correct idea or understanding of the condition in which I found the recruiting business. . . . The great and urgent demands of the government to fill up the ranks of our depleted army . . . were seized upon . . . to perpetrate forgeries and frauds upon the Government and soldiers, the extent and enormity of which I believe are unparalleled in the history of the world."[16]

Bounty brokers focused on New York City for several reasons. The government imposed larger draft quotas on New York, Pennsylvania, and the New England states than on states to the west. The larger populations in the Eastern states justified the higher quotas; also the Western states had met their quotas during the Militia Draft period of 1862, whereas the eastern states had not. It was also much easier to find public transportation from New York City to nearby localities where higher bounties were offered. In addition, most immigrants entered the country through New York City, and their papers were processed at Castle Garden, a former opera house converted into a central immigration depot in 1855. There the new arrivals, each eager to find a friendly face, were easily taken in by offers of jobs, housing assistance, transportation, or simply a drink and friendly conversation at the local tavern. The increasing presence of bounty brokers at Castle Garden and the openness of their activities caused the general agent of immigrant commissioners to publish a notice in the *New York Times*, asking individuals who expected friends or relatives from Europe to leave their addresses at his office, so that new arrivals could be sent quickly on their way. "If this is done," he wrote, "the liability of emigrants [sic] to be swindled or led astray by vagabonds, who constantly infest every locality in the vicinity of Castle Garden may be avoided."[17]

In most cases of fraudulent conscription a broker lured an immigrant without assistance. Usually he pretended to be a concerned individual, offering to help the newcomer but eventually treating him to liquor or soda that had been heavily drugged. When the profits seemed worth the risk, however, brokers worked in pairs, kidnapping three or four men at a time. Such, at least, was the case with James Johns and his friends. The kidnapping was carried off so cleverly that Consul Archibald might never have been aware of it had not J.T. Brown, examining physician in Wilmington, Delaware, informed him of the fraud.[18]

The four men, all blacks, were natives of St. Vincent in the West Indies and had been hired as laborers on a ship sailing for New York City. After the ship docked, an American black came on board and inquired about sailing times and passenger rates. Striking up a conversation with the four, he asked them to request a brief shore leave and accompany him to a local tavern. Once the men were away from the ship, their newly found friend disappeared. Two white men soon arrived and, despite the sailors' apprehensions, lured them into a nearby house and drugged them with liquor. The next day the abductors took the sailors to

Philadelphia but, apparently dissatisfied with the bounties offered, pushed on to Wilmington. Johns's friends were inducted under false names to avoid detection; Dr. Brown rejected Johns because he was missing an ear. Each of the inductees received a bounty, but the brokers took the money as payment for helping the men enlist. They also returned Johns to Philadelphia, where they abandoned him, penniless. A passerby took pity on the sailor and provided shelter for several days and transportation money to New York City. By the time Johns arrived back at his ship, Archibald had received Brown's letter and contacted Johns for a statement.[19]

Subsequent investigation revealed that men fitting the descriptions of the bounty brokers did not live at the address where the sailors had been taken. Moreover, the local provost marshal in Wilmington denied every assertion Dr. Brown and Johns had made. According to him, the sailors arrived alone at the recruiting station, were sober, and claimed they abandoned their ship in order to join the army and receive the bounty. On the basis of this statement, the War Department refused to discharge the men. Responding to the investigative report, Burnley almost called the provost marshal a liar. "I feel satisfied," he wrote, "that if a full and fair investigation had been made of this case, instead of a reference to the enlisting officer, the War Department would have come to a different conclusion respecting it."[20]

Just before he left the United States for England, Lyons informed Lord Russell that Archibald and Edwards were handling the bulk of fraudulent immigrant enlistments because brokers concentrated their activities in New York City. Archibald's problems were compounded by his dealings with the navy, which was less willing than the army to cooperate with consular efforts. "I must do General Dix the justice to say he has & does, now, all in his power to help our poor people out of difficulty," Archibald told Lyons, "I wish I could speak as [well] of naval [personnel]. This navy in which Secretary Welles persists, is enslaving the naval recruits, on the representation of their recruiting agents here."[21] Even Russell became concerned about naval recruiting practices: "The excesses of the U.S. Navy encouraged by Mr. Welles are much to be feared . . . but I trust you and Mr. Stuart will contrive with Mr. Seward & his President to keep things straight." [22]

According to LaFayette Baker, naval personnel made it easy for bounty brokers to bring in recruits: of the seven naval recruiting stations in New York City, three were located behind "public drinking saloons of the lowest and vilest character." To him it seemed as if taverns were "necessary appendages to a [naval] recruiting depot." [23] Once recruiting officers accepted an inductee, they sent him to the USS *North Carolina*, a receiving ship docked in New York harbor. Officers there quickly moved him on to another destination within two or three days. [24]

Naval officers did everything in their power to frustrate consular investigations. They refused to allow consuls to board receiving ships or to question the men. If a consul presented evidence of a fraudulent enlistment, he was often greeted with insult and ridicule. When Vice-Consul Edwards inquired about the forced induction of John Maggs, the officer in charge "treated my request very rudely and dismissed [me] in a very uncourteous manner, intimating that the despatch, which I have received from Your Lordship . . . was 'not genuine.'" Other officers loudly told a story about a naval captain who "didn't care a d——— for the consul anyhow. I write this," Edwards concluded, "solely to illustrate some of the difficulties in the way of dealing with these cases." [25]

The most tragic forced enlistment into the navy involved Michael Quinn, a newly arrived Irish immigrant. Quinn and Rose, his sister-in-law, arrived in the United States in 1863 on their way to join Quinn's brother in California but discovered they had only enough money for one person to continue on to the West Coast. Michael urged Rose to complete the journey while he stayed in New York City to await passage money from his brother. Almost as soon as Rose left, a bounty broker befriended and drugged Quinn. Unaware of what was happening, Quinn was inducted into the navy and kept in the brig for two days before being handcuffed to a fellow recruit and sent to join the Western Flotilla.

On the train between Chicago and Cairo, Illinois, Quinn's

partner devised a plan of escape: he and Quinn would go into the toilet compartment, slip off the handcuffs, and jump out the window. The plan went awry almost immediately. Quinn's hand was too large to slip through the handcuffs, and they caught when he jumped from the train. As the farmer who found him informed Consul Archibald, Quinn's "leg is cut to the bone and the flesh stripped off about four inches long [and] his left arm is so strained that he cannot use it; but that is not as dangerous as inward bruises. His bowels, they are the worst."

In Quinn's case the evidence was too blatant to be ignored. A naval investigation resulted in a discharge, and Admiral Andrew Foote, in charge of recruiting, ordered the naval officers responsible to the Western Flotilla. In time Quinn made it back to New York City, where Archibald arranged passage to California.[26]

The United States government did not condone the entrapment of immigrants into the Union military; still, it did little to discourage the practice until the close of the war. In fact, in 1862 Seward sent a circular to all American embassies and consulates in Europe, extolling the opportunities for employment in the United States. While it did not emphasize the military, it mentioned military service as one of several options. Then in 1864 Congress passed the Contract Labor Law. Originally suggested by Seward, the act authorized private persons and companies to bring foreign nationals to the United States as laborers. Under its provisions immigrants could be required to pledge all or part of their wages for one year to pay their travel expenses to the New World. The act was not designed to expand the military, but stipulations in many contracts conformed very closely to military salary and subsistence scales. Conscripted immigrants often noted that the promised jobs paid between $11 and $16 dollars a month, and they were to be supplied with food, housing, and all equipment necessary to complete their work.[27]

Even before Congress authorized the importation of foreign labor, Russell raised questions about the recruiting activities of Americans in the British Isles, especially in Ireland. Charles

Francis Adams asserted that most of the agents were attempting to obtain workers for American companies and not recruits for the military, and he even produced statements and letters from companies explaining their need for laborers and the conditions of employment. Since recruiting laborers from one country to another was not a violation of international law, there was little Russell could do to stop American agents. Still, he informed Lyons to have the Northern consuls be on the lookout for possible attempts to conscript these "workers." In his opinion, too many of Ireland's unskilled poor were being encouraged to immigrate to the United States.[28]

It was the forced induction of Thomas Tully (sometimes spelled Tulley) and six fellow Irish immigrants that finally caused the Lincoln administration to curb bounty brokering activities. Indeed, the treatment of Tully and his colleagues became a matter of public notoriety in Boston, and in Great Britain it created tremendous resentment against American recruiting practices.[29]

The case began in Ireland in 1864 when a man named Finney contracted with 120 Irishmen to come to America as railroad workers.[30] Each man agreed to work for $10 dollars a month until their ship passage was paid; after he would receive a full salary of $11 or $13. Room, board, and clothing was to be provided.[31]

Finney arranged steerage passage for the men on the *Nova Scotia*, and on February 25, 1864, the ship left Liverpool for the United States. The trip was uneventful, except that one of the Irishmen overheard Finney say "that [the men] had better be prepared to take the musket when they land," and he hoped to make thirty thousand dollars on "this trip."[32] On March 9, the *Nova Scotia* docked at Portland, Maine, where the Irish workers caught the train for Boston. Only 113 men made the train trip; seven remained behind in Portland.

When the men arrived in Boston, Finney took them to a vacant building on Bunker Hill Street. They were given no food the first day and served only whiskey on the second. Then Finney informed them that the promised jobs "were not yet ready" but that they could enlist in the army—he recommended the 28th Irish Regiment. While he spoke, police arrived and blocked the doors so the men could not leave.[33] The commotion brought out neighbors, who forced their way into the building and rescued those men who had not already enlisted. At a protest meeting held later, it was pointed out that the man behind the whole scheme was Jerome G. Kidder. Finney was merely his agent; but all the same, both men were described as "notorious brokers." One speaker claimed that Kidder had no intention of providing employment for the men and that, given the current bounty of between seven hundred and eight hundred dollars for each man, he hoped to clear between eighty thousand and ninety thousand dollars from their enlistments. Shortly thereafter, Kidder announced that he had offered the men jobs at the Charleston Water Works but that they had refused to take them.[34]

The fate of the men who escaped the clutches of Finney and Kidder is unknown, but they probably left the neighborhood to escape recruiting agents. Kidder and Finney's dreams of a fortune did not materialize; indeed, they may have lost money. According to Consul Lousada, only eight or ten men enlisted. Finney even had the impudence to visit the consulate—"A more villainous specimen of humanity . . . I have rarely seen"—and inquire if the men could be sued for breach of contract under British law. He also told Consul Lousada that he was going to the "Secretary in Washington to reclaim the fares of those who had not enlisted."[35]

Meanwhile, in Portland, the seven immigrants who had remained behind—Thomas Tully, Michael Byrne, James Higgins, Michael Moran, Edward Cassidy, Thomas Burke, and Martin Hogan—were encountering difficulties of their own. When the *Nova Scotia* had landed, several strangers had offered liquor to the seven Irishmen and, after giving them a number of drinks, called in the police to arrest them for public drunkenness. According to Tully, the spokesman for the group, the men spent the next thirty hours in jail without food and water. The chief of police offered to release them if they would enlist, but they refused; Tully demanded to see the British consul, John Henry Murray. The chief denied the request and threatened to keep the men confined without food or drink for sixty days. Finally, in desperation, they consented and were marched to the recruiting office. Tully later stated that he agreed to enlist only to get released from jail and have an opportunity to contact the British consul. At the recruiting office, the examining physician refused to pass the men, but the recruiting officers enlisted them anyway and assigned them to Company D of the 20th Maine Infantry. Each man received two hundred dollars of his bounty, but the police and recruiting agents forced them to purchase "junk items" they were selling.[36]

As soon as he was able, Tully contacted Consul Murray, who immediately asked the local provost marshal to detain the men in Camp Barry, the rendezvous outside Portland. By the time the provost marshal's order arrived, the men were already on their way to the Army of the Potomac.[37]

Urged on by Murray from Portland and by Tully, who wrote appeals from the fighting front, Lyons demanded an immediate investigation. He also insisted on the removal of the men from the combat zone so there could be no chance of their being injured or killed. The War Department ignored the latter request but quickly initiated an investigation. Usually investigations began several months after being requested; the Tully investigation was held two weeks after the men left for the front.

The investigation was cursory at best, but it differed from others of its type. Instead of merely gathering written evidence from recruiting officials and commanding officers, the War Department sent an examining board to Portland, where it questioned police officers and recruiting officials. Police denied withholding food and water and swore under oath that Tully demanded release to enlist and get the bounty. The recruiting officers maintained that the men were sober and signed the enlistment papers willingly and agreed without hesitation to purchase the items offered them. Reviewing the report of the investigation, the War Department recommended against discharge.[38]

The decision infuriated Lyons, and he refused to accept it as final. Soon after, Tully became ill and was sent to a hospital in Washington. Lyons arranged a meeting and obtained a statement from him declaring the entire testimony given at Portland to be false. When military officials discovered that Tully had been in contact with the legation, they immediately sent him to a hospital in Philadelphia. But, using Tully's statement as a basis, Lyons demanded another hearing in Portland. This time, however, he insisted that the Irishmen be present to testify on their own behalf and that they be represented by legal counsel.[39] Shortly afterward, Lyons contracted typhoid fever and suffered a physical breakdown and Chargé d'affaires Burnley took over the direction of the legation.

Both the State and the War departments accepted Lyons's demands. The army returned six of the Irishmen to Portland but, according to Tully, army personnel mistreated them at every step of their journey. While in Washington, D.C., the men were confined to Old Capitol Prison, and from there they were sent to Portland in handcuffs and under guard. The second investigation took place in early August. The police and recruiting officers stuck by their original testimony and did not waiver from their conviction that the seven had been inducted legally. Of the Irishmen, only Tully, Higgins, and Moran testified and, according to Consul Murray, their statements were confused and inconsistent. The soldiers' lawyer, although he charged three hundred dollars, was of little help to his clients. In early October the War Department again refused to discharge Tully and his comrades. Giving his own impression of the investigation, Murray concluded: "There is evidently false swearing somewhere though not more perhaps than is to be expected where there is an allegation of fraud and the interested persons are examined as witnesses."[40]

At Burnley's urging the men were kept in Portland until the matter could be referred to the Foreign Office. In his letter transmitting the full report of the investigation, Burnley noted that Seward had agreed with the War Department's decision. Burnley considered Seward's opinion of little value because, according to him, it was based on a summary and not the complete report. In England, Russell turned the report over to

Crown lawyers, who disagreed with the American decision and insisted that the entire affair was "a plot of the recruiting officers and the police." Still, the War Department refused to reverse itself and returned the men to the front.[41]

The fortunes of the seven Irishmen varied. Thomas Burke met his death in the Battle of the Wilderness on May 8, 1864, before the second investigation was held. On the same day, Edward Cassidy was wounded, and there is nothing further in his record. No record exists for Martin Hogan. Michael Byrne deserted after the group was returned to Maine and probably fled to Canada. Michael Moran and James Higgins became prisoners of war after being sent back to the front. Paroled in March 1865, they received discharges in June. Tully reenlisted at the end of the war and served as a private at various Western posts until 1869. He entered a soldier's home in Leavenworth, Kansas, in 1890, and died there in 1898.[42]

In the midst of the Tully investigations, Seward remarked to Lyons on the "good relations" between Britain and the United States. The comment took Lyons by surprise: "I could not take quite so complacent a view as Mr. Seward. . . . Perhaps I attach too much importance to cases of impressment which are the labour of my life. It is not true that British Subjects suffer more in these respects than Frenchmen or other Foreigners though it would be natural they should. They suffer rather less than American citizens, of course."[43]

Regardless of what he said, Seward knew that fraudulent enlistments remained a point of contention between the two nations, and he sought to ease the situation. In August 1864 he persuaded the War Department to hold all men claiming to be foreign nationals at their rendezvous until their cases were resolved. The same month, he approved new regulations relative to contracts with immigrants: every new arrival who enlisted in the army had to renounce his former allegiance and declare his intention to become an American citizen, and all records concerned with his enlistment were to be forwarded to the Central Recruiting Board in Washington. Feeling a sense of elation, Burnley wrote to Russell: "If these rules and regulations are consistently carried out, I have no doubt that they will tend to [lessen] many of the evils which have arisen latterly in Ireland."[44]

Still, it took one more incident for the Lincoln administration to tighten its regulations. In January 1865, the *Great Western* arrived at New York City with ninety-six Irishmen, supposedly brought to work at the Bliss, Ward, and Rose glass factory. After they passed through immigration, the men were sequestered in a private room, plied with liquor, and encouraged to enlist. Sixty-two men enlisted, and those who refused were set at liberty without employment. When Consul Archibald inquired into the matter, General Dix agreed that the enlistments were questionable. However, all the regulations had been complied with; further, it would not have been feasible to seek discharges because the men had been shipped out immediately and were assigned to various military units in Virginia and the further South.[45]

Shortly after the *Great Western* incident, the immigration service issued orders forbidding ships carrying immigrants to be boarded by private individuals before they were docked. In an amendatory act to the Enrollment Act of 1863 passed March 3, 1865, Congress stipulated that any individual or military officer who forcibly or fraudulently enlisted another person could, upon conviction, be fined up to one thousand dollars and imprisoned for two years.[46] This provision, and the end of the war, eliminated bounty brokers from the recruiting scene. For some, their activities had been lucrative. Throughout the war, Federal, state, and local governments had paid close to $600,000,000 in bounties. How much of this money fell into the hands of brokers is unknown, but as early as March 1864, General Dix estimated they were pocketing eight-tenths of all bounty money paid.[47]

The fraudulent induction of British nationals into the Union army gave Southern sympathizers in Parliament their chance to criticize Northern action and to demand punishment for the United States. The blatant conscription of Tully and his comrades even brought denunciations of Lyons and accusations of ineptness on his part. Defending his minister, Russell declared, "I can only say for Lord Lyons that he has continually remonstrated . . . with Mr. Seward. . . . Nothing has given him greater vexation and distress of mind than these proceedings. I say nothing about myself except that I have seconded the efforts of Lord Lyons." When the Earl of Clanricarde, a staunch Confederate sympathizer, demanded war because of fraudulent conscriptions in the Union, Russell, aware of what went on behind the scenes, responded quickly and to the point. He admitted that the number of Britons inducted in the North was larger than in the South, but he pointed out that the Lincoln administration was keeping the door open to negotiation and was attempting to cope with the situation. Conversely, when the consuls remonstrated in the South, they "were sent away altogether. . . . If war is our only remedy," Russell concluded, "we must go to war with both belligerents."[48] In his view, war with either the Union or the Confederacy was untenable; in the matter of conscription, one side was as guilty as the other.

12
At War's End

Being a prisoner of war under any circumstances is a traumatic experience. For an alien conscripted into the Confederate army and then captured by Union forces, the predicament was more distressing: first he had been compelled to fight for a nation and a cause in which he had little or no interest, and then, because the Federal government required an oath of allegiance before releasing any prisoner, he was forced to take an oath to a nation even though he was not one of its citizens.

Wilkins, the only consul in Union-held portions of the Mississippi Valley, encountered this problem shortly after the battles of Forts Henry and Donelson in February 1862, and by the end of the year he had received two hundred applications from British subjects requesting release from prisoner of war camps. When he sought direction from Lyons, the foreign minister suggested that Wilkins "exert all his influence unofficially in [the prisoners'] favor. I do not feel justified . . . to apply officially for their liberation as a matter of right." But as the numbers grew, Lyons appealed for an established policy from the War Department. He hoped the department would devise an oath of neutrality similar to the one Seward had designed for arrested British civilians in 1861, which would permit alien soldiers to subscribe it rather than to take an oath of allegiance.[1]

At first the War Department tried to evade the issue, declaring it would deal only with specific cases. The department, wrote Assistant Secretary Wolcott, received daily requests from prisoners of war who claimed they had been forced to fight unwillingly, and "it refused to take action in such cases."[2]

Even though Lyons submitted specific names and requested releases for these individuals, the War Department procrastinated. In every case it insisted on proof, other than the claimant's word, of his alienage and his forceful conscription. As

Lyons and several of the consuls realized, such evidence was almost impossible for a prisoner of war to obtain, and slowly they became aware that most prisoners who claimed foreign citizenship had little chance of freedom before the end of the war. Finally, in desperation, Lyons appealed to the War Department to allow these men to take an oath of neutrality to prevent them from being exchanged and possibly thrown into the fighting again.[3]

Lyons approached the prisoner of war issue halfheartedly. From the beginning he had realized that British citizens in the Southern army would find it difficult or impossible to prove their forced enlistment. As Seward informed him in 1863, "cases of a similar character are constantly occurring [and] it is inexpedient to grant release at present." The burden of proof lay with the prisoner and placed nearly impossible conditions on him. Lyons also empathized with the War Department's reluctance to free prisoners on a declaration of alienage alone because he knew that such a policy could work against its strategy of depriving the Confederacy of soldiers. In the end he merely informed his consuls to present only those cases in which proof was incontestable. To forward applications made merely on the basis of personal statements, he concluded, would "cause irritation and prejudice any cases having outstanding claims."[4]

Even after the fighting ended, the War Department continued to demand oaths of allegiance from men held as prisoners of war. As late as August 1865 Frederick Bruce, Lyons's replacement at the legation, appealed for the release of British subjects still imprisoned. As one of them reported from the prisoner of war camp on Johnson's Island in Lake Erie, Confederates were being released at the rate of two hundred to three hundred a day, but he remained because he refused to take the oath of allegiance.[5] The record does not indicate whether the holdouts finally swore allegiance to the United States, but given the unyielding attitude of the War Department it seems likely they did.

With the ending of the war, the Foreign Office assessed the work of its legation in Washington and the British consuls in the Union and Confederacy. Lord Russell said little about the Northern consuls and, instead, focused on those in the South. Possibly his concern lay there because of the total collapse of communications between Britain and the Confederacy and because of the expulsion of the consuls in 1863. He was also more aware of Southern consular problems because the Southern consuls had corresponded frequently with the Foreign Office, whereas consuls in the North had worked through the legation. Most of Russell's comments dealt with the expulsion of the Southern consuls. Unlike Lyons, who blamed both Walker and Fullarton, Russell directed his enmity at Fullarton alone. While he approved of the consul's efforts to keep British subjects out of the Southern army, he thought Fullarton's statement advising these men "to desert their colors at the moment of action" was unjustifiable. Had Benjamin communicated Fullarton's comment to the Foreign Office, Russell would have "thought it right to reprimand and even dismiss the consul who had acted in so improper a manner."[6]

Viewing Russell's attitude with historical hindsight, it appears somewhat harsh. The burden of preventing forced conscriptions into the Confederate army fell on Walker and Fullarton, and neither had experience or training as a consul or a diplomat. Each was named to his post as a matter of expediency, and, in his anxiety to avoid any problems with the Richmond government over exequaturs, Russell overlooked the appointees' lack of experience. And Walker and Fullarton found themselves dealing with situations that would have challenged even trained diplomats.

In retrospect, George Moore at Richmond deserves as much criticism, or even more. Having been a consul since 1836, his experience was more extensive,[7] but ill health and a dislike of Richmond caused him to foist most of the work off onto Cridland. When Moore was finally forced to assume total responsibility, he showed as little diplomatic skill as his fellow-consuls to the South. Because his involvement came just as public pressure to expel the consuls reached its height, he probably would not have been able to prevent his own expulsion at any rate.

Another drawback for the Southern consuls was their inability to seek advice from either Lyons or the Foreign Office at the time their difficulties were occurring. Between 1861 and 1863, communication with the world outside the Confederacy was erratic at best; after that date it became even more difficult. The increasing effectiveness of the blockade and doubts about the abilities of individual blockade runners to get through, left occasional British men-of-war the only sure means for the consuls to contact London or Washington. Dates of receipt stamped on Walker's correspondence to the Foreign Office between 1863 and 1865 indicate that his letters arrived six to eight weeks after they had been written. Before the war it usually took two weeks for a letter from Charleston to reach London.[8] The inability to communicate quickly with their superiors forced both Walker and Fullarton to act without direction.

On the matter of conscription, consuls in the South had to deal with two governmental entities, the individual states and the State Department at Richmond. After the passage of the Union's Enrollment Act of 1863, the Federal government handled the issue of alien conscription. Thus, consuls in the North could refer their insolvable problems to the legation, which offered solutions or took over the more difficult cases.

The ease with which Northern consuls confronted issues can be attributed to direction from the legation. Communication between the Northern consuls and the legation was rapid and constant, and as a result, policies were uniform.

The Northern consuls also had the advantage of experience. A few had only recently taken up their posts in the United States, but, at the beginning of the war, the average length of service for Northern consuls was ten years. Archibald's experience as consul was not as extensive, but his long career in Newfoundland politics made up for his lack of consular training.[9]

Finally, Seward's willingness to understand concerns about the treatment of British citizens paved the way to solving individual problems, which improved relations as the war continued. Lord Lyons reported to the Foreign Office Seward's efforts to resolve difficult issues as best he could within the departmentalized structure of the American government. Whereas Seward's cooperation served the Union well, the South's growing hostility toward Britain worked against it. By expelling the consuls and cutting all communications with Britain, the South became its own worst enemy in achieving its diplomatic objectives.

The end of the war brought a number of changes within the consular corps and at the legation. The majority of the consuls retained their posts and continued their usual duties; Archibald, Bunch, Cridland, and Walker were exceptions and received significant recognition from the Foreign Office.

Archibald remained consul general at New York until his retirement in 1882, but he was appointed to the British delegation that settled the Alabama claims in Geneva, Switzerland, in 1872. This British-American commission drew up a settlement of outstanding claims between the United States and Great Britain as a result of the Civil War. Undoubtedly, Archibald's role as consul gave him deep awareness about the validity of claims filed by British citizens.[10]

Russell named Bunch as consul general of Cuba in 1864, and two years later reassigned him to the same position in Colombia. The promotion came as a result of Bunch's role in gaining Confederate consent to the Declaration of Paris in 1861 and as a result of Lyons's efforts on his behalf. "I hope I am not doing wrong in saying," Lyons wrote to Russell as early as 1862, "that it would be very painful to me personally, if, in consequence [of the withdrawal of Bunch's exequatur] he should find himself in a worse position professionally than that in which he now stands, as consul at Charleston." Lyons went on to extol Bunch as a "valuable public servant" and the only reliable source on information on events in the South. "My object is to lay before you my own personal desire," he concluded, "that if not a gainer, he may at least not be a loser, professionally, by what has occurred." Informing Lyons of his new position, Bunch acknowledged the foreign minister's support: "Had it not been for your warm recommendation . . . I might, very probably, have been 'left out in the cold.'"[11]

Cridland and Walker were appointed to full consulships. After long years as vice-consul, Cridland became consul at Mobile in 1865.[12] Over Lyons's objections, Russell named Walker consul at Charleston at the same time. Still retaining some the animosity he felt toward Walker during the war, Lyons opposed the appointment, but Russell felt some obligation because Walker "has been acting as [consul] with great vigilance and ability." As evidence of Walker's diligence, Russell pointed out that he had sold his home and personal possessions following his expulsion and had remained in Charleston to look after British interests. Walker, moreover, had paved the way for his own advancement by persuading Union military authorities to recognize him as consul when Charleston fell into Northern hands.

Although Russell conferred the post on Walker, the terms of the appointment indicated a decline in Charleston's position as a listening post for events in the South. Whereas Bunch had been restricted to consular duties only, Walker was permitted "to trade." His duties became chiefly commercial and did not stipulate any "special considerations" as did Bunch's.[13]

These postwar appointments recognized important wartime roles or responsibilities of the consuls, for each in his own way gave advice that helped discourage either diplomatic recognition of the South or attempts at mediation. Because the Foreign Office regarded the consular corps as distinct from the diplomatic, Russell probably would have denied any influence on the consuls' part; still, a comparison of consular correspondence with events taking place in England indicates their influence.

The crisis point in British-American relations came in the late summer and autumn of 1862. In August, Prime Minister Palmerston, Chancellor of the Exchequer Gladstone, and Russell were slowly coming to the conclusion that an offer of mediation to both the Union and the Confederacy would be a humanitarian gesture sanctioned by international practice and would also serve British interests by making available supplies of raw cotton. Yet, in November, the British cabinet rejected just such a proposal. On October 30, 1862, Napoleon III communicated a suggestion to Russia and Great Britain that along with France they formally propose a six-month armistice, during which time the Union blockade would be withdrawn and the belligerents would attempt to reach a peaceful settlement, with the powers serving as mediators. Russia rejected the proposition outright. Britain also declined but left the impression it might consider such a proposal in the future. The fortunes of war began to favor the Union, especially after Gettysburg and Vicksburg, and further suggestions for joint intervention and mediation were never made.[14]

The most persuasive arguments against mediation were made in Britain by George Cornewell Lewis, secretary for war, in a number of memoranda to the cabinet and in letters to the *Times* of London. Lewis contended that mediation would lead to diplomatic recognition, an honor the Confederacy did not deserve. Lee's recent defeat at Antietam and the Union's continued ability to hold New Orleans, the South's major port, indicated weaknesses on the Confederacy's part and raised doubt that it could maintain its independence. The force of Lewis's argument was strengthened by a letter from Consul Cridland, stating that morale in Richmond was a its lowest ebb, inflation so rampant that average citizens found the price of food beyond their reach, and drunkenness and robbery so common that many people "carry all their possessions on their persons to keep them safe."[15]

Lewis also claimed that England could expect to gain little diplomatic advantage from a mediation effort and that all honor would be placed in the hands of "our copartner" (France). That the Confederacy would not be inclined to give England credit is borne out by Bunch's letters, which were the best source of information the Foreign Office received on Southern attitudes toward England. A reading of his comments indicates a lack of sincerity in the initial declarations of appreciation for English government and culture and a growing resentment slowly turning to outright hostility. By the fall of 1862, anti-British feeling had grown to such proportions that Bunch could only relate to his government: "We have nothing to expect from the good will of the South."[16] Given Southern antagonism toward Britain, the Confederacy, in all probability, would have given France full credit for a successful mediation effort.

If England had little to gain because the growing enmity of

the South, she had more to fear from the Northern reaction to a mediation proposal, claimed Lewis. Interference in the American conflict would almost certainly lead to a war, and Britain would have to confront the growing American army and the Union navy, now almost as strong as Britain's. In all likelihood the Union would attack Canada, and the logistics of transporting a military force to North America would be formidable. Almost simultaneously with the presentation of Lewis's argument, Consul Archibald warned that any attempt at mediation would bring war. "The present conjuncture of affairs demonstrates the wisdom of abstinence from recognition or mediation," he wrote. "It will give scope for political combinations, in which unscrupulous men will not hesitate, if practicable, to embroil this country in a war with England in order to promote their projects of reconstruction of the Union. I cannot help feeling that there has not yet been a time when it would be more important than at the present . . . to adhere to the observance of strict neutrality."[17] That Archibald's thoughts made an impression on the Foreign Office is evident. His letter was stamped "confidential" and circulated among members of the cabinet.

Even Lyons became involved in the argument against mediation. On leave in England as the issue was coming to head, he urged caution, but caution gave way to outright opposition sometime between his departure from England and his arrival in the United States in early November 1862. Lincoln's dismissal of General George B. McClellan and recent Republican losses in the congressional elections fostered the change in Lyons's attitude. McClellan's dismissal, surmised Lyons, indicated Lincoln's capitulations to the radical element of his party and the probability of his caving in to their future demands. If mediation were suggested, radical Republicans would in turn insist on war as a means of regaining popular support and remaining in power. Even if war were not an outcome, an offer of mediation at the present time would be rejected and would weaken any subsequent offers the powers might make. "All things considered," the minister concluded, "my own opinion certainly is that the present moment is not a favourable one for making an offer of mediation."[18] The input of Lyons and his consuls considered as isolated statements, might appear to have had little impact, yet taken together and coming about the same time, they strengthened Lewis's argument that mediation was not in Britain's best interest in the fall of 1862.

In addition to recommending a policy of restraint, throughout the war, Lyons kept the Foreign office aware of Seward's efforts to solve contentious issues. It was fortunate for both the United States and England that Lyons and Seward became warm and cordial friends. When Lyons informed Russell in 1861 that he regarded Seward as an inappropriate choice for secretary of state, he could hardly have guessed that two years later he would write: Seward "has so much vanity, personal and natural, that he seldom makes a favourable impression at first. When one comes really to know him, one is surprised to find much to esteem and even to like in him."[19]

Informing Seward of his departure from his post as minister in March 1865, Lyons concluded his letter by saying, "I must therefore bid you farewell. I do so with much gratitude for the kindness you showed me for many years, . . . I trust that when all these troubles are overpast, you will remember not altogether without satisfaction the official as well as the private relations which we maintained during the trying time we went through."[20]

During his years in Washington, Lyons had maintained caution, discretion, and a steadiness of purpose that garnered respect for him personally and for his country. Although not as outgoing as the other foreign ministers in Washington, he impressed Seward as being more trustworthy. His lack of flamboyance did not detract from his sincerity. Lyons never expressed his distaste for slavery publicly, but undoubtedly it came out in the many private conversations between the minister and secretary of state. Their mutual desire to prevent a British-American war and their growing ability to work in cordiality and to appreciate each other's viewpoints created a friendship between the two men. This was evident in Seward's response to Lyons's announcement of his departure: "I have never desponded of my country, of emancipation of her slaves, and of her resumption of her position as an agent of peace, progress, and civilization, interests which I never fail to believe are common with all branches of the British family. So I have had no doubt that, when this dreadful war shall be ended, the United States and Great Britain would be reconciled and become better friends than ever. I have thought that you are entitled to share in these great successes, as you have borne so great a part of the trials of the war."[21]

Nor did Russell overlook Lyons's achievements. Ill when he left the United States, Lyons spent several months recuperating in England. After he regained his health, Russell appointed him ambassador to Turkey, which was considered a prime British diplomatic post in the nineteenth century. Two years later Lyons was named ambassador to France, where he remained until his retirement in 1887.

Lyons was replaced by Sir Frederick Bruce, a man of wide experience who as minister to China had gained the Lincoln administration's respect by refusing to grant British registration to Confederate ships in Asian waters. Bruce, however, never developed a rapport with the State Department and with Seward. He arrived in Washington the week of Lincoln's assassination and the attack on Seward. Because the secretary was bedridden for the next several months, Bruce worked chiefly with Frederick Seward, assistant secretary, and clerks in the State Department. Then, in 1867, approximately two years after his arrival in the United States, Bruce suddenly died while on a trip to New York City.[22]

If Archibald's correspondence to the British legation and the Foreign Office is any indication, consular duties became less concerned with wartime issues during the early months of 1865. His last correspondence over the enforced conscription of immigrants dealt with the *Great Western* affair in January. From then on, his duties became routine: reports of marriages, deaths, and the increases in shipping. He also informed the Foreign Office about the search for a fugitive from justice, the granting of passports, and problems in aiding destitute Britons stranded in the United States.[23]

Nevertheless, Archibald and his fellow consuls reflected on the war and the changes it had brought. Always pro-Union, Archibald praised the Union's military success in 1865 and reminded his superiors that he had predicted it. From Charleston, Henry Pinckney Walker remarked on the economic impact of emancipation and the anxiety caused by the presence of large numbers of free blacks and black troops in Charleston. He implied that racial attitudes in the nation would have to undergo significant alteration before social calm was achieved. In Boston, Francis Lousada marvelled at America's ability to enhance its industrial and agricultural might while carrying on a conflict of such magnitude as its Civil War. What each consul saw depended on his vantage point: military advance, necessity for social and political change, and economic improvement. Still, no matter what they perceived, Archibald, Walker, and Lousada acknowledged that the country had developed into a major power and would never be the same.[24] And although they never said so, the return to regular consular duties undoubtedly made their workdays less challenging than they had been before war's end.

Notes

1. THE FOREIGN SERVICE ON THE EVE OF THE WAR

1. Middleton, *British Foreign Policy*, 214-53; Lord Lyons to his sister Minna, Feb. 21, 1861, Lyons Papers; Platt, *Cinderella Service*, 21.

2. Middleton, *British Foreign Policy*, 253; Platt, *Cinderella Service*, 43; Robert Bunch to Lyons, Aug. 17, 1861, and Lyons to Bunch, Jan. 2, 1861, both in Lyons Papers.

3. U.S. State Department, "Exequaturs" and "Index to Exequaturs"; U.S. Congress, *House Executive Documents*, 38 Cong., 2 sess. (1864-65), 209-10.

4. The conclusions in this paragraph are based on a listing of foreign consuls in the Confederacy in the *Official Records* and on correspondence during the Civil War between foreign consuls and the State Department. *OR, Navies*, ser. 2, 3:12; U.S. State Department, "Notes from Foreign Consuls in the United States to the Department of State, 1789-1906," and "Notes to Foreign Consuls in the United States from the Department of State, 1853-1906."

5. Middleton, *British Foreign Policy*, 244-53; Kennedy, *American Consul*, 127-41.

6. Russell, *My Diary North and South*, 44-45.

7. See the exequaturs for George Moore (consul for Virginia), Nov. 16, 1858, and for John E. Wilkins (consul at Chicago), Dec. 8, 1855, in U.S. State Department, "Exequaturs."

8. During a consul's annual leave, usually one month, the vice-consul in charge of a consulate normally received 50 percent of a consul's monthly salary. Middleton, *British Foreign Policy*, 245, 253; Platt, *Cinderella Service*, 21;

Lyons to Lord John Russell, June 12, 1862, and Frederick Bernel to Lyons, May 6 and 9, 1861, all in Lyons Papers.

9. Frederick Cridland to Confederate State Department, Sept. 16, 1862, Confederate State Department, "Records"; William Stuart [chargé d'affaires] to William H. Seward, June 26, 1862, U.S. State Department, BL-SD; *OR, Navies*, ser. 2, 3:12.

10. Platt, *Cinderella Service*, 19; Middleton, *British Foreign Policy*, 248-52; Stuart, *American Diplomatic and Consular Practice*, 292-94.

11. Bunch to Lyons, Apr. 19, 1861, Lyons Papers; Archibald, *Archibald*, 108-19; Russell, *My Diary North and South*, 44-45.

12. Lyons to Denis Donohoe, June 4, 1862, Lyons Papers. Consuls who protested too often about low salaries were drummed out of the service; at least this was the case with Charles Tulin, consul at Mobile. Given a small salary increase following complaints about his wages, Tulin protested again and was dismissed. Tulin to Lyons, Aug. 20 and Sept. 8, 1859, Feb. 11, Apr. 10, and Dec. 6, 1860, all in Lyons Papers.

13. The official exchange rate between the pound sterling and the dollar set in 1842 was $4.84 to £1; it remained in effect until 1873. It is unknown whether consuls received their salaries in pounds sterling or dollars; if in pounds, they faced the added disadvantage of losing money in the exchange transaction, because not all banks exchanged at the official rate. Hepburn, *History of Currency*, 62-63.

14. Platt, *Cinderella Service*, 43; Middleton, *British Foreign Policy*, 253.

15. Platt, *Cinderella Service*, 24; Edmund Molyneux to Lyons, May, n.d., 1862, and Edward Archibald to Lyons, Dec. 28, 1863, both in Lyons Papers.

16. Molyneux to Lyons, Dec. 2, 1861, Apr. 8, and May, n.d., 1862, and Lyons to Bunch, Apr. 12, 1861, all in Lyons Papers.

17. The Foreign Office considered reopening the Cincinnati consulate in 1861 to give British nationals faster access to consular protection, but the consul at New York City and the legation staff discouraged such a move. As a result, British citizens in the Midwest seeking consular services during the war had to travel either to the East Coast or to St. Louis. Lyons to Archibald, Oct. 5 and 29, 1861, Archibald to Lyons, Oct. 7 and Nov. 23, 1861, and Lyons to Russell, June 13, 1861, all in Lyons Papers.

2. THE CONSULS

1. Bunch to Lyons, May 22, 1860, Lyons Papers.

2. Archibald to Lyons, Apr. 10, 1860, Lyons Papers; Archibald to Spencer Ponsonby [clerk, Foreign Office], Nov. 2, 1857, and Ponsonby to Archibald, Nov. 20, 1857, both in Archibald, *Archibald*, 101-4; Platt, *Cinderella Service*, 36.

3. Bunch to Lyons, Apr. 11, 1860, Lyons Papers.

4. Lyons recommended upgrading the status of the New York consulate in 1861, but final action did not occur until two years later. Lyons to Archibald, Oct. 29, 1861, and Archibald to Lyons, Feb. 6, 1863, both in Lyons Papers.

5. Archibald, *Archibald*, 20; Bemis, *Diplomatic History*, 302-4.

6. Unless otherwise noted, information about consular appointments is

taken from the exequatur files or from Herslet, *Foreign Office List*. Entries are listed by date in the exequatur files, alphabetically in the *Foreign Office List*.

7. Bunch to Lyons, Mar. 21, 1861, Lyons Papers; Lyons to Russell, Dec. 4, 1861, in Bourne and Watt, *British Documents*, 5:165; Walther, *Fire-Eaters*, 145.

8. Seward to Lyons, Nov. 15, 1861, Lyons Papers.

9. Booker to Russell, May 10, 1861, FO5/785, and Nov. 18, 1863, FO5/911.

10. Bernel to Russell, Apr. 20 and 21, FO5/784; Bernel to Russell, Sept. 22, 1862, FO5/874.

11. Moore to Russell, June 11, 1861, FO5/786.

12. Bonham, *British Consuls in the Confederacy*, 186.

13. Lyons to Russell, Dec. 4, 1860, FO5/740.

14. Lyons to Russell, June 10 and Dec. 27, 1861, and Lyons to Archibald, Sept. 17, 1861, all in Lyons Papers; Lyons to Russell, Dec. 4, 1860, Bourne and Watt, *British Documents*, 5:164-65; Russell to Lyons, Dec. 21, 1860, and Palmerston to Lyons, Jan. 10, 1861, both in FO5/754; Lyons to Lynn, Mar. 21, 1861, FO5/761.

15. Lyons to Russell, Mar. 2, 1861, Lyons Papers.

16. White, "United States in the 1850s," 531-34; Crook, *North, South, and Powers*, 34-35.

17. "Benjamin" to "Dear Sir," Aug. 11, 1860, Archibald to "Sir," Aug. 14, 1860, and Archibald to Lyons, Aug. 14, 1860, all in Lyons Papers; Archibald, *Archibald*, 143-45; Allen, *Britain and United States*, 460.

18. Mure to Russell, Dec. 13, 1860, FO5/744.

19. Bunch to Russell, Dec. 5, 1860, FO5/745; Bunch to Lyons, Dec. 6, 1860, Lyons Papers; "Despatch from British Consul"; Blumenthal, "Confederate Diplomacy," 153; White, *Rhett*, 196; Crook, *North, South, and Powers*, 22-23. The reprint of Bunch's report to Russell in the *American Historical Review* is dated Dec. 15, 1860, a date cited by a number of historians. It may be a misprint, however. The manuscript copy in FO5/745 is dated Dec. 5. Further indication that the interview took place on Dec. 5 is Bunch's letter to Lyons on Dec. 5, 1860, informing the minister of the conversation.

20. Foreign Office to Lyons, July 27, 1861, FO5/758.

21. Lyons to Russell, Mar. 12, 1861, and Lyons to Bunch, Apr. 13, 1861, both in Lyons Papers; Bourne and Watt, *British Documents*, 5:185.

22. Bunch to Russell, Nov. 23, 1860, FO5/745.

23. Bunch to Lyons, Dec. 8, 1860, and Apr. 19, 1861, Lyons Papers; Bunch to Russell, Feb. 28, 1861, FO5/780; Bunch to Russell, Mar. 10, 1862, FO5/843.

24. Molyneux to Russell, Nov. 28, Dec. 13 and 22, 1860, all in FO5/744; Mure to Russell, Dec. 13, 1860, FO5/745; Mure to Lyons, Feb. 15, 1861, Lyons Papers; Bernel to Russell, Mar. 4, 1861, F05/784; Ellsworth, "British Consuls," 149.

25. Kortwright to Russell, May 13, 1861, FO5/787; Lyons to Russell, May 13, 1864, FO5/949; Lonn, *Foreigners in the Confederacy*, 412-13.

26. Bunch to Russell, Jan. 4, 1861, FO5/780.

27. Archibald to Russell, Apr. 6 and 9, 1861, Archibald to Lyons, Apr. 5 and 6, 1861, all in FO5/762; Archibald to Lyons, Apr. 8, 1861, Lyons Papers.

28. Archibald to Russell, Apr. 24, 1861, FO5/762; Archibald, *Archibald*, 119-28.

29. Bunch to Lyons, Dec. 8, 1860, Lyons Papers; Bunch to Russell, Mar. 21, 1861, FO5/780; Russell, *My Diary North and South*, 82; Crook, *North, South, and Powers*, 201-2; Owsley and Owsley, *King Cotton Diplomacy*, 21.

30. Mure to Russell, June 18, 1861, FO5/788; Magee to Lyons, May 26, 1861, Magee to Russell, July 19, 1861, and Fullarton to Russell, Aug. 18, 1861, all in FO5/786; Bunch to Russell, Sept. 4, 1861, FO5/781; Lyons to Russell, May 4, 1861, Lyons Papers.

31. Bunch to Russell, June 12 and Sept. 28, 1861, both in FO5/780; Jenkins, *Britain and the War*, 1:149-50; Ellsworth, "Russell and British Consuls," 35-36.

32. Bunch to Russell, Oct. 28, 1861, FO5/781; Mure to Russell, May 31, 1861, FO5/784; Lynn to Russell, Aug. 25, 1861, FO5/788; Molyneux to Russell, Dec. 4, 1861, and Magee to Russell, Aug. 21, 1861, both in FO5/786; Russell, *My Diary North and South*, 127-28; Owsley and Owsley, *King Cotton Diplomacy*, 47-48.

33. Bunch to Russell, June 21, 1862, FO5/780; Bunch to Russell, Oct. 21, 1862, FO5/844; Cridland to Russell, Oct. 29, 1862, FO5/845. See also Archibald to Russell, Sept. 24, 1861, FO5/842.

34. See Archibald to Russell, May 1, 1862, FO5/849; Bunch to Russell, Sept. 5 and Nov. 9, 1861, FO5/781; Molyneux to Russell, Nov. 20, 1861, FO5/786; and Henry Pinckney Walker to Russell, Jan. through June 1864, passim, FO5/906, 968, and 969; Russell, *My Diary North and South*, 338-39.

3. THE FOREIGN MINISTER

1. Laughton, "Edmund Lyons," and Hamilton, "Richard Bickerton Pemell Lyons," 355-59.

2. Ibid; Gallas, "Lyons and Civil War," 6.

3. Seward to Lyons, May 27, 1861, and Russell to Lyons, June 3, 1861, both in FO5/755; Beale, *Diary of Bates*, 148, 205; Jenkins, *Britain and the War*, 1:29-30, 44; Allen, *Britain and United States*, 454.

4. Quoted in Jenkins, *Britain and the War*, 1:44.

5. Lyons to Minna, June 4, 1861, Lyons Papers.

6. Lyons to Minna, Jan. 22, 1864, Lyons Papers; Russell, *My Diary North and South*, 55.

7. Lyons to Minna, Jan. 26, July 4 and 20, and Aug. 23, 1861, all in Lyons Papers.

8. Herslet, *Foreign Office List*, Stuart entry; Jenkins, *Britain and the War*, 2:109-10, 362-65; Brauer, "Slavery Problem," 463; Allen, *Britain and United States*, 482.

9. Willson, *Friendly Relations*, 212-13.

10. Newton, *Lord Lyons*, 1:137.

11. Archibald to Lyons, Feb. 21, 1865, and Jan. 2, 1866, both in Lyons Papers. Lyons returned to England in Dec. 1864.

12. Bunch to Lyons, Feb. 14 and Mar. 21, 1861, both in Lyons Papers.

13. Lyons to Russell, Mar. 18, 1861, FO5/761; Lyons to Russell, June 4, 1861, quoted in Newton, *Lord Lyons*, 1:42.

14. Archibald to Russell, May 18, 1861, FO5/778; Archibald to Russell, Nov. 5, 1862, FO5/782; Archibald to Lyons, Dec. 17, 1860, and Lyons to Archibald, Feb. 15, 1862, both in Lyons Papers; C.F. Adams, "British Proclamation," 226; Archibald, *Archibald*, 125-27.

15. Head to Edwin Morgan, Apr. 25, 1861, Seward to Lyons, May 3, 1861, Lyons to Russell, Apr. 27, 1861, and Lyons to Lousada, Apr. 27, 1861, all in FO5/763; Lyons to Archibald, June 7, 1861, Lyons Papers; Lyons to Seward, May 3, 1861, BL-SD.

16. Lyons to Russell, Dec. 10, 1860, Lyons Papers; Lyons to Russell, May 20, 1861, FO5/764; Lyons to Russell, May 21, 1861, Bourne and Watt, *British Documents*, 5:225; C.F. Adams, "British Proclamation," 201-02; Newton, *Lord Lyons*, 1:38-39.

17. Lyons to Russell, Apr. 23, 1861, Lyons Papers; Lyons to Russell, Dec. 4, 1860, FO5/740; Lyons to Russell, Jan. 27, 1863, FO5/875; Lyons to Russell, May 30 and June 8, 1861, both in Bourne and Watt, *British Documents*, 5:225, 245; O'Rourke, "Diplomacy of Seward," 52; Brauer, "Slavery Problem," 458-59; Ferris, *Desperate Diplomacy*, 39; McPherson, *Ordeal by Fire*, 301-2.

18. Russell, *My Diary North and South*, 255; Lyons to Minna, Apr. 27, 1861, Lyons Papers; Lyons to Russell, Dec. 18, 1860, FO5/740.

19. Lyons to Russell, Apr. 15, 1861, FO5/762; Lyons to Russell, Feb. 4 and May 16, 1861, and Lyons to Bunch, Dec. 12, 1860, all quoted in C.F. Adams, "British Proclamation," 203, 230-31; Lyons to Russell, May 12, 1861, Lyons Papers; Gallas, "Lyons and Civil War," 42.

20. Lyons to Russell, Apr. 8, 1862, Lyons Papers; Bemis, *Diplomatic History*, 332-35.

21. Lyons to Russell, Mar. 30 and May 6, 1861, both in FO5/763; O'Rourke, "Diplomacy of Seward," 51; Walpole, *Life of Russell*, 2:344; Jenkins, *Britain and the War*, 1:112; Carroll, *Mercier*, 50-51.

22. Baker, *Works of Seward*, 5:56; Bancroft, *Life of Seward*, 299; Jenkins, *Britain and the War*, 2:109, 193-94; O'Rourke, "Diplomacy of Seward," 49.

23. Ferris, *Desperate Diplomacy*, 8. Comments disapproving of American government and society are contained in almost any travel account written by an Englishman in the nineteenth century. Good examples are found in Russell, *My Diary North and South*, and Trollope, *Domestic Manners of Americans*.

24. Lyons to Russell, Mar. 3 and 12, 1861, both in FO5/761; Lyons to Russell, Apr. 1, 1861, FO5/762; Lyons to Russell, May 20, 1861, Bourne and Watt, *British Documents*, 5:223; Lyons to Russell, Feb. 16, 1861, and Lyons to Minna, Mar. 4, 1861, both in Lyons Papers; Gallas, "Lyons and Civil War," 41.

25. Lyons to Russell, Mar. 3 and 12, 1861, both in FO5/761; Lyons to Russell, Apr. 1, 1861, FO5/762; Lyons to Russell, May 20, 1861, Bourne and Watt, *British Documents*, 5:223; Lyons to Russell, Feb. 16, 1861, Lyons Papers; Gallas, "Lyons and Civil War," 41.

26. Lyons to Minna, Mar. 4, 1861, Lyons Papers; Van Deusen, *Seward*, 302

27. Lyons to Mrs. Seward, Feb. 3, 1860, and Lyons to Seward, June 20, 1860, both in Seward Papers; Lyons to Russell, Feb. 4, 1861, FO5/760; Lyons to

Russell, Apr. 15, 1861, Lyons Papers; Newton, *Lord Lyons*, 1:36-37; Hendrick, *Lincoln's War Cabinet*, 150-51; Allen, *Britain and United States*, 461-62; Bancroft, *Life of Seward*, 150. An excellent discussion of Seward's foreign policy in the early months of 1861 is found in Van Deusen, *Seward*, 288-306.

28. Lyons to Russell, Jan. 7 and June 3, 1861, both in FO5/755; Lyons to Head, May 22, 1861, Lyons Papers; Winks, *Canada and United States*, 23-24. Archibald was informed of the plot by George Manning; the complete Archibald-Manning correspondence is found in Bourne and Watt, *British Documents*, 5:236-38.

29. Seward believed that unionism was strong enough in the South to cause a reunification of the country if the United States was threatened by a foreign power. Although Seward's "Thoughts" remained a private matter between the secretary and the president and did not become public knowledge until 1890, Seward was making similar comments to friends and confidants in the capital. Russell the journalist reported Seward's boast about foreign war at an entertainment given by the Brazilian ambassador. For further explanation see Van Deusen, *Seward*, 282-84, and Taylor, *Seward*, 150-53; Russell, *My Diary North and South*, 331.

30. Lyons to Russell, May 20, 1861, Lyons Papers; Palmerston to Lyons, Feb. 20, 1861, FO5/754; Russell to Lyons, Apr. 6 and 20, 1861, Lyons to Russell, Nov. 12, 1860, all in Russell Papers; Gallas, "Lyons and Civil War," 54.

31. Lyons to Russell, May 2, 1861, FO5/763; Jenkins, *Britain and the War*, 1:191; Van Deusen, *Seward*, 195-97; Lyons to Mrs. Seward, Feb. 3, 1860, and Lyons to Seward, June 20, 1860, both in Seward Papers.

32. Russell to Lyons, Mar. 14, 1863, Russell Papers.

33. Lyons to Russell, June 17, 1861, FO5/766; Lyons to Russell, July 20 and Aug. 1, 1861, both in Lyons Papers.

34. Affidavit signed by Edmund Allen to John Henry Murray [consul at Portland, Maine], Jan. 13, 1862, FO5/846; Winks, *Canada and United States*, 109-10, 147; Gallas, "Lyons and Civil War," 107; Milne, "Lyons-Seward Treaty," 512-13; Beale, *Diary of Bates*, 314-15.

35. Lyons to Russell, July 3, 1863, FO5/890; Welles, *Diary of Welles*, 1:328, 409; Newton, *Lord Lyons*, 1:80-82.

36. Quoted in Hendrick, *Lincoln's War Cabinet*, 248-49; Jenkins, *Britain and the War*, 1:134.

37. Lyons to Russell, May 27, 1861, FO5/764; Lyons to Russell, May 2, 1861, quoted in C.F. Adams, "British Proclamation," 227; Seward to Adams, Feb. 5, 1862, U.S. Congress, *Senate Executive Documents*, 37 Cong. 3 sess., (1862-63), 21-22; Van Deusen, *Seward*, 298. Van Deusen has an enlightening discussion of the reason that lay behind Seward's show of bellicosity; see especially 303-5.

38. Van Deusen, *Seward*, 297-98; Lyons to Russell, May 23, 1861, FO5/764.

4. THE UNWELCOME CONSUL

1. More detailed discussions of privateering and Confederate raiders can be found in Bemis, *Diplomatic History*, 368-69, 377-81; Randall and Donald,

Civil War and Reconstruction, 364-65, 446-48; McPherson, *Ordeal by Fire*, 173-75, 342-43.

2. Congress did authorize Lincoln to issue letters of marque and reprisal in 1863, but none were applied for.

3. Russell to Lyons, May 4, 1861, Russell Papers.

4. Temple, "Seward," 7:38; Trescot, "Confederacy and the Declaration of Paris," 23:833-34; Duberman, *Adams*, 269; Bonham, *British Consuls*, 24-25; *Charleston Mercury*, Aug. 9, 1861.

5. McPherson, *Ordeal by Fire*, 175.

6. Russell to Lyons, Dec. 14, 1861, FO5/758; Henry Adams to Charles Francis Adams, Jr., Sept. 7, 1861, Ford, *Adams Letters*, 1:41; U.S. Congress, *House Executive Documents*, 37 Cong., 3 sess. (1862), 50-52; Jenkins, *Britain and the War*, 1:40-41, 127-28; Duberman, *Adams*, 271; C.F. Adams, "Negotiation of 1861," 23-84.

7. The Seamen Law required state authorities to seize and jail black sailors while their ships were in South Carolina ports. Repealed in 1856, it was reintroduced in the legislature in 1859. Bunch visited and wrote letters to Harleton Read, chairman of the committee on the "coloured population," arguing that black British seamen, knowing they were unwelcome, would remain on their ships, so the bill was unnecessary; besides, Bunch wrote, it would cause enmity between Britain and South Carolina at a time when the state was seeking friends abroad. Apparently impressed, Read played a leading role in defeating the bill. Bunch to Read, Nov. 18, 1859, Bunch to Lyons, Nov. 28, Dec. 23, 1859, and Dec. 20, 1860, and Lyons to Bunch, Feb. 10, 1862, all in Lyons Papers; Bunch to Russell, Jan. 21, 1861, FO5/780; Foreign Office to Bunch, Feb. 3, 1860, FO5/745; Bonham, *British Consuls*, 20, 25-26; Jenkins, *Britain and the War*, 1:115-16; C.F. Adams, "British Proclamation," 199; Freehling, *Prelude to Civil War*, 111-18; Sutherland, "Southern Fraternal Organizations," 592.

8. Lyons to Russell, July 1, 1861, Lyons Papers; Lyons to Bunch, July 5, 1861, and Lyons to Russell, July 12, 1861, both in Bourne and Watt, *British Documents*, 5:260, 263.

9. Lyons to Bunch, July 5, 1861, Bourne and Watt, *British Documents*, 5:263; Lyons to Bunch, July 6, 1861, Lyons Papers; Russell to Lyons, May 25, 1861, Russell Papers. The Davis administration was aware that consent to the declaration did not imply diplomatic recognition or a first step toward it. Still, Confederate leaders believed their action obligated England and France to receive Confederate commissioners if they wished to raise issues connected with the blockade. Russell's later refusal to receive James Mason caused extreme bitterness against Britain in the South. J. Davis, *Rise and Fall of Confederate Government*, 2:343-50, 371-82.

10. Bunch to Lyons, May 25, 1860, and Aug. 16, 1861, both in Lyons Papers; Bunch to Lyons, Aug. 16, 1861, Bourne and Watt, *British Documents*, 5:303-4. Bunch's statements about Trescot are found in the 1860 letter.

11. Trescot, "Declaration of Paris," 827-29; Lyons to Russell, Sept. 2, 1861, FO5/770.

12. Lyons to Russell, Aug. 27, 1861, FO5/770; Trescot, "Declaration of Paris," 829-30; Jenkins, *Britain and the War*, 1:139.

13. U.S. Congress, *Senate Executive Documents*, 37 Cong. 2 sess. (1861-62),

130-32; *OR, Armies*, ser. 2, 2:643-65; C.F. Adams to Russell, Sept. 3, 1861, and Lyons to Russell, Aug. 16, 1861, both in Bourne and Watt, *British Documents*, 5:296, 298-99; Bonham, *British Consuls*, 30-31.

14. Seward to Adams, Aug. 17, 1861, *OR, Armies*, ser. 2, 2:651; Lyons to Bunch, Aug. 17, 1861, Lyons Papers; Henry Adams to Charles Francis Adams, Jr., Sept. 7, 1861, Ford, *Adams Letters*, 1:41-42. A copy of Bunch's passport and instructions to Mure, both dated Aug. 7, 1861, are found in Bourne and Watt, *British Documents*, 5:299-300.

15. The version reported in the *Tribune* differs from the copy actually confiscated. The newspaper inserted the words that appear in parentheses; the other copy contained only blank lines. Seward to Adams, Aug. 17, 1861, in U.S. Congress, *Senate Executive Documents*, 37 Cong., 2 sess. (1861-62), 133; *New York Tribune*, Aug. 21, 1861.

16. Lyons to William Mure, Aug. 17, 1861, Mure to Lyons, Aug. 22, 1861, Lyons to Archibald, Oct. 10, 15, and 18, 1861, Archibald to Lyons, Oct. 18, 1861 and Nov. 1, 1861, and Edmund Hammond to Lyons, Sept. 21, 1861, all in Lyons Papers; Robert Mure to Archibald, Sept. 12, 1861, *O.R., Armies*, ser. 2, 2:69.

17. Bunch to Lyons, Aug. 31 and Sept. 30, 1861, both in Lyons Papers; Bunch to Lyons, Sept. 30, 1861, Bourne and Watt, *British Documents*, 5:317; Bunch to Foreign Office, Aug. 5, 1861, U.S. Congress, *Senate Executive Documents*, 37 Cong., 2 sess. (1861-62), 155-57; Russell to Lyons, Sept. 13, 1861, in Newton, *Lord Lyons*, 1:52.

18. Bunch to Lyons, Sept. 30 and Oct. 6, 1861, Hammond to Lyons, Nov. 3, 1860, and Jan. 20, 1861, all in Lyons Papers; Bunch to Lyons, Oct. 31, 1861, Bourne and Watt, *British Documents*, 5:356; Russell to Lyons, Oct. 28, 1861, in FO5/757. The sending of private letters in consular dispatch bags continued to be a problem. In Nov. 1861 Federal authorities confiscated two diplomatic pouches containing private letters. Among the letters in the first, only two were addressed to officials in London; there was no official correspondence in the second bag. The incidents caused Lyons to remark, "The consuls in the South do not behave well about forwarding private letters" and to threaten severe measures if they continued to disobey instructions. Lyons to Russell, Nov. 25, 1861, in Newton, *Lord Lyons*, 1:58. Also see correspondence between Lyons and Russell in FO5/773; U.S. Congress, *Senate Executive Documents*, 37 Cong., 2 sess. (1861-62), 174; Archibald to Lyons, July 17, 1861, and Lyons to Seward, Oct. 23, 1861, both in BL-SD; Seward to Lyons, Oct. 24, 1861, and April 5, 1862, both in SD-BL.

19. The correspondence between Seward, Adams, Russell, and Lyons on the Bunch affair is voluminous. A good selection is found in House of Commons, *Correspondence . . . Bunch's Exequatur*. Copies of some letters in that publication also appear in U.S. Congress, *Senate Executive Documents*, 37 Cong., 2 sess. (1861-62), in the Lyons Papers, and in FO5/756-58, 769-77, and 870. See also Seward to Adams, Aug. 17, Sept. 3, and Oct. 23, 1861, all in U.S. Congress, *Senate Executive Documents.*, 37 Cong., 2 sess. (1861-62), 130-31, 150, and 164-66; Russell to Adams, Nov. 25, 1861, Law officers of the Crown to Russell, Sept. 17, 1861, both in Bourne and Watt, *British Documents*, 5:305-6 and 344-45. The most detailed secondary account is Bonham, *British Consuls*,

20-47. On the issue of extraterritoriality see Adams to Russell, Nov. 21, 1861, U.S. Congress, *House Executive Documents*, 37 Cong., 3 sess. (1862), 3-5.

　　20. Lyons to Russell, Oct. 28, 1861, *Correspondence . . . Bunch's Exequatur*, 15; Adams to Russell, Nov. 21, 1861, U.S. Congress, *Senate Executive Documents*, 37 Cong., 3 sess. (1862) 3-5.

　　21. Van Deusen, *Seward*, 337-41; Crook, *North, South, and Powers*, 57.

　　22. As early as May 1861, Seward lodged a formal complaint about Bunch's illegal use of his diplomatic pouch and the issuing of passports to American citizens of British birth. Lyons to Bunch, Oct. 31, 1861; Lyons to Russell, Dec. 31, 1861, both in Lyons Papers.

　　23. Lyons to Russell, Dec. 6, 1861, FO5/776; U.S. State Department, "Exequaturs" and "Index to Exequaturs"; Ferris, *Desperate Diplomacy*, 110-11; Bonham, *British Consuls*, 45-46.

　　24. Lyons to Stuart, July 19, 1862, Lyons Papers.

　　25. Lyons to Russell, Dec. 31, 1861, Bourne and Watt, *British Documents*, 6:28.

　　26. *New York Herald*, June 16, 1862.

　　27. The warship did not actually dock in Charleston harbor. After receiving permission to pass through the blockade, the vessel sailed as far as Fort Sumter and sent word that it had messages for the consul. Either the consul took a small craft to the ship or a detail was sent into the city. The ship then retired beyond the blockade, where it remained until it returned for the consul's responses. Seward to Lyons, Feb. 6, 1862, SD-BL; U.S. Congress, *House Executive Documents*, 37 Cong. 3 sess. (1862), 253; Courtemanche, *No Need of Glory*, 112; *Charleston Mercury*, Feb. 5, 1863.

　　28. Lyons to Russell, Oct. 15, 1861, Lyons Papers.

　　29. U.S. Congress, *House Executive Documents*, 38 Cong., 2 sess. (1864-65), 325-26, 353-54.

　　30. Lyons to Russell, Oct. 28, 1861, *Correspondence . . . Bunch's Exequatur*, 15-16.

　　31. Earl Cowley to Russell, Sept. 10, 1861, Bourne and Watt, *British Documents*, 5:302; Jenkins, *Britain and the War*, 1:136; Crook, *North, South, and Powers*, 88-89.

　　32. Lyons to Russell, Aug. 19 and Oct. 14, 1861, both in Lyons Papers; Lyons to Russell, Oct. 26, 1861, FO5/773; Jenkins, *Britain and the War*, 1:186; Ferris, *Desperate Diplomacy*, 110; Van Deusen, *Seward*, 299-300.

　　33. Lyons to Russell, June 25, 1861, FO5/766; John A. Kennedy to Seward, June 20, 1861, and N.A. Garrett to Simon Draper, Aug. 23, 1861, both in *O.R.*, *Armies*, ser. 2, 2:46, 644.

　　34. Bunch to Russell, Apr. 19, 1861, quoted in C.F. Adams, "British Proclamation," 205-12; Bunch to Russell, Feb. 28, 1861, FO5/780; Bunch to Russell, July 9, 1861, FO5/781; Bunch to Russell, May 5, 1862, FO5/843; Ellsworth, "Russell and the British Consuls," 38.

　　35. Bunch to Russell, Feb. 28, 1861, FO5/780; Bunch to Russell, Mar. 10, 1862, FO5/843; C.F. Adams, "British Proclamation," 205-8.

　　36. Bunch to Lyons, Mar. 21, 1861, Lyons Papers; Bunch to Russell, Dec. 13, 1862, FO5/844; C.F. Adams, "British Proclamation," 208-10.

37. Lyons to Russell, Oct. 28, 1861, Bourne and Watt, *British Documents*, 5:332-33.

38. Bunch to Lyons, Aug. 17, 1861, Lyons to Bunch, Sept. 20, 1861, and Feb. 20, 1862, all in Lyons Papers; Middleton, *British Foreign Policy*, 247; Bancroft, *Life of Seward*, 199.

39. Bunch to Lyons, Dec. 8, 1861, Lyons to Bunch, Nov. 27 1861, and Jan. 2, 1862, all in Lyons Papers.

5. ARBITRARY ARRESTS AND PROPERTY RIGHTS

1. Sprague, *Freedom Under Lincoln*, 158-59.
2. Neely, *Fate of Liberty*, 3-31.
3. Sangston, *Bastiles of the North*, 54.
4. Seward to Lyons, Jan. 7, 1862, Gideon Welles to Seward, Jan. 4, 1862, and Commander Maxwell Woodhull to Welles, Dec. 17, 1861, all in U.S. Congress, *House Executive Documents*, 37 Cong., 3 sess. (1862), 242-43.
5. Neely, *Fate of Liberty*, 26.
6. Archibald to Lyons, Jan. 23, 1861, and Archibald to Frederick Monson, Sept. 20, 1861, both in Lyons Papers; Seward to Lyons, Nov. 19 and 21, 1861, both in SD-BL; Archibald, *Archibald*, 107.
7. Archibald to Lyons, Sept. 20, 1861, Lyons Papers; Archibald to Russell, Sept. 2 and 13, 1862, both in FO5/842; Archibald to Russell, June 29, 1861, FO5/778; Archibald to Russell, Oct. 7, 1861, FO5/779.
8. Lyons to Russell, Sept. 13 and 30, 1861, both in Lyons Papers.
9. The volume entitled *Treatment of Suspected and Disloyal Persons, North and South* in *O.R., Armies*, ser. 2, vol. 2, contains case summaries for all persons arrested in 1861 and early 1862.
10. Ibid., 305, 415-25, 547, 627-35. See also Lyons to Seward, June 29 and Sept. 22, 1861, both in BL-SD; Seward to Lyons, June 21, 1861, SD-BL; Lyons to Bunch, June 21, 1861, Lyons Papers; Neely, *Fate of Liberty*, 25-26.
11. *O.R., Armies*, ser. 2, 2:982-1008.
12. Ibid., 711-12.
13. Ibid., 171, 311.
14. Ibid., 627-35.
15. Kortwright to Russell, Sept. 2, 1861, FO5/787; Archibald to Lyons, Sept. 11, 1861, Lyons Papers.
16. Russell to Lyons, Sept. 28, 1861, Bourne and Watt, *British Documents*, 5:310.
17. Although Lincoln defended his policy early in the war, his best statement on the issue was made to Erastus Corning in 1863. See Basler, *Works of Lincoln*, 6:260-69.
18. Lyons to Russell, Oct. 14, 1861, FO5/771 [also in BL-SD]; Seward to Lyons, Oct. 14, 1861, U.S. Congress, *Senate Executive Documents*, 37 Cong., 2 sess. (1861-62), 170-71; Seward to Lyons, Oct. 24, 1861, SD-BL; *New York Times*, Oct. 21, 1861.
19. Seward to Lyons, Jan. 13, 1862, Bourne and Watt, *British Documents*, 6:39-40.

20. U.S. Congress, *Senate Executive Documents*, 37 Cong., 3 sess. (1862), 27-32.
21. Neely, *Fate of Liberty*, 62.
22. Lyons to Seward, Feb. 21 and Apr. 4, 1863, Statement of J. M. Vernon, Feb. 12, 1863, and Seward to Lyons, June 22, 1863, all in U.S. Congress, *House Executive Documents*, 38 Cong., 1 sess. (1863-64), 513-14, 545, and 638; Archibald to Lyons, Sept. 4, 1862, FO5/841; Archibald to Lyons, Feb. 6, 1864, BL-SD; Lyons to Russell, Feb. 21, 1862, Lyons Papers.
23. Lyons to Seward, June 3, 1862, Lyons Papers; Butler to Coppell, May 11, 1862, *O.R., Armies*, ser. 3, 2:126-27.
24. Butler to Coppell, June 7, 1862, *OR, Armies*, ser. 3, 2:209-10. Letters on the Butler-Coppell controversy can be found in several sources; however, the most complete information is contained in *O.R., Armies*, ser. 3, 2:115-17, 124-30, 154-60, 178, and 497-505.
25. Lyons to Russell, May 16, 1862, quoted in Newton, *Lord Lyons*, 1:87.
26. Lyons to Wilkins, Nov. 15, 1864, Lyons Papers; Hinton to Fullarton, Oct. 11, 1862, "Savannah Consulate Papers," Duke; William Argill to Archibald, Oct. 12, 1861, and Archibald to Russell, Oct. 18, 1861, both in FO5/779.
27. Lyons to Wilkins, Jan. 9 and Dec. 27, 1862, both in Lyons Papers.
28. Lyons to Russell, Sept. 9, 1861, and Lynn's article, both in FO5/770; Lyons to Russell, Nov. 29, 1861, quoted in Newton, *Lord Lyons*, 1:59.
29. Stuart to Coppell, Oct. 30, 1862, FO5/838.
30. Bernal to Lyons, Oct. 22, 1861, and Lyons to Seward, Mar. 19 and Apr. 15, 1862, all in *O.R., Armies*, ser. 2, 2:900-903. See also the case of John Turner in Turner to Bernal, Feb. 12, 1863, and Bernal to Lyons, Feb. 13, 1863, both in BL-SD.
31. Molyneux to Lyons, Dec. 2, 1861, Lyons Papers; Statement of Allan Fullarton, Sept. 9, 1865, BL-SD.
32. ——— to Fullarton, Jan. 25, 1865, Statement of Allen Fullarton, Sept. 9, 1865, statement of William Tasker-Smith, Sept. 8, 1865, and Frederick Bruce to Seward, Nov. 2, 1865, all in BL-SD. All correspondence and papers regarding the Molyneux claim, including letters from Union army officers to the War Department, are found in FO5/1233.
33. John Sullivan to Archibald, July 30, 1861, "Savannah Consulate Papers," Duke.
34. McRae to Bunch, Apr. 3, 1861, Bunch to McRae, Apr. 4, 1861, Bunch to Lyons, Apr. 4, 1861, and Lyons to Russell, Apr. 13, 1861, all in FO5/762.
35. Molyneux to Lyons, Feb. 2, 4, 9, and 11, 1861, all in FO5/786; Molyneux to Lyons, Feb. 20, 1861, FO5/761; Lyons to Russell, Feb. 11, 1861, FO5/760; Brown to Molyneux, Dec. 10, 1861, "Savannah Consulate Records," Emory.
36. Russell, *My Diary North and South*, 173-74; Mure to Russell, Jan. 31, Mar. 25, and Aug. 14, 1861, all in FO5/788; Mure to Lyons, Jan. 16, 1860, Lyons Papers.
37. Mure to Randall Hunt, July 9, 1861, Mure to Russell, July 17, 1861, Hunt to Mure, July 17, 1861, Lyons to Russell, Aug. 3, 1861, and Lyons to Mure, Aug. 3, 1861, all in FO5/768; Russell to Lyons, Aug. 20, 1861, FO5/758;

Lyons to Russell, Oct. 12, 1861, FO5/771; Mure to Lyons, July 16, 1861, Lyons Papers; Lyons to Seward, Jan. 2, 1862, BL-SD.

6. SEARCHING FOR STIRRUP AND EDWARDS

1. In November 1862, United States naval officials estimated Stirrup's age at nineteen; thus, he would have been either seventeen or eighteen in early 1861. Edwards, testifying under oath in 1867, gave his age as sixteen at the time of his abduction. Samuel Dupont to Gideon Welles, Nov. 14, 1862, FO5/839; testimony of Samuel Edwards, *U.S. v. Clark.*

2. Lyons to Molyneux, July 25, and Nov. 21, 1860, and Lyons to Russell, Nov. 24, 1860, all in FO5/740; Lyons to Russell, Dec. 3, 1860, and Molyneux to Lyons, May 5, 9, and July 20, 1860, all in Lyons Papers; Lyons to Russell, Dec. 24, 1860, in FO5/740.

3. For a discussion of kidnapping in the slave states see, Ira Berlin, *Slaves Without Masters,* 99-100, 160-64.

4. Finkelman, "Kidnapping of John Davis"; Cattrell, *Judicial Cases,* 5:422, 504, 540.

5. Cattrell, *Judicial Cases,* 1:161; Edwardsville *Spectator,* June 8, 1823.

6. Edwards's testimony, *U.S. v. Clark.* Edwards's statement, somewhat embellished by the reporter, was also published in the *Savannah News and Herald,* May 7, 1867

7. The official report noted Sampson's death during the incident. The kidnapping was reported to Bahamian officials by the captain of the *Lazer,* which indicates that he may not have been involved in the scheme; but, because the scuffle on the *Hebe* and the firing of bullets could hardly have gone unnoticed, the captain may have reported the incident to avoid being suspected of involvement. W.J.C. Bayley to Lyons, Apr. 13, 1861, BL-SD; Edwards's testimony, *U.S. v. Clark; Savannah News and Herald,* May 7, 1867.

8. Clark's name appears as both "Clark" and "Clarke" in court records, correspondence, and newspaper reports. The signature on his bail bond, posted at the time of his arrest, does not contain a final "e." See Clark's bail bond, *U.S. v. Clark.*

9. Edwards's testimony, *U.S. v. Clark.*

10. Ibid.

11. Bayley to Lyons, Apr. 13, 1861, BL-SD.

12. Lyons to Seward, Apr. 29, 1861, and Seward to Lyons, Apr. 30, 1861, both in BL-SD; Lyons to Fullarton, Apr. 29, 1861, "Savannah Consulate Records," Emory.

13. Stirrup to "Dear Uncle," n.d., and Stuart to Seward, Sept. 24, 1862, both in BL-SD.

14. Russell to Lyons, Sept. 12, 1862, FO5/821; Lyons to Russell, Dec. 5, 1862, Seward to Lyons, Nov. 25, 1862, Welles to Seward, Nov. 25, 1862, Dupont to Welles, Nov. 14, 1862, Dupont to "Dear Sir," Nov. 18, 1862, Dupont to A.S. Clarey, June 9, 1862, and memorandum of Judge Burritt, Dec. 5, 1862, all in FO5/839; Stuart to Seward, Sept. 24, 1862, BL-SD; Seward to Stuart, Oct. 8, 1862, SD-BL; Coulter, *Confederate States of America,* 354; Porter, *Naval History,* 61, 77; W.W. Davis, *Civil War and Reconstruction,* 158.

15. Seward to Lyons, Dec. 29, 1862, and Lyons to Seward. Jan. 6, 1863, both in BL-SD; Lyons to Russell, Jan. 7, 1863, Seward to Lyons, Dec. 29, 1862, A.P. Wolcott to Seward, Dec. 27, 1862, Lyons to Seward, Jan. 6, 1863, and Lyons to Russell, Jan. 7, 1863, all in FO5/874; Saxon to Edwin Stanton, Feb. 4, 1863, and Lyons to Russell, Feb. 16, 1863, both in FO5/877.

16. Archibald to Lyons, Apr. 15, 1863, and Lyons to Russell, Apr. 21, 1863, both in FO5/882. A copy of the Archibald-Lyons letter is also found in "Savannah Consulate Papers," Duke.

17. Lyons to Fullarton, Apr. 30, 1863, P. Thweatt to Fullarton, June 12 and 25, 1863, G.W. Crawford to Fullarton, June 16, 1863, and C.H. McCann to Fullarton, July 7, 1863, all in "Savannah Consulate Papers," Duke; Fullarton to Lyons, May 14, 1863, and Lyons to Russell, May 29, 1863, both in FO5/885.

18. See chapter 9 on the expulsion of the consuls. Owsley and Owsley, *King Cotton Diplomacy*, 489-90; Bonham, *British Consuls*, 210-58.

19. Long to Edwards, Aug. 20, 1865, "Savannah Consulate Records," Emory.

20. Long to Tasker-Smith, May 19, 1866, ibid.

21. Tasker-Smith to Russell, June, n.d., 1865, FO5/1031.

22. *Savannah News and Herald*, May 15, 1867.

23. Ibid., May 7, 1867; *U.S. Statutes at Large*, 3:450, 600; W.E.B. Du Bois, *Suppression of Slave-Trade*, 118-21.

24. Edwards's testimony, *U.S. v. Clark*; *Savannah News and Herald*, May 7, 1867; Tasker-Smith to "Sir," May 9, 1867 (draft), "Savannah Consulate Papers," Duke.

25. *Savannah News and Herald*, May 11, 15, 1867; Tasker-Smith to "Dear Sir," May 16, 1867 (draft), "Savannah Consulate Papers," Duke. A copy of the bail bond is found in *U.S. v. Clark*.

26. U.S. *Statutes at Large*, 9:22.

27. "Opinion of the District Court and Reasons for Remanding the above Case to the Circuit Court," filed Dec. 7, 1867, *U.S. v. Clark*.

28. The circuit court did take up the case in April 1868 but only subpoenaed witnesses on behalf of Clark. There is nothing in the court record or in the newspapers to indicate that the witnesses appeared or that the court dealt with the case between Apr. 1868 and Nov. 1870. "Circuit Court Subpoenas," Apr. term, 1868, *U.S. v. Clark*.

29. *U.S. v. Clark*; *Savannah Morning News*, Nov. 19, 1870.

30. Ibid.

31. Normally Erskine would have heard the case along with Chief Justice Salmon P. Chase, whose circuit district included Georgia; however, by an act of Congress in 1846, the presence of a Supreme Court justice was not required, and inasmuch as Chase suffered a number of minor strokes during the fall of 1870, the court probably proceeded without him. *U.S. Statutes at Large*, 9:22; Blue, *Chase*, 313-14.

32. Roberts, *Brown*, 45, 70; Fortson, "John Erskine," 180.

33. Edwards's testimony, *U.S. v. Clark*; Bayley to Lyons, Apr. 13, 1861, BL-SD; Memorandum of Judge Burritt, Dec. 5, 1862, FO5/839; Wallace, *Carpet-Bag Rule*, 16.

34. Edwards's testimony, *U.S. v. Clark*; *U.S. Statutes at Large*, 3:600.
35. Tasker-Smith to "Sir," May 18, 1867 (draft), "Savannah Consulate Papers," Duke.
36. Newton, *Lord Lyons*, 1:138-42; Brian Jenkins, *Britain and the War*, 2:381.
37. "Statement of Expenses," in *U.S. v. Clark*.

7. CONSULAR PROBLEMS IN THE SOUTH

1. Lyons to Russell, Feb. 24, 1862, Lyons Papers.
2. Lyons to Russell, Dec. 31, 1861, Bourne and Watt, *British Documents*, 6:28.
3. Lyons to Russell, Feb. 24, 1863, Lyons Papers; Russell to Lyons, Jan. 18, 1863, FO5/818.
4. The best survey of journalistic antagonism toward the consuls is found in Bonham, *British Consuls*, 210-15; Lyons to Russell, n.d., Lyons Papers. This letter is found among several others written in Jan. 1862 and was probably written in that month.
5. Murray to Russell, Mar. 23, 1863, FO5/869.
6. Bunch to Lyons, Mar. 2, 1862, Lyons Papers; Walker to Gen. John Porter Hatch, Mar. 15, 1865, FO5/1030.
7. Bunch to Lyons, June 10, 1861, and Lyons to Bunch, Aug. 5, 1862, both in Lyons Papers.
8. Bunch to Lyons, June 4, 1861, FO5/766; Lyons to Rear Admiral Alexander Milne, Nov. 24, 1861, and Lyons to Bunch, Nov. 24, 1861, both in Lyons Papers; Courtemanche, *No Need of Glory*, 26-29. Federal forces freed the *Alliance* after they captured Beaufort in November 1861.
9. Lyons to Russell, Jan. 24, 1862, and Lyons to Bunch, Aug. 5, 1862, both in Lyons Papers.
10. Bunch to Lyons, Jan. 25 and 28, 1862, both in Lyons Papers.
11. Bunch to Stuart, Aug. 20, 1862, and Lyons to Stuart, Aug. 26 and Oct. 3, 1862, all in Lyons Papers.
12. Lyons to Russell, Mar. 2 and 6, 1863, Lyons to Walker, Mar. 12, Apr. 2, and Aug. 26, 1863, all in Lyons Papers; Lyons to Russell, Apr. 7 and 21, 1863, both in FO5/881.
13. Walker to Lyons, Mar. 23, 1863, Lyons Papers; Walker to Lyons, Mar. 23, 1863, FO5/881. Both letters have the same date, but their contents are different.
14. Lyons to Seward, Feb. 26, 1863, BL-SD; Walker to Benjamin, June 15, 1863, Benjamin to Walker, June 18, 1863, and Walker to Russell, June 22, 1863, all in FO5/906; Walker to Lyons, Apr. 21, 1863, FO5/882; Lyons to Russell, Apr. 7, 1863, FO5/881.
15. Seward to Stuart, June 23, 1862, Francis H. Ruggles to Seward, and Ruggles's report on Goolrick, both dated July 3, 1862, all in U.S. Congress, *House Executive Documents*, 37 Cong., 3 sess. (1862), 263-64, 268-72.
16. Seward to Stuart, June 23, 1862, SD-BL; Seward to Stuart, July 12, 1862, U.S. Congress, *House Executive Documents*, 37 Cong., 3 sess. (1862), 267.

17. Stuart to Seward, June 25, 1862, U.S. Congress, *House Executive Documents*, 37 Cong., 3 sess. (1862), 265-66.
18. Cridland to Stuart, Aug. 2, 1862, Lyons Papers; Jenkins, *Britain and the War*, 2:131-42.
19. Lyons to Seward, Jan. 16, 1863, BL-SD.
20. Lyons to Russell, Jan. 5, 7, and 14, 1861, Lyons to Charles Lubuzan, Jan. 24, 1861, all in FO5/759; Bonham, *British Consuls*, 151-52.
21. Russell, *My Diary North and South*, 143; Lyons to Russell, March 6, 1863, Lyons Papers.
22. Walsh to Magee, Nov. 11, 1862, and Magee to Walsh, Nov. 14, 1862, both in Confederate State Department, *Correspondence . . . British Consuls*, 24-25; Lyons to Russell, Jan. 3, 1863, Lyons Papers.
23. N.B. Hitchcock to Magee, Apr. 8, 1863, *Correspondence . . . British Consuls*, 27; Lyons to Russell, Jan. 30 and Feb. 13, 1863, both in Lyons Papers; Bonham, *British Consuls*, 155.
24. Lyons to Russell, Jan. 30, Feb. 3, 13, and Mar. 6, 1863, all in Lyons Papers; Lyons to Russell, Feb. 3, and Mar. 10, 1863, both in FO5/789; Russell to Lyons, Feb. 14, 1863, FO5/868; Lyons to Seward, Mar. 1 and 3, 1863, both in U.S. Congress, *House Executive Documents*, 38 Cong., 1 sess. (1863-64), 516-18; Seward to Welles, Mar. 3, 1863, U.S. Navy Department, "Letters Received . . . Navy"; Seward to Lyons, Mar. 3, 1863, FO5/878; Lyons to Seward, Mar. 4, 1863, BL-SD.
25. Magee to Lyons, Mar. 25, 1863, Lyons to Magee, May 12, 1863, and Seward to Lyons, June 4, 1863, all in FO5/886; Lyons to Russell, Mar. 6, 1863, FO5/879; Lyons to Russell, June 30, 1863, Lyons Papers; Seward to Lyons, June 3, 1863, SD-BL.
26. Benjamin to Mason, June 11, 1863, *O.R., Navies*, ser. 2, 3:696-802; Lyons to Russell, Nov. 17, 1863, quoted in Newton, *Lord Lyons*, 1:122. Despite his resentment of Lyons's influence in the Magee affair, Benjamin did rely on him for personal favors. In 1864, he asked Lyons to forward a letter and draft to his wife in Paris, and he assured the foreign minister that only family matters were discussed in the letter. Benjamin to Lyons, July 12, 1864, Lyons Papers.
27. Shorter to Benjamin, Mar. 28, 1863, and Benjamin to Shorter, Apr. 4, 1863, Confederate State Department, "Records"; Bonham, *British Consuls*, 157.
28. Lyons to Russell, Mar. 6, 1863, and Lyons to Moore, Apr. 30, 1863, both in Lyons Papers; Lyons to Moore, Mar. 11, 1863, FO5/880; Lyons to Seward, May 2, 1863, BL-SD.
29. Extracts from the *Richmond Whig*, May 18 and 19, 1863, and Benjamin to Mason, June 11, 1863, both in *Correspondence . . . British Consuls*, 14, 21-22; Richardson, *Messages and Papers*, 2:498-505.
30. Franklin Buchanan to Stephen Mallory, June 4, 1863, circular to Foreign Consuls, June 10, 1863, Benjamin to Mason, June 11, 1863, and Russell to Mason, Aug. 19, 1863, all in *Correspondence . . . British Consuls*, 14-21, 23.
31. Dabney Maury to Benjamin, June 13, 1863, and Cridland to Benjamin, June 13, 1863, both in Confederate State Department, "Records."

32. Cridland to Russell, Sept. 3, 1863, Cridland to Benjamin, Feb. 6, 13, and 20, 1864, and Benjamin to Cridland, Feb. 29, 1864, all in FO5/970.

8. CONSCRIPTION, CONFEDERATE STYLE

1. Mure to Lyons, July 19, 1861, and clipping from *New Orleans Picayune*, July 6, 1861, both in Lyons Papers.

2. Mure to Russell, May 3, 1861, FO5/788; Mure to Lyons, May 7, 1861, Lyons Papers; Lyons to Russell, July 20, 1861, FO5/768; W.H. Hunt to Coppell, Sept. 30, 1861, FO5/775. Consuls of other nations also brought pressure on Governor Moore to end the conscription of their citizens. See Mejan, French consul at New Orleans, to Moore, July 11, 1862, *O.R., Armies*, ser. 1, 15:776.

3. Coppell to Russell, Jan. 3, Feb. 13 and 19, 1861, all in FO5/848; Coppell to Lyons, Oct. 1, 1861, Lyons Papers.

4. Lyons to Mure, June 20, 1861, Lyons to Russell, Mar. 10 and 31, 1861, all in Lyons Papers; Foreign Office to Lyons, Aug. 7, 1861, FO5/756; Bunch to Russell, Nov. 20, 1861, FO5/781.

5. Lt. Col. Henry L. Webb to Major Edmund Turner, Jan. 21, 1863, *O.R., Armies*, ser. 1, 15:966; Lonn, *Foreigners in the Confederacy*, 386ff, 431, 434-35.

6. *O.R., Navies*, ser. 2, 3:12.

7. Magee to George Randolph, Oct. 22, 1862, FO5/839; Thomas Wright to Fullarton, Aug. 7, 1863, "Savannah Consulate Papers," Duke.

8. Lonn, *Foreigners in the Confederacy*, 29-30, 386ff; U.S. Bureau of the Census, *Eighth Census*, xxx-xxxi, 620-23.

9. Cridland to Lyons, Feb. 19, 1862, Lyons Papers; Cridland to Russell, Mar. 25, 1862, FO5/846.

10. J.B. Jones, *Rebel War Clerk's Diary*, 1:217.

11. Bunch to Randolph, Oct. 28, Nov. 7, and Nov. 18, 1862, Bunch to Campbell, Nov. 11, 1862, and Bunch to Russell, Nov. 20, 1862, all in FO5/844; Campbell to Bunch, Dec. 15, 1862, and Walker to Russell, Feb. 7, 1863, both in FO5/906.

12. Moore, *Conscription and Conflict*, 16, 59-60; Lonn, *Foreigners in the Confederacy*, 391; Coulter, *Confederate States of America*, 313-28; *O.R., Armies*, ser. 4, 2:164.

13. Some historians regard the Confederate conscription laws as failures. Exemptions caused opposition from the populous, and governors tried to obstruct enforcement; still, the Confederate's draft was more successful than the Union's. Draftees comprised 20 percent of the Confederate army, whereas only 8 percent of the men in the Union army had actually been drafted. Lonn, *Foreigners in the Confederacy*, 394-96; McPherson, *Ordeal by Fire*, 182-83.

14. *O.R., Armies*, ser. 4, 1:1096, 2:77, 163; Moore, *Conscription and Conflict*, 114-16, 127, 207-8.

15. The following certificate of nationality, dated Sept. 18, 1862, is found in "Savannah Consulate Records," Emory: "I hereby declare that I have reason to believe, after careful examination, that the bearer, John Mangan, a native of Ireland, is a Subject of Her Brittanick Majesty, who has never forfeited his claim to the protection of the Queen, by becoming a Subject or a Citizen of any

foreign State. Given under my Hand and Seal of Office, at the City of Charleston, this 18th day of September 1862. [signed] H. Pinckney Walker, British Vice-consul." See also Moore, *Conscription and Conflict*, 60-61.

16. *O.R., Armies*, ser. 4, 2:164; Lonn, *Foreigners in the Confederacy*, 387.

17. Alexander Pratt to Fullarton, Oct. 25, 1862, and Bunch to Benjamin, May 13 and 18, 1862, all in Confederate State Department, "Records"; Magee to Randolph, Aug. 4 and 20, 1862, Randolph to Magee, Sept. 16, 1862, G.W. Magee to James Magee, Aug. 26, 1862, General Orders no. 68 (Sept. 17, 1862) and General Orders no. 82 (Nov. 3, 1862), all in *O.R., Armies*, ser. 4, 2:67, 70 84, 85; Magee to Stuart, Sept. 6, 1862, FO5/838; *Mobile Sun* quoted in Moore, *Conscription and Conflict*, 60-61.

18. Russell to Lyons, Oct. 10, 1862, FO5/821; Russell to Lyons, Nov. 27, 1862, FO5/822; Foreign Office to Lyons, Oct. 10, 1862, FO5/758; Bunch to Benjamin, Nov. 12, 1862, and Lyons's instructions on enlistments to the Southern consuls, July 31, 1861, both in FO5/744; Lynn to Lyons, Feb. 26, 1863, and Lyons to Lynn, May 12, 1863, both in FO5/885; Lonn, *Foreigners in the Confederacy*, 409-10; Owsley and Owsley, *King Cotton Diplomacy*, 479.

19. Walker to Russell, June 20 and July 6, 1863, both in FO5/907; Cridland to Russell, July 13, 1863, FO5/908; Bonham, *British Consuls*, 222-26; Lonn, *Foreigners in the Confederacy*, 389-90; Owsley and Owsley, *King Cotton Diplomacy*, 479.

20. William Gray to Fullarton, Sept. 10, 1863, "Savannah Consulate Records," Emory; Lonn, *Foreigners in the Confederacy*, 189.

21. Walker to Russell, Apr. 6, 9, May 4, and Oct. 22, 1863, all in FO5/902; Walker to Lyons, Apr. 7, 1863, FO5/906.

22. Lynn to Patrick Walsh, June 19, 1863, and Walsh to Lynn, July 15, 1863, both in FO5/909; General William Hardee to Fullarton, Jan. 22, 1863, "Savannah Consulate Records," Emory.

23. Weems to Fullarton, Oct. 30, 1862, "Savannah Consulate Records," Emory.

24. Wayne to Fullarton, July 3, 1863, ibid.

25. Bunch to Russell, Dec. 22, 1862, FO5/844.

26. Magee to Stuart, Oct. 27, 1862, FO5/839; Cridland to ———, July 10, 1861, FO5/768; Lyons to Russell, Feb. 2, 1863, FO5/909; Lynn to Lyons, Dec. 13, 1862, and Aug. 12, 1863, both in FO5/876; statement of James Hurley, Mar. 15, 1863, FO5/886.

27. Walker to Fullarton, July 10, 1863, "Savannah Consulate Records," Emory; Lynn to Russell, Dec. 27, 1863, FO5/907; Walker to Russell, Nov. 1 and 28, 1864, both in FO5/969; Moore to Lyons, Mar. 5, 1863, FO5/879.

28. Fetherston to Fullarton, Oct. 23, 1862; see also Thomas Hogan to Fullarton, n.d., both in "Savannah Consulate Papers," Duke; Molyneux to Russell, Nov. 12, 1862, FO5/849.

29. Moore to James Seddon, Apr. 24, 1863, FO5/883; Lynn to General Theophilus Holmes [Confederate], Apr. 13, 1863, FO5/909; Kelly to Fullarton, Nov. 11, 1862, "Savannah Consulate Records," Emory; Moore to Lyons, Apr. 9, 1863, FO5/883.

30. Magee to Stuart, Oct. 27, 1862, FO5/839; Magee to Russell, Nov. 17,

1862, FO5/848; Magee to Randolph, Sept. 24, 1862, FO5/839; Coppell to Lyons, Mar. 10, 1863, FO5/880. A copy of Nelson's certificate of exemption, dated Jan. 24, 1863, is found in Confederate State Department, "Records."
31. Cridland to Stuart, Oct. 18, 1862, FO5/839; Thomas, *Confederate Nation*, 149, 191-92.
32. Randolph to Magee, Sept. 16, 1862, *O.R., Armies*, ser. 4, 2:84; Randolph to Magee, n.d., FO5/839; John B. Weems to Fullarton, Nov. 7, 1862, and Randolph to Fullarton, Nov. 11, 1862, both in "Savannah Consulate Records," Emory.
33. Moore to Lyons, Feb. 25 and 26, 1863, both in FO5/879.
34. Moore to J.B. Caldwell, May 5, 1863, Confederate State Department, "Records."
35. Moore to Benjamin, Feb. 16, 1863, Moore to Lyons, Feb. 16, 1863, Benjamin to Moore, Feb. 18, 1863, and Lyons to Moore, Mar. 22, 1863, all in FO5/879; Moore to Benjamin, Feb. 16, 1863, Confederate State Department, "Records."
36. John O'Connell to Fullarton, Sept. 15, 1863, "Savannah Consulate Papers," Duke; Russell to Lyons, May 9 and 21, 1863, both in FO5/870.

9. EXPELLING THE SOUTHERN CONSULS

1. Russell, *My Diary North and South*, 5, 11, 12, 298-300.
2. Ibid., 86.
3. Crook, *North, South and Powers*, 253, 288, 329; Long, *Civil War Day by Day*, 70, 81, 984; Russell, *My Diary North and South*, 82, 86; Rawley, *Turning Points*, 97-115.
4. Bunch to Russell, Sept. 4 and 28, 1861, both in FO5/781; Benjamin to Molyneux, Jan. 31, 1862, "Savannah Consulate Records," Emory; Walker to Russell, Aug. 27, 1863, FO5/907.
5. Mason to Benjamin, Aug. 6, 1863, *O.R., Navies*, ser. 2, 3:858; Moore to Lyons, Mar. 21, 1863, FO5/881.
6. Lyons to Russell, Apr. 25, 1862, Lyons Papers; Moore to Russell, Jan. 15, 1863, FO5/909; Jones, *Rebel War Clerk's Diary*, 1:217.
7. Bunch to Lyons, Dec. 3, 1859, Lyons Papers; Bunch to Russell, Mar. 20 and July 5, 1861, both in FO5/781; Bunch to Russell, Mar. 19, 1862, FO5/843; Bunch to Russell, Dec. 13, 1862, FO5/844.
8. Walker to Russell, Aug. 21, 1863, FO5/907; Walker to Russell, Mar. 21, 1864, FO5/968; Cridland to Russell, Nov. 16, 1863, FO5/908.
9. Bonham, *British Consuls*, 210-15. See also Owlsey and Owlsey, *King Cotton Diplomacy*, 467-70.
10. U.S. Congress, Senate, *Journal . . . Confederate States*, 1:286, 294, 2:143-44, 5:317, 322, 333-34, 421-24, 464-67, and 6:516.
11. Benjamin to Mason, Oct. 31, 1862, and Benjamin to Foreign Consuls, June 10, 1863, both in *O.R., Navies*, ser. 2, 3:587, 795-96; Cridland to Lyons, Apr. 21, 1862, Lyons Papers; circular to Foreign Consuls, June 10, 1863, *Correspondence . . . British Consuls*, 28-29; Benjamin to Walker, June 10, 1863, FO5/906.

12. See chapter 7 for detail on Benjamin's refusal to accept Cridland as acting consul.

13. Moore to Russell, June 11, 1861, FO5/786.

14. Moore to Benjamin, Feb. 16, 1863, *Correspondence . . . British Consuls*, 8-9. Copies of this letter are also found in Confederate State Department, "Records," and in FO5/879.

15. Benjamin to Moore, Feb. 20, 1863, FO5/879; also found in *Correspondence . . . British Consuls*, 9-10.

16. Moore to Lyons, Mar. 21, 1863, FO5/881.

17. Benjamin to Mason, June 6, 1863, and Lt. Col. George M. Edgar to Captain R.H. Catlett, May 25, 1863, both in *Correspondence . . . British Consuls*, 5-9, 12-13; Richardson, *Messages and Papers*, 2:495-98; *O.R., Navies*, ser. 2, 3:786-92.

18. Moore to Caldwell, May 5, 1863, *Correspondence . . . British Consuls*, 13-14.

19. Benjamin to Moore, June 5, 1862, ibid., 11-12. Davis's letter patent is found in the same source, 10-11.

20. Moore to Lyons, June 6, 1863, and Moore to Russell, June 9, 1863, both in FO5/909.

21. Proclamation of Governor Brown, July 17, 1863, and General Order no. 16, both in *O.R., Armies*, ser. 4, 2:639-42.

22. Fullarton to Brown, July 22, 1863, *Correspondence . . . British Consuls*, 41-42. Copies of this letter are also found in *O.R., Armies*, ser. 4, 2:657-58 and in Confederate State Department, "Records."

23. Brown to Fullarton, Aug. 8, 1863, "Savannah Consulate Records," Emory. See also *O.R., Armies*, ser. 4, 2:698-701.

24. Fullarton to Brown, Aug. 17, 1863, and Brown to Fullarton, Aug. 26, 1863, both in *O.R., Armies*, ser. 4, 2:729-30, 755-58.

25. Walker to Jordan, June 13, July 17, and Aug. 4. 1863, and Walker to Russell, Sept. 11, 1863, all in FO5/907; Walker to "Sir," June 26, 1863, "Savannah Consulate Records," Emory; Beauregard to Gen. John Cooper, Aug. 20, 1863, Confederate State Department "Records."

26. Walker to Russell, June 13 and 22, 1863, both in FO5/906; Walker to Benjamin, July 17, 1863, Confederate State Department, "Records"; Bonham, *British Consuls*, 129-31.

27. Walker to Bonham, Sept. 2, 10, 1863, Bonham to Walker, Sept. 11, 1863, and Walker to Russell, Sept. 11 and 12, 1863, all in FO5/907; Bonham, *British Consuls*, 130-31.

28. Benjamin to Fullarton and Benjamin to Walker, both Oct. 8, 1863, both in *Correspondence . . . British Consuls*, 38-39; Owsley and Owsley, *King Cotton Diplomacy*, 491-92.

29. W.C. Davis, *Jefferson Davis*, 486-87, 544-45; Eaton, *Jefferson Davis*, 172-73; David Potter, "Jefferson Davis and the Political Factors in Confederate Defeat," in Donald, *Why the North Won*, 105-7; Patrick, *Davis and His Cabinet*, 34-35.

30. Lynn to Lyons, Mar. 22 and Dec. 26, 1863, both in FO5/948; Bonham, *British Consuls*, 184.

31. Benjamin to Slidell, Oct. 8, 1863, *O.R., Navies*, ser. 2, 3:922-27. See also Richardson, *Messages and Papers*, 2:576-83, and *Correspondence . . . British Consuls*, 31-38.

32. Lyons to Russell, Nov. 17, 1863, and Lyons to Admiral Milne, Aug. 30, 1863, both in Lyons Papers; Lyons to Russell, Mar. 19, 1863, FO5/879; Lyons to Russell, June 16, 1863, FO5/887; Newton, *Lord Lyons*, 1:122.

33. Lyons to Russell, Nov. 17, 1863, Lyons Papers.

34. Meade, *Benjamin*, 113-14; Patrick, *Davis and His Cabinet*, 201-22. The most recent biography of Benjamin is Evans, *Benjamin*.

35. Crook, *North, South, and Powers*, 331-32; Jenkins, *Britain and the War*, 2:15-17.

36. Cridland to Russell, June 9, 1862, FO5/846; Benjamin to Davis, Oct. 8, 1863, *O.R., Navies*, ser. 2, 3:926-29.

37. Lyons to Russell, June 16, 1863, Lyons Papers; Moore to Russell, June 9 and July 21, 1863, both in FO5/909.

38. Fullarton to Benjamin, Oct. 15, FO5/909; Citizens of Savannah to Benjamin, Oct. 15, 1863, Confederate State Department, "Records"; Benjamin to Fullarton, Oct. 19 and Nov. 10, 1863, both in "Savannah Consulate Records," Emory; Bonham, *British Consuls*, 251.

39. W.C. Cosins to Sir Frederick Bruce, Aug. 16, 1865, FO5/1233; statement of Allan Fullarton, Sept. 6, 1865, BL-SD; Bonham, *British Consuls*, 252-53.

40. Walker to Russell, Jan. 2 and Apr. 20, 1864, both in FO5/968; Bonham, *British Consuls*, 252-53.

41. Davis to Bonham, Sept. 19, 1864, *O.R., Armies*, ser. 4, 3:671; Walker to Russell, Jan. 2, 14, 30, May 27, and June 6, 1864, all in FO5/968; Walker to Russell, July 7, 10, 19, Aug. 8, 13, 22, Sept. 19, Nov. 10, and Dec. 31, 1864, all in FO5/969.

42. Jenkins, *Britain and the War*, 2:315; Lyons to Russell, Jan. 18, 1864, Lyons Papers; Lyons to Russell, Jan. 18, 1864, FO5/943; Lyons to Russell, Mar. 18, 1864, FO5/946; U.S. Congress, *House Executive Documents*, 38 Cong., 2 sess. (1864-65), 568; Cridland to Benjamin, Feb. 6, 13, and 20, 1864, and Benjamin to Cridland, Feb. 29, 1864, all in FO5/970. See chapter 7 for details on the Cridland-Benjamin correspondence.

43. Crook, *North, South and Powers*, 356-57.

10. CONSCRIPTION, UNION STYLE

1. Shannon, *Organization and Administration*, 1:308; 2:128; Murdock, *One Million Men*, 24-25, 178, and 308.

2. The development of conscription procedures in the North are fully discussed in three recent works: Murdock, *Patriotism Limited*; Murdock, *One Million Men*; and Geary, *We Need Men*.

3. Archibald to Russell, Apr. 26, 1861, FO5/778.

4. Lyons to Bernal, Aug. 28, 1861, Lyons Papers.

5. Seward to Lyons, July 15, and Oct. 5, 1861, both in SD-BL; Seward to Lyons, Dec. 11, 1861, U.S. Congress, *House Executive Documents*, 37 Cong., 3

sess. (1862), 240-42; Lyons to Seward, Dec. 9, 1861, BL-SD. A complete record of the correspondence on the issue of minors is found in SD-BL, Apr. through Dec., 1861, passim.

6. Lyons to Russell, Feb. 15, 1862, Lyons Papers; Lyons to Russell, Apr. 27, 1862, FO5/882; Lyons to Seward, Apr. 18, 1862, BL-SD; Seward to Lyons, Apr. 3, 1862, SD-BL; Seward to Stanton, May 30, 1862, Lyons to Seward, May 24, 1862, and Stanton to Seward, June 8, 1862, all in U.S. War Department, "Letters Received by the Secretary of War, from the President, Executive Departments, and War Department Bureaus, 1862-1870"—cited hereafter as "Letters Received . . . War"; Edward S. Canby to Seward, Apr. 14, 1865, and Report of Col. H.S. Gansevoort, Apr. 14, 1864, both in FO5/948.

7. Stuart to Russell, Aug. 8, 12, and 15, 1862, all in Bourne and Watt, *British Documents*, 6:77-79; Geary, *We Need Men*, 81.

8. Stanton to Salomon, Aug. 12, 1862, *O.R., Armies*, ser. 3, 2:369; Murdock, *One Million Men*, 308.

9. Stuart to Russell, Aug. 15, 1862, House of Commons, *Correspondence . . . Civil War*, 15-16; memorandum dated Aug. 20, 1862, and Stuart to Seward, Sept. 6, 1862, both in BL-SD.

10. Report of H. Percy Anderson, Sept. 18, 1862, and Stuart to Russell, Sept. 18, 1862, both in House of Commons, *Correspondence . . . Civil War*, 15-16, 23, 25, 33-37.

11. Wilkins to Lyons, Sept. 6, 1861, and Feb. 10, 1863, both in FO5/880.

12. Stuart to Seward. Sept. 6, 1862, U.S. Congress, *House Executive Documents*, 37 Cong., 3 sess. (1862), 286-87.

13. Shannon, *Organization and Administration*, 2:103; Murdock, *One Million Men*, 6-7; Geary, *We Need Men*, 115; *U.S. Statues at Large*, 12:597-600.

14. Lyons to Russell, Feb. 24, 1863, Lyons Papers.

15. Seward to Stuart, Oct. 24 and Dec. 12, 1862, and Memorandum dated Oct. 23, 1861, all in SD-BL; Lyons to Russell, Dec. 20, 1862, FO5/840; Lyons to Russell, Apr. 24, 1862, FO5/882.

16. Wilkins to Lyons, Dec. 24, 1862, and Jan. 15, 1863, both in Lyons Papers; Russell to Lyons, Aug. 17, 1863, FO5/872.

17. Stanton to Salomon, Aug. 12, 1862, *O.R., Armies*, ser. 3, 2:369; Seward to Stuart, Aug. 20., 1862, SD-BL.

18. Kortwright to Russell, Jan. 18, 1864, FO5/970; Hamilton Gamble to Brigadier General Gray, Sept. 18, 1862, FO5/905; Seward to Stuart, Oct. 24, 1862, SD-BL; Lonn, *Foreigners in the Union Army and Navy*, 443; Winks, *Canada and United States*, 194.

19. Russell to Lyons, Apr. 3, 1863, FO5/869.

20. Proclamation of May 8, 1863, in Basler, *Works of Lincoln*, 6:203-4; Russell to Lyons, May 11 and June 6, 1863, both in FO5/883.

21. Russell to Lyons, Aug. 10, 1863, FO5/871; Lyons to Bernal, Mar. 1, 1864, Lyons Papers. The State Department's attitude toward individuals who left the country to avoid the draft remained resolute throughout the war. As a result of Lincoln's proclamation, three naturalized Prussians returned to their homeland, where they were immediately seized and put into the army. When they appealed on the basis of their American citizenship, Seward instructed

the U.S. minister to Prussia not to intercede on their behalf. Seward to Norman Judd, June 6, 1863, U.S. Congress, *House Executive Documents*, 38 Cong., 1 sess. (1863-64), 1021.

22. Lyons to Russell, May 3, 1864, FO5/949; George Dundas to Lyons, Apr. 10, 1862, in Lyons Papers; Russell to Lyons, Nov. 4, 1864, FO5/941; Russell's comment about Adams is quoted in Allen, *Britain and United States*, 492.

23. Lyons to Seward, June 27 and July 1, 1863, both in BL-SD; Lyons to Russell, July 24, 1863, in FO5/891; Lyons to Kortwright, Feb. 10, 1864, Lyons Papers; Murdock, *One Million Men*, 309.

24. Lyons to Kortwright, Aug. 13, 1863, Lyons Papers.

25. Quoted in Murdock, *One Million Men*, 313.

26. J.S. Shaw to Lyons, July 12, 1863, and Affidavit of G.W. Miller, Aug. 20, 1864, both in BL-SD.

27. Lousada to Lyons, July 22, 1863, Lyons Papers.

28. Kortwright to Lyons, Aug. 4 and 5, 1863, and "Extract from Consul at Philadelphia on Refusal of Enrolling Officers to Recognize Statements of Alienage," n.d. but sent to the State Department in November 1863, all in BL-SD. For Lincoln's proclamation see Basler, *Works of Lincoln*, 6:451-52.

29. Edwards to Lyons, Aug. 11, 1864, BL-SD; Wilkins to Lyons, Feb. 22, 1864, Lyons Papers.

30. Dickson to his parents, Jan. 21, 1865, BL-SD.

31. Patrick Flynn to Commanding Officer, Jan. 10, 1865, Patrick Flynn to "Dear Brother," Mar. 10, 1865, John Flynn to "Dear Brother," Feb. 20, 21, and Mar. 2, 1865, and Frederick Bruce to Seward, Apr. 20, 1865, all in BL-SD.

32. Lyons to Seward, Aug. 13, 1864, Joseph Burnley to Seward, Sept. 29, 1864, Statement of Luke Riley, n.d., enclosure in Burnley to Seward, Apr. 10, 1865, all in BL-SD.

33. The Federal bounty at the beginning of the war was one hundred dollars payable upon discharge. Congress raised the bounty to three hundred dollars in 1864 (four hundred dollars for veterans) and provided for installment payments. Murdock, *One Million Men*, 160-61; Randall and Donald, *Civil War and Reconstruction*, 328-29.

34. *New York Times*, Aug. 25, 1864. It is beyond the scope of this study to explain the bounty brokerage system in detail, but there are a number of excellent discussions. See Shannon, *Organization and Administration*, 2:69-141; Murdock, *Patriotism Limited*, 107-15; Murdock, *One Million Men*, 259-83.

35. L. Baker, *History of Secret Service*, 396, 407; Murdock, *One Million Men*, 255-58; statement of Charles Jackson, n.d., attached to Lyons to Seward, July 30, 1864, BL-SD; Lousada to Lyons, Dec. 5, 1863, FO5/899; *New York Times*, Aug. 28, 1864.

36. Russell to Lyons, May 7, 1864, Russell Papers; Lyons to Russell, May 3, 1864, FO5/849; Perkins to Lyons, Oct. 28, 1864, BL-SD.

37. Lyons to Seward, June 25, July 4, Aug. 20, and 22, 1864, all in BL-SD.

38. Statement of John Davis, Sept. 7, 1864, and Lyons to Seward, Nov. 19, 1864, both in BL-SD.

39. F.W. Mcdonald to Lyons, Sept. 4, 1863, Stuart to Seward, Sept. 12, 1863, Seward to Stanton, Sept. 17, 1863, Brig. Gen. Isaac Quinby to Provost

Marshal General James B. Fry, Sept. 1, 1863, S.P. Smith to Col. P.P. Brown, Sept. 25, 1863, Quinby to D.F. Van Buren, Sept. 28. 1863, Scroogs to Quinby, Sept. 5, 1863, and P.H. Watson to Seward, Oct. 16, 1863, all in "Letters Received . . . War."

40. Lyons to Russell, May 3, 1864, FO5/949; Edwards to Lyons, June 6, 1864, and Lyons to "Sir James," Aug. 1, 1864, both in Lyons Papers.

41. Lonn, *Foreigners in the Union Army and Navy*, 472; Raney, "Recruiting and Crimping," 30.

42. Canby to Seward, Mar. 21, 1864, and Stanton to Seward, May 30, 1864, both in U.S. War Department, "Letters Sent by the Secretary of War to the President and Executive Departments, 1863-1870"—cited hereafter as "Letters Sent . . . War"; Seward to Lyons, Aug. 3, 1864, Bruce to Seward, Oct. 9, 1865, and statement of Anne Cunningham, Feb. 9, 1866, all in BL-SD; Lyons to Seward, Aug. 5, 21, and 22, and Seward to Lyons, Aug. 8, 1864, all in FO5/959.

43. Seward to Lyons, Nov. 4, 1864, SD-BL; Lonn, *Foreigners in the Union Army and Navy*, 474-75; Winks, *Canada and United States*, 187.

44. Burnley to Mrs. Verner, Sept. 30, 1864, Burnley to Seward, Oct. 23, 1864, and Burnley to Russell, Jan. 27, 1865, all in FO5/1014; statement of Charles Jackson, enclosure in Lyons to Seward, July 30, 1864, and E.M. Jackson to "Honored Sir," June 24, 1865, all in BL-SD.

45. Lyons to Russell, Nov. 3, 1863, quoted in Newton, *Lord Lyons*, 1:121; Shannon, *Organization and Administration*, 2:78; Owsley and Owsley, *King Cotton Diplomacy*, 497-98; Lonn, *Foreigners in the Union Army and Navy*, 469-70; BL-SD, Jan. 1, 1862 through Apr. 15, 1865, passim.

46. Edwards to Lyons, Aug. 11, 1864, BL-SD; Lyons to Russell, Aug. 19, 1864, and Lyons to Kortwright, Feb. 17, 1864, both in Lyons Papers.

47. Statement of Michael Holmes, Aug. 25, 1864, statement of Jeremiah Riordan, n.d., 1864, Narcisse Villiard to Lyons, Nov. 4, 1865, Lyons to Seward, Nov. 20, 1864, and Burnley to Seward, Aug. 24, 1864, all in BL-SD; Seward to Lyons, June 3, 1862, SD-BL; Catherine Garvin to Lyons, Oct. 14, 1863, Pierrepont Edwards to Lyons, Sept. 15, 1863, Lyons to Seward, Oct. 17, 1863, and Seward to Stanton, Oct. 23, 1863, all in "Letters Received . . . War."

48. Lyons to Archibald, Apr. 15, 1864, Lyons Papers.

11. PREYING ON THE INNOCENT

1. Nevins, *War for the Union:* 3:220-21; Paludan, *"People's Contest,"* 284-85; Randall and Donald, *Civil War and Reconstruction*, 483-84.

2. Hamer, "Luring Canadian Soldiers," 152-53; Winks, *Canada and the United States*, 105.

3. Hamer, "Luring Canadian Soldiers," 153; Head to Lyons, Oct. 10, 1861, Bourne and Watt, *British Documents*, 5:320-21; Colonel R.A. Booker to Head, Oct. 7, 1861, and Lyons to Russell, Oct. 17, 1861, both in FO5/771; Lyons to Russell, Oct. 24, 1861, FO5/773.

4. Russell to Lyons, Nov. 4, 1864, FO5/941; Archibald to Lyons, Feb. 22, 1864, BL-SD; Raney, "Recruiting and Crimping," 28; Winks, *Canada and United States*, 197.

5. Quoted in Murdock, *Patriotism Limited*, 177.

6. Hamer, "Luring Canadian Soldiers," 155.

7. Burnley to Seward, Nov. 16, 1864, FO5/963; Burnley to Seward, Sept. 16, 1864, and Seward to Burnley, Sept. 19, 1864, both in U.S. Congress, *House Executive Documents*, 38 Cong., 2 sess. (1864-65), 708, 712; Burnley to Seward, Jan. 18 and 23, 1864, both in FO5/903; C.F. Dunbar to Lousada, Dec. 5, 1863, FO5/899; Lousada to Lyons, Apr. 5, 1864, FO5/947; Raney, "Recruiting and Crimping," 26-27.

8. Casey to Archibald, Apr. 15, 1865, BL-SD.

9. Statement of James Fitzgerald, Dec., no day, 1864, BL-SD.

10. Thomas Thomas to Lyons, May 27, 1864, and Charles E. Lloyd to "dear wife," Oct., no day, 1863, both in BL-SD; Raney, "Recruiting and Crimping," 25-26; Paludan, " *People's Contest*," 284; Murdock, *One Million Men*, 228-29; Winks, *Canada and United States*, 184

11. Statement of James Conway, Oct. 24, 1864, and Burnley to Seward, Nov. 18, 1864, both in BL-SD.

12. Fitzgerald statement, Dec., no day, 1864, and Burnley to Seward, Nov. 16, 1864, both in BL-SD; Raney, "Recruiting and Crimping," 30-32; Winks, *Canada and United States*, 194.

13. Wister to John A. Dix, quoted in Newton, *Lord Lyons*, 1:113.

14. Moore to Lyons, n.d., and Lyons to Seward, Feb. 3, 1863, both in BL-SD.

15. Winks, *Canada and United States*, 193.

16. Baker, *History of Secret Service*, 408.

17. *New York Times*, Nov. 9, 1863; Archibald to Lyons, Nov. 12, 1863, BL-SD; Seward to Lyons, Feb. 11, 1863, SD-BL; Sutherland, *Expansion of Everyday Life*, 110.

18. Brown to Archibald, Oct. 23, 1864, BL-SD.

19. Statement of James Johns re Adam Johnson, Edward Barber, and John Smith, Oct. 26, 1864, enclosure in Archibald to Lyons, Oct. 26, 1864, both in BL-SD.

20. Burnley to Seward, Feb. 1, 1865, BL-SD.

21. Archibald to Lyons, Apr. 10, 1864, Lyons Papers.

22. Russell to Lyons, June 13, 1863, Russell Papers.

23. Baker, *History of Secret Service*, 399.

24. Statement of Thomas Godfrey, Aug. 12, 1863, enclosure in Stuart to Seward, Aug. 18, 1863, both in BL-SD.

25. Lyons to Seward, Aug. 17, 1864, U.S. Congress, *House Executive Documents*, 38 Cong., 2 sess. (1864-65), 328; Edwards to Lyons, Aug. 16, 1864, Lyons Papers.

26. Statement of Michael Quinn, July 13, 1863, Jeremiah Pittenger to Archibald, Feb. 25, 1863, affidavit of Edgar Jones, July 9, 1863, and Lyons to Seward, Mar. 18, 1863, all in BL-SD; William Radford to Hiram Paulding, Mar., 19, 1863, Seward to Welles, Mar. 19, 1863, statement of John Quinn, Mar. 6, 1863, Charles Hawley to Paulding, Mar. 9, 1863, and Foote to Paulding, Feb. 13, 1864, all in "Letters Received . . . Navy"; Lonn, *Foreigners in the Union Army and Navy*, 467.

27. Lyons to Archibald and Lousada, both Apr. 9, 1864, both in FO5/947;

Owsley and Owsley, *King Cotton Diplomacy*, 498-99; Murdock, *One Million Men*, 114-15; Randall and Donald, *Civil War and Reconstruction*, 483-84; McPherson, *Battle Cry of Freedom*, 324-25. Evidence proving that immigrant laborers were being mistreated and paid starvation wages caused Congress to repeal the Contract Labor Law in 1868. Van Deusen, *Seward*, 512-13.

28. There are a number of letters between Adams and Russell on this topic. See especially Adams to Seward, Nov. 27, 1862, and Apr. 24, 1863, Russell to Adams, Nov. 20, 1862, and Apr. 16, 1863, Adams to Russell, Apr. 18, 19, and 29, 1863, memorandum from McAndrew and Winn, Mar. 27, 1863, and Mr. Forbes to Adams, Apr. 29, 1863, all in U.S. Congress, *House Executive Documents*, 38 Cong., 1 sess. (1863-64), 11-12, 251, 259, 261, 273-74; Lyons to Archibald and Lousada, both Apr. 9, 1864, both in FO5/947. The Confederate government was also aware of Northern recruiting efforts and sent agents to uncover evidence incriminating the United States; however, the endeavor was unsuccessful. Owsley and Owsley, *King Cotton Diplomacy*, 495-96; L.Q.C. Lamar to Benjamin, Mar. 20, 1863, Benjamin to Mason, Apr. 28 and July 8, 1863, Benjamin to J.L. Capston, July 3, 1863, and J.E. Macfarland to Benjamin, all in *O.R., Navies*, ser. 2, 2:719, 753, 792, 828-29.

29. Lyons to Seward, Apr. 7, 1864, "Letters Received . . . War"; Russell to Lyons, May 27, 1864, FO5/939; Archibald to Russell, Mar. 18, 1864, FO5/966.

30. None of the sources mention Finney's first name. Correspondence on the Tully case is extensive and repetitious. Duplicate copies of letters between the consulates at Portland, Boston, the British legation, and the State Department can be found in the Lyons Papers; BL-SD; SD-BL; "Letters Sent . . . War"; "Letters Received . . . War"; FO5/959; FO5/946; and FO5/957. The most complete file was published by the order of the House of Commons, *Correspondence Respecting the Enlistment of British Subjects in the United States Army*, which includes all correspondence from Mar. to Aug. 1864. Foreign Office Records (FO5/1287) contain copies of all letters from Aug. to Nov. 1864, when the case was concluded.

31. Extract from *Boston Courier*, n.d., enclosure no. 1 in Lousada to Russell, Mar. 15, 1864, *Correspondence Respecting Enlistments*.

32. "Committee Report," enclosure no. 7 in Lyons to Russell, Apr. 9, 1864, ibid.

33. Extract from *Boston Courier*, n.d., enclosure no. 1 in Lousada to Russell, Mar. 15, 1864, ibid.

34. Enclosure no. 2 in Lousada to Russell, Mar. 15, 1864, ibid.

35. Lousada to Lyons, Mar. 21, 23, and 25, and Lyons to Russell, Apr. 8, 1864, all in ibid.

36. Tully to Lyons, Mar. 13, 1864, Murray to the mayor of Portland, Mar. 14, 1864, both in ibid.; Tully to Lyons, Apr. 27, 1864, FO5/949; Murray to Lyons, Mar. 14, 1865, BL-SD.

37. Murray to Lyons, Mar. 17, 1864, BL-SD; J.W.T. Gardiner to Murray, Mar. 15, 1864, and Lyons to Seward, Mar. 19, 1864, both in *Correspondence Respecting Enlistments*.

38. Lyons to Seward, Apr. 7, 1864, Letters Received, War; Examining Committee Report, Apr. 2, 1864, statement of John W. Collins, Apr. 1, 1864, state-

ment of John Todd, Apr. 1, 1864, statement of Harrison Cole, Apr. 1, 1864, statement of J.H. Berrick, Apr. 4, 1864, statement of Alonzo Wentworth, Mar. 31, 1864, statement of William Foster, Mar. 31, 1864, and C.S. Dana to Seward, Apr. 18, 1864, all in *Correspondence Respecting Enlistments*. The testimonial statements are all enclosures in Lyons to Russell, Apr. 19, 1864, *Correspondence Respecting Enlistments*.

39. Tully to Lyons, Apr. 23, 1864, statement of Thomas Tully, May 9, 1864, and Lyons to Seward, Apr. 22, 23, and 25, 1864, all in *Correspondence Respecting Enlistments*.

40. Tully to Murray, June 30, 1864, in House of Commons, *Further Correspondence Respecting the Enlistment of British Subjects in the United States of America*; Murray to Lyons, Aug. 15 and Sept. 20, 1864, and Seward to Burnley, Oct. 6 and 12, all in BL-SD.

41. Burnley to Seward, Oct. 10, 1864, Seward to Lyons, Nov. 26, 1864, and Burnley to Russell, Oct. 10, Nov. 14 and 25, 1864, all in FO5/1287.

42. U.S. War Department, "Service Records . . . "; U.S. Interior Department, "Pension Records. . . ."

43. Lyons to Russell, July 29, 1864, Lyons Papers.

44. Burnley to Russell, Sept. 9, 1864, FO5/960; Lyons to Russell, Aug. 23, 1864, FO5/959; Lyons to Seward, Aug. 22, 1864, U.S. Congress, *House Executive Documents*, 38 Cong., 2 sess. (1864-65), 688-90.

45. Archibald to Burnley, Jan. 15 and Feb. 3, 1865, Archibald to Dix, Jan. 18, 1865, Investigative Report of Dix, Jan. 15, 1865, statements of John Ware and Edward Mortimer, both Jan. 14, 1865, and of James O'Brien, Jan. 19, 1865, all in FO5/1014; Russell to Bruce, Apr. 7, 1865, FO5/1010.

46. Burnley to Russell, Jan. 30, 1865, FO5/1014; Burnley to Russell, Mar. 13, 1865, FO5/1016.

47. Bruce to Lord Stanley, Jan. 17, 1867, FO5/1104; Geary, *We Need Men*, 16; Lonn, *Foreigners in the Union Army and Navy*, 438-39.

48. *New York Times*, June 25, 1864; Winks, *Canada and the United States*, 191-92; Bonham, *British Consuls*, 254.

12. AT WAR'S END

1. Wilkins to Lyons, May 1 and Nov. 10, 1862, and Lyons to Russell, May 5, 1862, all in Lyons Papers.

2. Lyons to Seward, June 12, 1862, Frederick Seward to Lyons, June 14, 1862, and Wolcott to Seward, June 18, 1862, all in U.S. Congress, *House Executive Documents*, 37 Cong., 3 sess. (1862), 261.

3. Wilkins to Lyons, Nov. 10, 1863, Lyons to Wilkins, Dec. 4, 1863, Seward to Lyons, Nov. 30, 1863, and Lyons to Seward, Dec. 4, 1863, all in FO5/898; Edwards to Lyons, Aug. 21, 1864, Lyons Papers.

4. Seward to Lyons, Nov. 30, 1863, Lyons to Seward, Dec. 4, 1863, and Lyons to Wilkins, Dec. 4, 1863, all in FO5/898; Lyons to Russell, Dec. 7, 1863, Lyons Papers.

5. Thomas Bean to Archibald, May 15, 1865, Bruce to William Hunter, June 20, 1865, and Bruce to Seward, Aug. 25, 1865, all in BL-SD.

6. Bonham, *British Consuls*, 255-56.

7. Herslet, *Foreign Office List*, Moore entry.

8. Walker to Russell, FO5/906 and FO5/968, passim.

9. Herslet, *Foreign Office List*, Murray entry.

10. Archibald, *Archibald*, 201.

11. Lyons to Russell, Feb. 25, 1862, and Bunch to Lyons, Oct. 12, 1864, both in Lyons Papers.

12. Cridland to Lyons, Apr. 16, 1865, Lyons Papers; Cridland to Russell, Apr. 17, 1865, FO5/1029.

13. Walker to Russell, Feb. 7 and Mar. 11, 1865, both in FO5/1030; Russell to Lyons, June 19, 1865, and Lyons to Russell, June 20, 1865, both in Lyons Papers; Russell to Bruce, Mar. 25, 1865, Russell Papers; Bruce to Seward, Sept. 30, 1865, BL-SD; and Walker to Gen. John P. Hatch, Mar. 15, 1865, FO5/1030.

14. The best discussions of this subject are found in Crook, *North, South, and Powers*, 245-53; and Jones, *Union in Peril*, 198-224.

15. Crook, *North, South, and Powers*; Jones, *Union in Peril*; Cridland to Russell, Nov. 16, 1862, FO5/908.

16. Bunch to Russell, Dec. 12, 1862, FO5/844.

17. Archibald to Russell, Nov. 8, 1862, FO5/782.

18. Lyons to Russell, Nov. 17, 1862, in Bourne and Watts, *British Documents*, 6:113-16.

19. Lyons to Russell, Aug., n.d., 1863, quoted in Newton, *Lord Lyons*, 1:117-18.

20. Lyons to Seward, Mar. 4, 1865, Seward Papers.

21. Seward to Lyons, Mar. 20, 1865, Lyons Papers.

22. Jenkins, *Britain and the War*, 2:363-64, 384-85; Herslet, *Foreign Office List*, Bruce entry.

23. Archibald to Foreign Office, passim, FO5/1023.

24. Archibald to Lyons, Feb. 21, 1865, Lyons Papers; Walker to Russell, Feb. 27, Mar. 25 and 27, 1865, all in FO5/1030; and Lousada to Russell, Jan. 31, 1865, FO5/1025.

Bibliography

MANUSCRIPT SOURCES

PRIVATE PAPERS

Lyons, Richard Bickerton Pemell. Papers. West Sussex Record Office, Chichester.

Pickens, Francis Wilkinson, and Milledge Luke Bonham. Papers. 1837-1920. Manuscript Division, Library of Congress, Washington, D.C.

Russell, John. Papers. Public Record Office, Kew (London).

Seward, William Henry. Papers. Microfilm, University of Wyoming, Library, Laramie.

COLLECTIONS AND DOCUMENTS

Confederate State Department. "Records of the Confederate States of America, 1861-1865." Manuscript Division, Library of Congress, Washington, D.C.

Great Britain, Foreign Office. "General Correspondence Before 1906, United States of America." Series 2 (1793-1905). Public Record Office, Kew.

"Savannah Consulate Papers, 1816-1875." Duke University Library, Durham, N.C.

"Savannah Consulate Records, 1859-1866." Emory University Library, Atlanta, Ga.

U.S. Interior Department. "Pension Records of Volunteer Soldiers Who Served in Organizations of the State of Maine—Co. D, 20th Maine Infantry." Record Group 94, National Archives, Washington, D.C.

U.S. Navy Department. "Letters Received by the Secretary of the Navy from the President and Executive Agencies, 1837-1886." Record Group 45, National Archives.

————. "Letters Sent by the Secretary of the Navy to the President and Executive Agencies, 1821-1866." Record Group 45, National Archives.

U.S. State Department. "Despatches of United States Ministers to France, 1789-1869." Record Group 59, National Archives.

———. "Exequaturs." Record Group 59, National Archives.

———. "Notes from Foreign Consuls in the United States to the Department of State, 1789-1906." Record Group 59, National Archives.

———. "Notes from the British Legation in the United States to the Department of State, 1791-1906." Record Group 59, National Archives.

———. "Notes to Foreign Consuls in the United States from the Department of State, 1853-1906." Record Group 59, National Archives.

———. "Notes to Foreign Legations in the United States from the State Department, 1834-1906." Record Group 59, National Archives.

U.S. War Department. "Letters Received by the Secretary of War, from the President, Executive Departments, and War Department Bureaus, 1862-1870." Record Group 107, National Archives.

———. "Letters Received by the Secretary of War, 1861-1866." Irregular Series. Record Group 107, National Archives.

———. "Letters Received by the Secretary of War, 1801-1870." Registered Series. Record Group 107, National Archives.

———. "Letters Sent by the Secretary of War to the President and Executive Departments, 1863-1870." Record Group 107, National Archives.

———. "Letters Sent by the War Department, 1800-1870." Military Books. Record Group 107, National Archives.

———. "Service Records of Volunteer Union Soldiers Who Served in Organizations from the State of Maine—Co. D, 20th Maine Infantry." Record Group 94, National Archives.

United States v. Frederick Clark, United States District Court Records, Southern District of Georgia. Record Group 21, National Archives, Federal Record Center, East Point, Ga.

PUBLISHED SOURCES

PRIVATE PAPERS, REMINISCENCES, AND DIARIES

Baker, George E., ed. *The Works of William Seward.* 5 vols. Boston, 1890.

Basler, Roy P., ed. *The Collected Works of Abraham Lincoln.* 9 vols. New Brunswick, N.J., 1953-55.

Beale, Howard K., ed. *The Diary of Edward Bates, 1859-66.* Washington, D.C., 1933.

Donald, David, ed. *Inside Lincoln's Cabinet: The Civil War Diaries of Salmon P. Chase.* New York, 1960.

Ford, Worthington Chauncey, ed. *A Cycle of Adams Letters, 1861-1865.* 2 vols. Boston, 1920.

Gooch, George P., ed. *The Later Correspondence of Lord John Russell, 1840-1878.* 2 vols. London, 1925.

Jones, J.B. *A Rebel War Clerk's Diary at the Confederate Capital.* 2 vols. Philadelphia, 1866.

Russell, John Earl. *Recollections and Suggestions, 1813-1873.* London, 1875.

Russell, William Howard. *My Diary North and South.* Ed. Eugene H. Berwanger. New York, 1988.

Sangston, Lawrence. *The Bastiles of the North.* Baltimore, 1863.

Seward, Frederick. *Reminiscences of a War-Time Statesman and Diplomat.* New York, 1916.

Trollope, Francis. *Domestic Manners of the Americans.* Ed. Donald Smalley. New York, 1949.

Welles, Gideon. *The Diary of Gideon Welles.* 3 vols. Boston, 1911.

COLLECTIONS AND DOCUMENTS

Bourne, Kenneth, and D. Cameron Watt, eds. *British Documents of Foreign Affairs: Reports and Papers from the Foreign Office Confidential Print.* 15 vols. Frederick, Md., 1981.

Cattrell, Helen T. *Judicial Cases Concerning American Slavery and the Negro.* 5 vols. Washington, D.C., 1926-37.

Confederate State Department. *Correspondence of the [Confederate] Department of State in Relation to the British Consuls Resident in the Confederate States.* Richmond, 1863.

"Despatch from the British Consul at Charleston to Lord John Russell, 1860." *American Historical Review* 18 (1913): 783-87.

Herslet, Edward, comp. *The Foreign Office List: A Complete British Diplomatic and Consular Handbook.* London, 1870.

House of Commons. *Correspondence Relating to the Civil War in the United States of America Presented to Both Houses of Parliament by Command of Her Majesty, 1863.* London, 1863.

———. *Further Correspondence Respecting the Enlistment of British Subjects in the United States Army.* London, 1864.

———. *Correspondence Respecting the Enlistment of British Subjects into the United States Army.* London, 1864.

———. *Correspondence Respecting Removal of the British Consuls from the So-Styled Confederate States of America.* London, 1864.

———. *Correspondence Respecting the Withdrawal by the Government* of the United States of Mr. Bunch's Exequatur as Her Majesty's Consul at Charleston, Presented to Both Houses of Parliament by Command of Her Majesty. London, 1862.

House of Lords. Correspondence on the Civil War in the United States. London, 1862.

Official Records of the Union and Confederate Navies in the War of the Rebellion. 26 vols. Washington, D.C., 1894-1922.

Richardson, James D., ed. A Compilation of the Messages and Papers of the Confederacy, Including the Diplomatic Correspondence, 1861-1865. 2 vols. Nashville, Tenn., 1906.

U.S. Bureau of the Census. Eighth Census of the United States: 1860, Population. Washington, 1864.

U.S. Congress. House of Representatives. House Executive Documents, 37 through 39 congresses (1861-65).

———. Senate. Journal of the Congress of the Confederate States of America, 1861-1865. 7 vols. Washington, D.C., 1904.

———. Senate Executive Documents, 37 through 39 congresses (1861-65).

U.S. Statutes at Large, 3, 9, and 12.

The War of the Rebellion: A Compilation of the Official Records of the Union and Confederate Armies. 128 vols. Washington, D.C., 1880-1901.

NEWSPAPERS

Charleston (South Carolina) Mercury, 1861-63.
Edwardsville (Illinois) Spectator, 1823.
New York Herald, 1861-65.
New York Times, 1861-65.
New York Tribune, 1861-65.
Savannah (Georgia) Daily News and Herald, 1867-70.

INDEXES AND GUIDES

Beers, Henry Putney. Guide to the Archives of the Government of the Confederate States of America. Washington, D.C., 1968.

Munden, Kenneth W., and Henry Putney Beers. Guide to Federal Archives Relating to the Civil War. Washington, D.C., 1962.

U.S. State Department. "Index to Exequaturs." Record Group 59, National Archives.

U.S. War Department. "Index to Compiled Service Records of Volunteer Union Soldiers Who Served in Organizations from the State of Maine." National Archives Microfilm Publication, M543.

————. "Indexes to Letters Received by the Secretary of War, 1861-1870." National Archives Microfilm Publication, M495.

SECONDARY ACCOUNTS

Adams, Charles Francis. "The British Proclamation of May, 1861." *Proceedings of the Massachusetts Historical Society* 49 (1915): 190-242.

————. "The Negotiation of 1861 Relating to the Declaration of Paris of 1856." *Proceedings of the Massachusetts Historical Society* 46 (1912): 23-84.

Adams, Ephraim Douglass. *Great Britain and the American Civil War.* 2 vols. New York, 1924.

Adams, Henry. *The Great Secession Winter of 1860-61 and Other Essays.* Ed. George E. Hochfield. New York, 1958.

Allen, H.C. *Great Britain and the United States: A History of Anglo-American Relations.* New York, 1955.

Archibald, Edith J. *Life and Letters of Sir Edward Mortimer Archibald, K.C.M., G.C.B.: A Memoir of Fifty Years Service.* Toronto, 1924.

Baker, LaFayette. *History of the United States Secret Service.* Philadelphia, 1868.

Bancroft, Frederic. *The Life of William H. Seward.* New York, 1900.

Beloff, Max. "Great Britain and the American Civil War." *History,* 33 (1952): 40-48.

Bemis, Samuel Flagg. *A Diplomatic History of the United States.* 5th ed. New York, 1965.

Berlin, Ira. *Slaves Without Masters: The Free Negro in the Antebellum South.* New York, 1974.

Blue, Frederick J. *Salmon P. Chase: A Life in Politics.* Kent, Ohio, 1987.

Blumenthal, Henry. "Confederate Diplomacy: Popular Notions and International Realities." *Journal of Southern History* 32 (1966): 151-71.

Bonham, Milledge L., Jr. *The British Consuls in the Confederacy.* Vol. 43, *Columbia University Studies in History, Economics, and Public Law.* New York, 1911.

Bourne, Kenneth. *Britain and the Balance of Power in North America, 1815-1908.* Berkeley, Calif., 1967.

————. *The Foreign Policy of Victorian England, 1830-1902.* Oxford, 1970.

Brauer, Kinley J. "British Mediation and the American Civil War: A

Reconsideration." *Journal of Southern History* 38 (1972): 49-64.

———. "The Slavery Problem in the Diplomacy of the American Civil War." *Pacific Historical Review* 46 (1977): 439-69.

Callahan, James Morton. *Diplomatic History of the Southern Confederacy.* New York, 1964.

Carroll, Daniel B. *Henri Mercier and the American Civil War.* Princeton, N.J., 1971.

Case, Lynn M., and Warren F. Spencer. *The United States and France: Civil War Diplomacy.* Philadelphia, 1970.

Coulter, E. Merton. *The Confederate States of America.* Baton Rouge, La., 1950.

Courtemanche, Regis A. *No Need of Glory: The British Navy in American Waters, 1860-1864.* Annapolis, Md., 1977.

Crawford, Martin. *The Anglo-American Crisis of the Mid-Nineteenth Century: The Times and America, 1850-1862.* Athens, Ga., 1987.

Crook, D.P. *The North, the South, and the Powers, 1861-1865.* New York, 1974.

Davis, Jefferson. *The Rise and Fall of the Confederate Government.* 2 vols. New York, 1881.

Davis, William C. *Jefferson Davis: The Man and His Hour.* New York, 1991.

Davis, William Watson. *The Civil War and Reconstruction in Florida.* Gainsville, Fla., 1964.

Donald, David, ed. *Why the North Won the Civil War.* New York, 1960.

Duberman, Martin. *Charles Francis Adams, 1807-1886.* Boston, 1961.

Du Bois. W.E.B. *The Suppression of the African Slave-Trade in the United States of America, 1638-1870.* New York, 1934.

Eaton, Clement. *Jefferson Davis.* New York, 1977.

Ellsworth, Edward W. "British Consuls in the Confederacy in 1862." *Lincoln Herald* 46 (1964): 149-54.

———. "Lord John Russell and the British Consuls in America in 1861." *Lincoln Herald* 46 (1964): 34-39.

Evans, Eli N. *Judah P. Benjamin: The Jewish Confederate.* New York, 1988.

Ferris, Norman. *Desperate Diplomacy: William H. Seward's Foreign Policy, 1861.* Knoxville, Tenn., 1976.

Finkelman, Paul. "The Kidnapping of John Davis and the Adoption of the Fugitive Slave Law of 1793." *Journal of Southern History* 56 (1990): 397-422.

Fortson, Blanton. "John Erskine," in vol. 6 of *Dictionary of American Biography* (New York, 1937), 180.

Freehling, William W. *Prelude to Civil War: The Nullification Controversy in South Carolina, 1816-1836.* New York, 1965.

Gallas, Stanley. "Lord Lyons and the Civil War, 1859-1864: A British Perspective." Ph.D. diss., University of Illinois, Chicago, 1982.

Geary, James W. *We Need Men: The Union Draft in the Civil War.* DeKalb, Ill., 1991.

Hamer, Marguerite. "Luring Canadian Soldiers into Union Lines During the War Between the States." *Canadian Historical Review* 27 (1946): 150-62.

Hamilton, John A. "Richard Bickerton Pemell Lyons," in vol. 12 of *Dictionary of National Biography* (Oxford, 1921-1922), 357-59.

Hendrick, Burton J. *Lincoln's War Cabinet.* Garden City, N.Y., 1961.

Hepburn, A. Barton. *A History of Currency in the United States.* New York, 1967.

Hernon, Joseph M., Jr. "British Sympathies in the American Civil War: A Reconsideration." *Journal of Southern History* 33 (1967): 356-67.

Hyman, Harold. *Heard Round the World: The Impact Abroad of the Civil War.* New York, 1969.

Jefferson, D.W. "Gladstone and the American Civil War." *Proceedings of the Leeds Philosophical and Literary Society* 6 (1951): 583-94.

Jenkins, Brian. *Britain and the War for the Union.* 2 vols. Montreal, 1974 and 1980.

Jones, Howard. *Union in Peril: The Crisis over British Intervention in the Civil War.* Chapel Hill, N.C., 1992.

Jones, Robert. "Anglo-American Relations: 1861-1865: Reconsidered." *Journal of the Illinois Catholic Historical Society,* 45 (1963): 36-49.

Jones, Wilbur D. "The British Conservatives and the American Civil War." *American Historical Review* 58 (1953): 526-43.

Kennedy, Charles Stuart. *The American Consul: A History of the United States Consular Service.* New York, 1990.

Laughton, John K. "Edmund Lyons," in vol. 12 of *Dictionary of National Biography* (Oxford, 1921-1922), 355-57.

Long, E.B. *The Civil War Day by Day: An Almanac, 1861-1865.* New York, 1971.

Lonn, Ella. *Desertion During the Civil War.* Gloucester, Mass., 1966.

——. *Foreigners in the Confederacy.* Chapel Hill, N.C., 1940.

——. *Foreigners in the Union Army and Navy.* Baton Rouge, La. 1951.

Lothrop, Thornton K. *William Henry Seward.* Boston, 1896.

McPherson, James. *Battle Cry of Freedom: The Civil War Era.* New York, 1988

——. *Ordeal By Fire: The Civil War and Reconstruction.* New York, 1982.

Meade, Robert Douthat. *Judah P. Benjamin: Confederate Statesman.* New York, 1943.

Merli, Frank J., and T.A. Wilson. "The British Cabinet and the Confederacy: Autumn 1862." *Maryland History Magazine* 65 (1970): 239-62.

Middleton, Charles Roland. *The Administration of British Foreign Policy, 1782-1846.* Durham, N.C., 1977.

Milne, A. Taylor. "The Lyons-Seward Treaty of 1862." *American Historical Review* 38 (1932): 511-25.

Monaghan, Jay. *Diplomat in Carpet Slippers.* Indianapolis, Ind. 1945.

Moore, Albert Burton. *Conscription and Conflict in the Confederacy.* New York, 1924.

Murdock, Eugene C. "New York's Civil War Bounty Brokers," *Journal of American History* 13 (1966): 259-78.

———. *One Million Men: The Civil War Draft in the North.* Madison, Wisc., 1971.

———. *Patriotism Limited, 1862-1863: The Civil War Draft and the Bounty System.* Kent, Ohio, 1967.

Neely, Mark E., Jr. *The Fate of Liberty: Abraham Lincoln and Civil Liberties.* New York, 1991.

Nevins, Allan. *The War for the Union: The Organized War. 1863-1864.* 4 vols. New York, 1959-71.

Newton, Thomas W.L. *Lord Lyons: A Record of British Diplomacy.* 2 vols. London, 1913.

O'Rourke, Sister Mary Martinece. "The Diplomacy of William H. Seward During the Civil War: His Policies As Related to International Law." Ph.D. diss., University of California, Berkeley, 1963.

Owsley, Frank Lawrence, and Harriet Chappell Owsley. *King Cotton Diplomacy: Foreign Relations of the Confederate States of America.* Chicago, 1959.

Paludan, Philip Shaw. *"A People's Contest": The Union and the Civil War, 1861-1865.* New York, 1988.

Patrick, Rembert W. *Jefferson Davis and His Cabinet.* Baton Rouge, La., 1944.

Platt, D.C.M. *The Cinderella Service: British Consuls since 1825.* Hamden, Conn., 1971.

Porter, David D. *The Naval History of the Civil War.* New York, 1886.

Randall, James G., and David Donald. *The Civil War and Reconstruction.* 2nd ed. Boston, 1961.

Raney, William F. "Recruiting and Crimping in Canada for the Northern Forces, 1861-1865." *Mississippi Valley Historical Review,* 10 (1923): 21-33.

Rawley, James. *Turning Points of the Civil War.* Lincoln, Nebr., 1966.

Reid, Robert. "William E. Gladstone's 'Insincere Neutrality' During the Civil War." *Civil War History* 15 (1969): 293-307.

Roberts, Derrell. *Joseph E. Brown and the Politics of Reconstruction*. University, Ala., 1973.

Sears, Louis. *John Slidell*. Durham, N.C. 1925.

––––––. "The London *Times*' American Correspondent in 1861: Unpublished Letters of William H. Russell in the First Year of the Civil War." *The Historical Outlook* 16 (1925): 150-57.

Shannon, Fred Albert. *The Organization and Administration of the Union Army, 1861-1865*. 2 vols. Gloucester, Mass, 1965.

Sprague, Dean. *Freedom under Lincoln: Federal Power and Personal Liberty Under the Strain of Civil War*. Boston, 1965.

Stuart, Graham. *American Diplomatic and Consular Practice*. New York, 1952.

Sutherland, Daniel E. "Southern Fraternal Organizations in the North." *Journal of Southern History* 53 (1987): 587-612.

––––––. *The Expansion of Everyday Life, 1860-1876*. New York, 1989.

Taylor, John M. *William Henry Seward: Lincoln's Right Hand*. New York, 1991.

Temple, Henry W. "William H. Seward, Secretary of State, March 5, 1861 to March 4, 1869," in vol. 6 of *The American Secretaries of State and Their Diplomacy*, ed. Samuel Flagg Bemis (New York, 1963), 106.

Thomas, Emory. *The Confederate Nation, 1861-1865*. New York, 1979.

Trescot, William H. "The Confederacy and the Declaration of Paris." *American Historical Review* 23 (1918): 826-35.

Van Deusen, Glyndon G. *William Henry Seward: Lincoln's Secretary of State, The Negotiator of the Alaska Purchase*. New York, 1967.

Wallace, John. *Carpet-Bag Rule in Florida*. Gainsville, Fla., 1964.

Walpole, Spencer. *The Life of Lord John Russell*. 2 vols. London, 1899.

Walther, Eric. *The Fire-Eaters*. Baton Rouge, La., 1992.

White, Laura. *Robert Barnwell Rhett: Father of Secession*. New York, 1931.

––––––. "The United States in the 1850's as Seen by British Consuls." *Mississippi Valley Historical Review* 19 (1933): 509-36.

Willson, Beckles. *Friendly Relations: A Narrative of Britain's Ministers and Ambassadors in America, 1791-1930*. Boston, 1934.

Winks, Robin W. *Canada and the United States: The Civil War Years*. Baltimore, 1960.

Index